Jonathan Edwards, Samuel Hopkins, and the Theological Ethics of Social Concern

Jonathan Edwards, Samuel Hopkins, and the Theological Ethics of Social Concern

Joseph W. Lee

Volume 6

A Series of Treatises on Jonathan Edwards

JE Society Press

WWW.JESOCIETY.ORG

Paperback Edition March 13, 2026
ISBN 979-8-9945933-0-1

A publication of JESociety Press
Visit https://www.jesociety.org

For permission requests and inquiries,
Email: rob@jesociety.org
Web: www.jesociety.org

PRAISE FOR THIS VOLUME

"Many thanks to Joseph Lee for this learned, thoughtful, and careful interpretation of the continuity of Hopkins with Edwards' understanding of benevolence, virtue, and ethics more generally. While most previous scholars have contended that Hopkins diverged from his teacher in fundamental ways, Lee demonstrates instead that Hopkins proved more consistent than his teacher had done in applying Edwardsean ethics to the issue of slavery."

Douglas A. Sweeney
Dean and Professor of Divinity
Beeson Divinity School

"Scholars and pastors have long wondered how Jonathan Edwards's principal disciple in the eighteenth century could have used the theology of slave-owning Edwards to lead a fight against slavery. Joseph Lee helps us all answer that question by this very helpful study."

Gerald McDermott
co-author, *The Theology of Jonathan Edwards*
(Oxford University Press)

"Jonathan Edwards owned slaves. This truth is shocking to most people and difficult to understand for all. On the other hand, one of Edwards's mentees, Samuel Hopkins, actively supported the abolition of slavery in the new nation, the United States of America. After establishing how Edwards's ethics are rooted in his virtue theory, Lee argues that Hopkins, a former slave owner, was more consistent than his mentor in applying Edwards's doctrine of benevolence in his advocacy for the abolition of slavery. This book makes an important contribution to the literature on Edwards's ethics, not just on the reality of his endorsement of slavery. Rather than a declension from one generation to the next, Edwards's theological heirs, including but not limited to Hopkins, significantly improved on his views on slavery."

Glenn R. Kreider
Editor in Chief, *Bibliotheca Sacra*
Professor of Theological Studies
Dallas Theological Seminary

"In this welcomed addition to Edwardsean studies, Joseph Lee enters the scholarly debate over the extent to which the virtue theory of Samuel Hopkins diverged from that of his "Doktorvater," Jonathan Edwards. A work rich in theological content and comprehensive in assessing multiple perspectives, this important revision of the "betrayal thesis" offers a salutary course correction, arguing for a congruence of ethical theories between Edwards and Hopkins. Of particular significance, Lee contends that Hopkins "faithfully applied Edwards's doctrine of benevolence" in his abolitionist stance. Lee may have his naysayers, but no serious scholar can now examine the virtue theories of Edwards and Hopkins without consulting this impressive work."

David Kling
Professor, Department of Religious Studies
University of Miami

"Clearly written, and thoroughly saturated in the sources, Joseph Lee's tightly argued study demonstrates the remarkable consistency between Edwards and Hopkins in their theocentric social vision. Far from 'betraying' Edwards's ethics, Hopkins largely reproduced and consistently applied them in his anti-slavery advocacy. Lee's volume is a wonderful study underscoring the unity of theology, political theory, and social concern in eighteenth-century America."

Robert Caldwell
Professor of Church History
Southwestern Baptist Theological Seminary

ABSTRACT

This project examines the virtue theories of Jonathan Edwards and Samuel Hopkins to provide evidence of congruence between the two figures. I argue that Hopkins was more consistent with Edwards's ethical theology by faithfully applying Edwards's doctrine of benevolence to advocate for the abolition of institutionalized slavery and the slave trade.

Chapter one provides the need for the study. It shows how scholars have portrayed Hopkins as diverging from Edwards's ethics. Claims of Edwards's ethical thought being solely philosophical and/or theocentric and Hopkins's ethics being pragmatic in nature have led to such claims.

Chapter two establishes the scholarly context for the study. It shows the need to view both Edwards's and Hopkins's virtue theories holistically, taking into account the philosophical, theocentric, and activist dimensions of their respective ethics.

Chapter three provides background information, giving rationale for Edwards's proslavery stance and Hopkins's abolitionism. It shows how slavery and the slave trade were largely unquestioned in prerevolutionary America and how antislavery sentiment started and began to grow in the Revolutionary years.

Chapter four examines Edwards's virtue theory in preparation for the comparative examination in chapter five. The philosophical, God-centered, and practical aspects of Edwards's ethics are established. Rationale for Edwards's agreement with slave-owning is also discussed in light of his doctrine of benevolence.

Chapter five provides a comparative examination of Edwards's and Hopkins's virtue theories. More specifically, it shows social and activist stimuli located in Edwards's doctrine of benevolence and Hopkins's agreement with Edwards by way of his doctrine of disinterested benevolence. Thus, evidence is provided that substantiates the claim of this study. The chapter concludes with a discussion of Hopkins's abolitionism in light of his doctrine of disinterested benevolence.

Chapter six provides a synopsis of this study and shows potential areas for further research.

Abbreviations

CEW	*Concerning the End for Which God Created the World*
CF	*Charity and Its Fruits*
DS	*A Dialogue Concerning the Slavery of the Africans*
DSS	*A Discourse Upon the Slave Trade and the Slavery of the Africans*
Misc	*"Miscellany"*
RA	*Religious Affections*
TH	*An Inquiry into the Nature of True Holiness*
TV	*The Nature of True Virtue*

Acknowledgments

This is a version of my PhD dissertation that was completed at Dallas Theological Seminary in Spring 2018. Pertinent sections have been updated with more current scholarship as deemed appropriate. The thesis and argumentation remain the same. I would like to thank Dr. Robert L. Boss (Director of the Jonathan Edwards Society) and JESociety Press for the opportunity to publish this version of my dissertation.

I continue to thank God for his great love and faithfulness to my family and me over the years. The completion of the original dissertation and the PhD program are a result of God's guidance, strength, and provision of family and friends, of whom there are too many to thank. As I look back on my time as a doctoral student, certain individuals made a significant impact:

I greatly appreciate the members of my dissertation committee. Dr. Glenn R. Kreider was a mentor and constant source of support throughout my ThM and PhD programs. His theological insights and the gracious giving of his time blessed me. I was encouraged by Dr. J. Lanier Burns and his interests in the areas of history, ethics, and race. And Dr. Barry D. Jones modeled well a concurrent love for the local church and the Christian academy. Thank you.

I was encouraged by Dr. Richard A. Taylor throughout my time in the PhD program for his expectations of scholarly excellence and support of me as a doctoral student. Likewise, Dr. Michael J. Svigel aided me with his academic support during my time in both the ThM and PhD programs. I learned a great deal due to his expertise in historical theology.

I am thankful for my friends at the DTS Book Center who provided joy, laughter, and friendship during my first two years in the PhD program. In like manner, I was encouraged by a number of PhD students, especially those in the Theological Studies Department, during my time in the program. Thank you to all.

Thank you to my in-laws, Dr. Patrick and Kathy Reece. They both faithfully loved and prayed for my family and me throughout my ThM and PhD programs. Mom Reece loved and encouraged her daughter and grandchildren during my times away and we were blessed as a result. Dad Reece provided constant encouragement, proofread a draft of the original dissertation, and provided valuable feedback.

My brother-in-law and sister, David and Stacie Kahm, gave love and family support, which helped make possible the completion of my ThM and PhD programs. Thank you for being family over these years.

The love that my parents, Paul and Yung Lee, gave cannot be overstated. Without their support, my time at Dallas Theological Seminary would not have been possible. Mom and dad helped sustain my family throughout all my years in the ThM and PhD programs. Their care for their daughter-in-law and grandchildren was a gift to me. Thank you. You both continue to be a blessing.

From the time they were young, my children, Tytus and Abby, saw their dad with his head buried in books and journal articles. I am thankful you gave dad the time to finish. And I am so proud of the young man and woman that you are becoming. Now that you are grown, I look forward to new memories together. I love you both.

Finally, to my wife, Mollie. Your love for the Lord and commitment to the "faith that was once for all delivered to the saints" (Jude 3, ESV) emboldens me. You truly are a picture of God's grace. Thank you for all of the years you sacrificed. I continue to look forward to the rest of our lives together. I love you.

Contents

Acknowledgments v

Chapter 1: Introduction 1

Need for the Study 3
Thesis of the Study 7
Method of the Study 7
A Note on the Scope of the Study 8
Conclusion 9

Chapter 2: New Divinity, Hopkins, and the Scholarly Context 11

Introduction to the New Divinity Movement and Hopkins 11
Primary Sources 20
Works on Edwards's Ethics 23
Works that Claim Divergence 33
Revisionist Works 38
Conclusion 50

Chapter 3: Historical Context 51

Eighteenth-Century Pre-Revolutionary America (Puritan America) 51
Eighteenth-Century Revolutionary America (Enlightened America) 80
Conclusion 95

Chapter 4: Edwards's Virtue Theory and the Issue of Slavery 97

Benevolence to Being in General 98
Self-Love 117

Benevolence, Charity, and Love 123
The Issue of Slavery 141
Conclusion 150

Chapter 5: A Comparative Analysis 151

Benevolence to God *and* Neighbor 152
Self-Regard and the Role of Happiness 161
Selfishness and Self-Enlargement 166
Social Concern and Activism 169
The Issue of Slavery 181
Conclusion 189

Chapter 6: Conclusion 191

Bibliography 193

Index 219

Chapter 1: Introduction

In his work on Jonathan Edwards's (1703–1758) ethics, Clyde Holbrook claimed that Edwards "was not a social reformer by direct intent, but his theological ethics of universal benevolence had a social outthrust which was later given expression in the antislavery crusade and 'humanitarianism' of Samuel Hopkins."[1] Hopkins's (1721–1803) commitment to social justice, namely the abolition of slavery and the slave trade, is well documented in the literature.[2] This activist zeal was driven by a desire for holiness, which for Hopkins was composed of Christian benevolence or love in connection to the law of God. Specifically, when one obeys the divine law, one produces holiness for "the law of God is the standard of all moral

[1] Clyde A. Holbrook, *The Ethics of Jonathan Edwards: Morality and Aesthetics* (Ann Arbor: University of Michigan Press, 1973), 95.

[2] For example, see Allan G. Hedberg, "Slavery," in *The Jonathan Edwards Encyclopedia*, ed. Harry S. Stout (Grand Rapids: Eerdmans, 2017), 535–36; Peter Jauhianen, "Samuel Hopkins and Hopkinsianism," in *After Jonathan Edwards: The Courses of New England Theology*, ed. Oliver D. Crisp and Douglas A. Sweeney (New York: Oxford University Press, 2012), 107–17; Douglas A. Sweeney and Allen C. Guelzo, eds., *The New England Theology: From Jonathan Edwards to Edwards Amasa Park* (Grand Rapids: Baker Academic, 2006), 149–52; Sherard Burns, "Trusting the Theology of a Slave Owner," in *A God Entranced Vision of All Things: The Legacy of Jonathan Edwards*, ed. John Piper and Justin Taylor (Wheaton, IL: Crossway Books, 2004), 145–71; Charles E. Hambrick-Stowe, "All Things Were New and Astonishing: Edwardsian Piety, the New Divinity, and Race," in *Jonathan Edwards at Home and Abroad: Historical Memories, Cultural Movements, Global Horizons*, ed. David W. Kling and Douglas A. Sweeney (Columbia: University of South Carolina Press, 2003), 121–36; David S. Lovejoy, "Samuel Hopkins: Religion, Slavery, and the Revolution," *New England Quarterly* 40, no. 2 (1967): 227–43.

rectitude or holiness."[3] For Hopkins, "the knowledge of the precepts of the moral law" is necessary since God's law "requires" holiness itself.[4] When one obeys the divine law, one expresses love; specifically "love to God and our neighbor, including ourselves."[5] According to Hopkins, this love "is the whole that is required; therefore, this is the whole of true holiness; it consists in this love, and in nothing else."[6] Hopkins is best known for his commitment to Christian benevolence and its activist expression. By using his doctrine of disinterested benevolence to fuel his opposition toward both institutionalized slavery and the slave trade, Hopkins's reputation as a social activist is warranted.

As Holbrook pointed out, Hopkins's activist impulse was deeply influenced by Edwards's understanding of benevolence. Holbrook also mentioned that Edwards did not directly engage in social reform. Similarly, other scholars in the past have argued that Edwards lacked social concern and activism in his theology. Edwards's condoning of institutionalized slavery gave reason for such positions.[7] So how did Edwards's understanding of benevolence influence Hopkins, given that Edwards was a slave owner, to advocate for the freedom of enslaved Africans? The nature of this influence and Hopkins's appropriation of Edwards's thought is a topic of debate in both New Divinity and Hopkinsian scholarship.[8] Claims of betrayal or divergence by Hopkins from Edwards's thought have a long history. Views arguing for a philosophical and/or theocentric bent in Edwards's virtue theory along with Hopkins's seeming pragmatism of his mentor's ethics have been consistently espoused for the last one hundred years. Only within the last forty-five years have the betrayal or divergence theses been challenged by revisionist works advocating either partial or full-fledged faithfulness for both the New Divinity disciples and Hopkins to Edwards's thought.

[3]Samuel Hopkins, "An Inquiry into the Nature of True Holiness," in *The Works of Samuel Hopkins, D.D.*, vol. 3 (Boston: Doctrinal Tract and Book Society, 1854), 13. More on Hopkins's understanding of the divine law will be discussed in chapter 5.

[4]Hopkins, *TH*, 14.

[5]Hopkins, *TH*, 14.

[6]Hopkins, *TH*, 14.

[7]Edwards's seeming lack of social concern and activism based on past theses will be dealt with in detail in chapter 2. By recognizing the necessity of viewing Edwards's moral philosophy and moral theology as a united whole to gain a holistic understanding of Edwards's ethical thought, evidence of activism substantiates needed revisionist accounts of Edwards's virtue theory.

[8]The New Divinity disciples were Edwards's theological heirs, establishing an Edwardsean intellectual and ecclesiastical tradition that would extend into the nineteenth century. A brief overview of the New Divinity movement/New England Theology will be provided in chapter 2.

Given the inconsistency of views of Hopkins's relationship to Edwards's ethical thought, particularly as it pertains to the issue of benevolence, this study provides a comparative examination of their respective virtue theories. Because the doctrine of benevolence was foundational for both figures in developing their respective views, an examination of Hopkins's doctrine of disinterested benevolence in relation to Edwards's doctrine of benevolence is key to comprehend their ethics holistically.

Need for the Study

There are a number of reasons why this study is needed. First, as aforementioned, there has been a long history of scholars putting forward a betrayal thesis, claiming divergence of the New Divinity disciples from Edwards's theology. In the mid-nineteenth century, representing the beginning of the first stage of the New England Theology's historiography, Edwards Amasa Park (Andover Seminary) established the New England Theology as a faithful theological development of Edwards's thought.[9] Contrarily, what would follow for over a century is a dominant model put forward by scholars of decline or betrayal by the New Divinity disciples to Edwards's theology. In describing the scholarly view of divergence, Douglas Sweeney explains, "While admirers have generally characterized the New England Theology as continuous, any changes being consistent with Edwards's own intentions, critics have tended to discover discontinuity, each development within the tradition viewed as a departure from Edwards's Calvinism."[10]

Views of the New England Theology's extreme moralism and systematic and/or metaphysical emphases were perpetuated.[11] Frank Hugh Foster is

[9]Douglas A. Sweeney, "Edwards and His Mantle: The Historiography of the New England Theology," *New England Quarterly* 71, no. 1 (1998): 97–101. I use Sweeney's historiography of the New England Theology as a guide for the following discussion on the scholarly context for the relationship between the New Divinity disciples and Edwards. Sweeney, "Edwards and His Mantle," 97–119.

[10]Sweeney, "Edwards and His Mantle," 100.

[11]In discussing the different versions of the betrayal thesis, Breitenbach explains, "The betrayal interpretation comes in a couple of versions. The first, and still the most common, characterizes the Edwardsians as arid metaphysicians and austere hyper-Calvinists who systematized Edwards's thought, but in so doing drained it of its warm and vital piety. These theological Doctors Rappaccini, killing what they hoped to protect, ultimately found themselves alone in their studies with the bloodless corpse of a rigid and unpopular Calvinism. The second version describes the New Divinity ministers as liberalizers and moralizers who were intent upon accommodating Edwards's Calvinistic creed to the humanitarian spirit of the day, even if that meant compromising the essentials of his faith." William Breitenbach, "Piety and Moralism:

representative of the second stage of the New England Theology's historiography as he continued the divergence theory with his *A Genetic History of the New England Theology*.[12] Joseph Haroutunian, then, cements the betrayal thesis in *Piety Versus Moralism*.[13] The impact of Haroutunian's betrayal thesis would be far reaching as it represented the consensus scholarly voice until recent revisionist accounts.[14]

Although scholars continue to represent variations of Haroutunian's thesis, recent nuanced interpretations suggest either the New Divinity's partial resemblance or full faithfulness to Edwards's thought.[15] Additional work to supplement the revisionist accounts is needed to achieve a more accurate picture of the New Divinity movement and thus, the New England Theology. Fortunately, recent revisionist accounts have focused on evidencing continuity between Edwards and his heirs. For example, Allen C. Guelzo asserts, The New Divinity's "preaching and teaching were, looked at in the long run, still the stuff of Calvinism given yet another working over. As such, the New Divinity was hardly more than a set of variations on certain Edwardsean themes."[16] A focused study on individuals within the tradition such as Hopkins is an effective way to reinforce needed revisionist perspectives.

Second, there continues to be very little work done in Hopkinsian scholarship. This is evidenced by the sparseness of dissertations written directly on Hopkins in the last seventy-five years.[17] Given the abundance of work

Edwards and the New Divinity," in *Jonathan Edwards and the American Experience*, ed. Nathan O. Hatch and Harry S. Stout (New York: Oxford University Press, 1988), 177–78. In chapter 2, the theses claiming change or divergence by the New Divinity disciples and Hopkins from Edwards's theology will be covered.

[12]Sweeney, "Edwards and His Mantle," 104–5; Frank Hugh Foster, *A Genetic History of the New England Theology* (New York: Garland, 1987).

[13]Sweeney, "Edwards and His Mantle," 107–10; Joseph Haroutunian, *Piety Versus Moralism: The Passing of the New England Theology* (New York: H. Holt, 1932).

[14]Sweeney, "Edwards and His Mantle," 108, 112, 114.

[15]Sweeney, "Edwards and His Mantle," 112–18. For examples of revisionist perspectives, see Joseph A. Conforti, *Samuel Hopkins and the New Divinity Movement: Calvinism, the Congregational Ministry, and Reform in New England Between the Great Awakenings* (Grand Rapids: Christian University Press, 1981); Breitenbach, "Piety and Moralism," 177–204; Allen C. Guelzo, *Edwards on the Will: A Century of American Theological Debate* (Middletown, CT: Wesleyan University Press, 1989).

[16]Guelzo, *Edwards on the Will*, 136.

[17]See John Gleim, "Topographies of Difference: Joseph Bellamy, Samuel Hopkins, and the Uneven Theological Development of Late-Puritan New England" (PhD diss., Fordham University, 2020); Peter Dan Jauhiainen, "An Enlightenment Calvinist: Samuel Hopkins and the Pursuit of Benevolence" (PhD diss., University of Iowa, 1997); Stephen Garrard Post, "Love and

being done in Edwardsean scholarship, it is surprising that a key source for better understanding Edwards's thought is seldom utilized. Examining the "reception of Edwards's ideas" and "how his ideas were transmitted, changed, and developed in the process of dissemination and reception" is a worthy task.[18] Thus, an analysis of Hopkins's appropriation of Edwards's ethical theology supplements a needed area of study.

Third, in light of the scarce number of works on Hopkins and similar to scholarship on the New England Theology, fewer works claim congruence between the two figures.[19] This is significant because Edwards has been portrayed as one void of social concern due to his theocentric commitments and philosophically oriented ethics. Similarly, Hopkins's legalistic tenor

Eudaemonism: A Study in the Thought of Jonathan Edwards and Samuel Hopkins" (PhD diss., University of Chicago, 1983); Joseph A. Conforti, "Samuel Hopkins and the New Divinity Movement, 1740–1820: A Study in the Transformation of Puritan Theology and the New England Social Order" (PhD diss., Brown University, 1975); Hugh Heath Knapp, "Samuel Hopkins and the New Divinity" (PhD diss., University of Wisconsin, 1971); Dick L. Van Halsema, "Samuel Hopkins, 1721–1803: New England Calvinist" (PhD diss., Union Theological Seminary, 1956). I am indebted to Marvin Hunn and Jeff Webster for generating a list that includes these works.

[18]Oliver D. Crisp and Douglas A. Sweeney, "Introduction," in *After Jonathan Edwards: The Courses of the New England Theology*, ed. Oliver D. Crisp and Douglas A. Sweeney (New York: Oxford University Press, 2012), 6.

[19]Jauhiainen's 1997 dissertation on Hopkins's appropriation of Enlightenment thought with Reformed doctrine is the only full-length monograph on Hopkins that argues for congruence between Edwards and Hopkins. See Jauhiainen, "An Enlightenment Calvinist." As it pertains to the topic of this study, Jauhiainen argues that Hopkins remained faithful overall to Edwards's understanding of genuine virtue. He provides evidence by concentrating primarily on Edwards's *The Nature of True Virtue* and Hopkins's *An Inquiry into the Nature of True Holiness*, sparsely interacting with other primary sources in examining their respective ethical theologies. Specifically, Jauhiainen argues that Hopkins was "consistent" overall with Edwards's doctrine of benevolence to Being in general. Jauhiainen, "An Enlightenment Calvinist," 236. I look to expand on Edwards's definition of benevolence in the *Two Dissertations*, in particular *TV*, by looking at how Edwards used the concept of benevolence in writings dealing with his ethical/moral theology (sermons/miscellany entries). While Edwards deals primarily with philosophical argumentation in *TV*, his moral thought is highlighted elsewhere. I will show parallels between the two figures stemming from the social and activist stimuli located in Edwards's doctrine of benevolence and Hopkins's appropriation thereof. More specifically, I will demonstrate that Hopkins derived social concern and activism from Edwards's doctrine of benevolence. This will result in a more complete understanding of Edwards's doctrine of benevolence and consequently, a more holistic understanding of his virtue theory. Thus, this study supplements Jauhiainen's revisionist work, providing additional evidence and new perspectives of not only Hopkins's overall faithfulness to Edwards's ethical thought, but also providing rationale for Hopkins's faithful application of Edwards's doctrine of benevolence to fight institutionalized slavery and the slave trade and consequently, Edwards's failure to apply his own doctrine by condoning institutionalized slavery. If Hopkins was indeed consistent with Edwards's understanding of ethics as an abolitionist, then a legitimate question is why Edwards condoned institutionalized slavery in light of his doctrine of benevolence.

and pragmatic bent in his ethical thought have been exaggerated, failing to consider his theocentric commitments and his view of self-regard in light of his doctrine of disinterested benevolence. By evidencing the foundational nature of Edwards's doctrine of benevolence for Hopkins's social concern and activism, specifically as it pertains to Hopkins's commitment for the abolition of both institutionalized slavery and the slave trade, Hopkins's congruence with Edwards's ethical theology is substantiated, thus providing helpful revisionist perspectives for both figures.[20]

Fourth, a fuller account of Edwards's doctrine of benevolence is needed. Scholars claiming divergence look at Hopkins's use of Edwards's *The Nature of True Virtue* in developing his doctrine of disinterested benevolence to show differences between the two figures. However, what is often missing is an explanation of Edwards's purpose for writing that particular work. Specifically, Edwards was responding to certain eighteenth century moral philosophers and intentionally used philosophical language and argumentation, giving a narrow definition of benevolence. As William C. Spohn notes, for both *TV* and *CEW*, "Edwards was responding to eighteenth-century deism, to Hutcheson and Shaftsbury, who maintained that morality could be explained adequately without reference to God."[21] A fuller understanding of Edwards's doctrine of benevolence arises from looking beyond *TV* to his sermons and miscellany entries, pointing to clear disinterested and activist principles that Hopkins drew from.

Finally, clarity on the topic of slavery is needed. Analyzing Hopkins's appropriation of Edwards's doctrine of benevolence elucidates both the tension and rationale of Edwards's proslavery stance and Hopkins's abolitionism

[20]Recent scholarship has provided a portrait of an Edwards who was indeed concerned for the needs of society. See for example Gerald R. McDermott, *One Holy and Happy Society: The Public Theology of Jonathan Edwards* (University Park, PA: Penn State University Press, 1992), 93–116, 137–76; Gerald R. McDermott and Ronald Story, eds., *The Other Jonathan Edwards: Selected Writings on Society, Love, and Justice* (Amherst: University of Massachusetts Press, 2015), 16–19; Ronald Story, *Jonathan Edwards and the Gospel of Love* (Amherst: University of Massachusetts Press, 2012), 51–121; Dane C. Ortlund, *Edwards on the Christian Life: Alive to the Beauty of God* (Wheaton, IL: Crossway, 2014), 55–73; Richard A. S. Hall, *The Neglected Northampton Texts of Jonathan Edwards: Edwards on Society and Politics*, vol. 52, Studies in American Religion (Lewiston, NY: Edwin Mellen Press, 1990), 41–330; Paul Ramsey, "Editor's Introduction," in *Ethical Writings*, vol. 8, *The Works of Jonathan Edwards* (New Haven, CT: Yale University Press, 1989), 1–121. These sources will be discussed in chapter 2 as the scholarly context for the study is established. Moreover, by showing Hopkins's congruence with Edwards's doctrine of benevolence, this study supplements the revisionist perspectives of Edwards as one who stressed the need to live a life of Christian love towards others.

[21]William C. Spohn, "Sovereign Beauty: Jonathan Edwards and the Nature of True Virtue," *Theological Studies* 42, no. 3 (1981): 399.

in light of Hopkins's appropriation of Edwards's ethical theology. Where Edwards failed to fully apply his doctrine of benevolence towards enslaved Africans, Hopkins succeeded by advocating for the abolishment of both institutionalized slavery and the slave trade.

Thesis of the Study

Contrary to theses that present Hopkins as betraying or diverging from Edwards's ethics, I contend that there is congruence between the two figures. Not only was Hopkins consistent with Edwards's understanding of benevolence but dependent as well, developing an impetus for social activism based on the social and activist stimuli located in Edwards's understanding of benevolence. This influenced Hopkins and his understanding of disinterested benevolence, which he used to advocate for the abolition of both the slave trade and institutionalized slavery. While Hopkins and Edwards aligned doctrinally, they diverged in practice regarding the issue of slavery. Thus, the thesis of this study is that Hopkins was more consistent with Edwards's ethical theology by faithfully applying Edwards's doctrine of benevolence to support the abolition of institutionalized slavery and the slave trade.

Method of the Study

The need for the thesis and method of this study are established in this introductory chapter. In chapter 2, I introduce the theological and ecclesiastical tradition Hopkins was a part of along with Hopkins himself to situate Hopkins in his intellectual and ministerial tradition. I then survey the seminal works, providing the scholarly context for the study to show the need to supplement recent revisionist works. In chapter 3, I survey the historical epochs of Edwards and Hopkins and their respective social, cultural, and intellectual milieus in preparation for chapters 4 and 5. This provides both historical context and highlights key influences for their respective positions on both slavery and the slave trade. In chapter 4, I specifically explore Edwards's virtue theory and proslavery stance. Accordingly, evidence shows clear disinterested and activist principles in his ethical thought, challenging claims that Edwards's theory was exclusively philosophical and/or theocentric, thereby inhibiting moral action. Edwards's failure to apply his doctrine of benevolence to enslaved Africans is also discussed. In chapter 5, I cover two areas. First, I explore Hopkins's virtue theory and abolitionist stance. The social and activist thrust of Hopkins's doctrine of disinterested benevolence is highlighted along with evidence of self-regard, correcting exaggerated depictions of Hopkins's idea of complete self-denial. His abolitionism in light of his understanding of disinterested benevolence is also discussed. Second, I provide evidence of Hopkins's congruence with Edwards's ethics. The evidence for congruency is established by demonstrating consistency in meaning from the primary sources.[22] In the end, Edwards's virtue theory was not the issue but Edwards himself.[23] Finally, in the conclusion I provide a synopsis of Hopkins's congruence with Edwards's ethical theology, the tension between Edwards's proslavery stance and Hopkins's abolitionism considering theological agreement, and comments regarding potential areas for further study.

A Note on the Scope of the Study

Scholars who have written on Hopkins have concentrated on different areas of study to understand Hopkins and his thought.[24] David S. Lovejoy probes how Hopkins used religious and theological convictions stemming from the Great Awakening along with Revolutionary ideology to establish a philosophy of equalitarianism, which he used to oppose slavery.[25] Joseph Conforti studies the social and intellectual contexts in order to understand Hopkins for the purpose of reassessing "the standard historical interpretation of the New Divinity movement."[26] Stephen Post also engages in a historical study, concentrating on "the field of American theological ethics" while focusing on Edwards and Hopkins and the issue of self-love.[27] Peter Jauhiainen "examines the convergence of and friction between Reformed theology and

[22]This will be accomplished by analyzing and expositing the pertinent primary source material.

[23]Justice was a natural expression of Christian benevolence for Edwards. The tension arises when looking at Edwards's proslavery stance. Because of social and pragmatic convictions, Edwards failed to apply his doctrine of benevolence to enslaved Africans by condoning institutionalized slavery. It is my contention that he was not fully aware of the wrong he was committing by promoting slavery due to the influences of his social and cultural milieu. Nonetheless, Edwards cannot be absolved of the wrong he committed.

[24]The following is not meant to be an exhaustive list but rather a representation of the different emphases scholars have focused on while studying Hopkins.

[25]Lovejoy, "Samuel Hopkins," 227–43.

[26]Conforti, *Samuel Hopkins and the New Divinity Movement*, vii.

[27]Stephen Garrard Post, *Christian Love and Self-Denial: An Historical and Normative Study of Jonathan Edwards, Samuel Hopkins, and American Theological Ethics* (Lanham: University Press of America, 1987), vii.

Enlightenment philosophy" in Hopkins's writings.[28] While most scholars engage social and religious histories to understand Hopkins's thought, I seek to make a theological contribution.[29] Specifically, the validation of Hopkins's agreement with and use of Edwards's doctrine of benevolence to advocate for the abolition of slavery and the slave trade dictates the parameters of this study.

Conclusion

Claims of Hopkins's departure from Edwards's ethics have been exaggerated due to misrepresentations of their virtue theories. As a result, revisionist views are needed to provide more balanced perspectives for both figures. Both had philosophical, theocentric, and activist commitments in their respective virtue theories. Showing this to be the case and examining their doctrines of benevolence will lead to a view of Hopkins maintaining the inherent integrity of Edwards's ethical theology. Thus, as Hopkins used his doctrine of disinterested benevolence to promote abolitionism, he more consistently applied Edwards's doctrine of benevolence.

[28]Jauhiainen, "An Enlightenment Calvinist," 1.

[29]This is not to say that scholars who have written on Hopkins completely neglect his theology but rather that the primary focus of this study is theological in nature as I examine Edwards's and Hopkins's ethical theologies and show parallels.

Chapter 2: New Divinity, Hopkins, and the Scholarly Context

In this chapter, I first provide an overview of the New Divinity movement to show Hopkins's intellectual and ministerial tradition. Second, pertinent sources are covered. These include: specific primary sources relevant for the study, secondary sources pertaining to Edwards's ethics, works that claim the New Divinity's and Hopkins's departure from Edwards's thought, and revisionist works that evidence activism in Edwards's ethics and Hopkins's agreement with Edwards. Doing so provides the scholarly context for the study, substantiating the need to probe Hopkins's use of Edwards's doctrine of benevolence to evidence congruence.

Introduction to the New Divinity Movement and Hopkins

The New Divinity Movement

The influence of Jonathan Edwards's life and thought was far-reaching on those he served during his time as a pastor. This influence directly shaped the theology of Edwards's immediate heirs, the New Divinity disciples.[1]

[1]Hopkins was part of the "first stage of the New England Theology." This first stage, immediately following Edwards's passing, was mainly represented by Joseph Bellamy (1719–1790) and Nathaniel Emmons (1745–1840) along with Hopkins. Bruce Kuklick, *Churchmen and Philosophers: From Jonathan Edwards to John Dewey* (New Haven, CT: Yale University Press, 1985), 43. For a representative list of early "Edwardseans," see Michael J. McClymond and Gerald R. McDermott, *The Theology of Jonathan Edwards* (New York: Oxford University Press, 2012), 601.

Hopkins was part of a theological movement that was foundational for the transmission of Edwardsean influence. This movement, known as New Divinity theology or "the New England Theology," makes up a distinctly "Edwardsean tradition or school of thought," which finds its origin in Edwards's theology.[2] Specifically, the New England Theology arose from Edwards's life and thought as the New Divinity disciples applied Edwards's theology to meet the needs of a changing social and political environment. Thus, the distinctive traits of the movement stem from certain intellectual, theological, and doctrinal concerns arising from Edwards's thought as their foundation.[3]

The impact of the New Divinity disciples was felt immediately, particularly in the life of the local church. Subsequent to Edwards's passing, the number of New Divinity pastors filling pulpits in New England grew exponentially up to the end of the eighteenth century.[4] As Jauhiainen explains, "Between 1765 and 1783, New Divinity candidates filled half of New England's ministerial vacancies. By 1792, the movement claimed fifty-eight ministers in Connecticut, more than one-third of the state's Congregational clergy, as well as all of its new clerical candidates," contributing to the popularity of the movement.[5] Like Edwards, these New Divinity pastors embraced revivalism and the promotion of pietistic living.[6] In a very real sense, they were Edwardsean apologists of the Great Awakening who "envisioned

[2]Douglas A. Sweeney and Allen C. Guelzo, "Introduction," in *The New England Theology: From Jonathan Edwards to Edwards Amasa Park*, ed. Douglas A. Sweeney and Allen C. Guelzo (Grand Rapids: Baker Academic, 2006), 15, n. 5; Douglas A. Sweeney, *Nathaniel Taylor, New Haven Theology, and the Legacy of Jonathan Edwards* (New York: Oxford University Press, 2003), 7–9. Specifically, New Divinity Theology and "the New England Theology" can be viewed as synonymous. Breitenbach notes, "New Divinity came eventually to be known as the New England Theology." William Breitenbach, "The Consistent Calvinism of the New Divinity Movement," *William and Mary Quarterly* 41 (1984): 244, n. 6.

[3]Oliver D. Crisp and Douglas A. Sweeney, "Introduction," in *After Jonathan Edwards: The Courses of the New England Theology*, ed. Oliver D. Crisp and Douglas A. Sweeney (New York: Oxford University Press, 2012), 1.

[4]David William Kling, *A Field of Divine Wonders: The New Divinity and Village Revivals in Northwestern Connecticut, 1792–1822* (University Park, PA: Pennsylvania State University Press, 1993), 19.

[5]Peter Dan Jauhiainen, "An Enlightenment Calvinist: Samuel Hopkins and the Pursuit of Benevolence" (PhD diss., University of Iowa, 1997), 2. Kling notes, "Samuel Hopkins, a patriarch of the New Divinity movement, calculated that the number of New Divinity clergy grew from a handful in 1756 to nearly fifty in 1773 and by 1797 topped the one hundred mark." Kling, *A Field of Divine Wonders*, 19. For Hopkins's remarks, see Stephen West, ed., *Sketches of the Life of the Late, Rev. Samuel Hopkins, D.D., Pastor of the First Congregational Church in Newport, Written by Himself; Interspersed with Notes Extracted from His Private Diary* (Hartford, CT: Hudson and Goodwin, 1805), 102–3.

[6]Kling, *A Field of Divine Wonders*, 24.

themselves as the guardians of evangelical Calvinism, the self-appointed heirs of Jonathan Edwards."[7]

Not only were the New Divinity disciples committed to promoting revivalism, salvation, and pious living, but theological training as well. They gave themselves to intense theological learning, spending between "thirteen to eighteen hours a day" studying and writing.[8] The emphasis on systematic theology was driven by a desire to train and prepare men well for ministerial service.[9] This desire for proper training of future clerics gave rise to the "schools of the prophets." Educated and trained clergy were highly valued as pastors. They were often the most learned individuals in society. The formal education centers of the day were Yale and Harvard, colleges "designed as clerical training schools" as graduates either continued to attend for additional theological training or sought apprenticeships to study under specific pastors.[10] The personal apprenticeships under New Divinity pastors came to be known as the "schools of the prophets." It became normative "for aspiring clergymen to reside with theoretically inclined ministers. Young men eager to absorb the essence of the religious life and to learn the secrets of the Awakening wanted to sit at the feet of the great revivalist theologians."[11] This resulted in the New Divinity disciples having a reputation for training future pastors.[12]

Moreover, the piety and revivalist emphases stemming from the Great Awakening, which the New Divinity disciples embodied, would prove to be vital for those seeking training from New Divinity men.[13] As a result, those taught were identified "with the clerical values and style that marked the pattern of the New Divinity ministry."[14] The fact that trainees lived with

[7]Kling, *A Field of Divine Wonders*, 25. The first two generations of New Divinity disciples span the approximate years of 1740–1790. The third generation New Divinity men were the leaders of the Second Great Awakening. Kling, *A Field of Divine Wonders*, 24, 26.

[8]Joseph A. Conforti, *Samuel Hopkins and the New Divinity Movement: Calvinism, the Congregational Ministry, and Reform in New England Between the Great Awakenings* (Grand Rapids: Christian University Press, 1981), 36.

[9]Conforti, *Samuel Hopkins and the New Divinity Movement*, 37.

[10]Kuklick, *Churchmen and Philosophers*, 45.

[11]Kuklick, *Churchmen and Philosophers*, 45.

[12]Kuklick, *Churchmen and Philosophers*, 45.

[13]Conforti, *Samuel Hopkins and the New Divinity Movement*, 24.

[14]Conforti, *Samuel Hopkins and the New Divinity Movement*, 25.

their New Divinity mentors certainly aided in the passing on of theological, ministerial, and pietistic concerns.[15]

Being both products and proponents of the Great Awakening, the New Divinity disciples placed priority on the systemization of theological truths for preparatory and apologetic reasons. The analyzing of theological problems would prove to be key in defending the Awakening against Old Light opponents.[16] The Old Lights accused New Divinity or New Light men of dealing with Christian truths in a metaphysical way. Specifically, New Divinity men became known as metaphysicians because of their "desire for consistency," which involved systemization of "biblical and rational truths."[17] Furthermore, Old Light men were against the Awakening due to fear of excessive emotionalism and consequent insincerity of religion. They accused the heirs of Edwards as delving into a "New Divinity" by straying away from the Calvinism embraced by the Old Lights.[18] Contrarily, the New Divinity disciples believed they were faithful heirs of Puritan Calvinism and preferred the title "Consistent Calvinists," embracing a high view of God's sovereignty coupled with human responsibility and the need for immediate repentance from sin.[19]

Concerning church membership, Old Light men advocated open membership to professing adults who lived piously along with their children.[20] New Lights, following Edwards's lead, wanted proof of genuine conversion not only by the testimony of one's life, but also by a genuine profession of faith.[21] The desire was to be a part of a pure church made up of the

[15]Conforti, *Samuel Hopkins and the New Divinity Movement*, 39.

[16]Conforti, *Samuel Hopkins and the New Divinity Movement*, 37. A third group in addition to Old Lights and New Lights is referred to by several different names: moderate Calvinists, old Calvinists, or moderate Old Lights. This third group aligned more with the ecclesial practices of the Old Lights, yet embraced the Puritan, orthodox theology of the New Lights. For concise discussions on this third group, see E. Brooks Holifield, *Theology in America: Christian Thought from the Age of the Puritans to the Civil War* (New Haven, CT: Yale University Press, 2003), 127–28; Mark A. Noll, *Christians in the American Revolution* (Grand Rapids: Christian University Press, 1977), 44.

[17]Holifield, *Theology in America*, 136.

[18]Holifield, *Theology in America*, 127.

[19]Holifield, *Theology in America*, 136.

[20]Holifield, *Theology in America*, 127.

[21]George M. Marsden, *Jonathan Edwards: A Life* (New Haven, CT: Yale University Press, 2003), 347. Specifically, the New Divinity disciples followed Edwards's divergence from his grandfather's (Solomon Stoddard) stance on halfway covenant membership. As Holifield explains, "Old Calvinists tended to like the halfway covenant – some preferred a Stoddardean

regenerate only.[22] Hence they emphasized the need to grow in personal holiness for sin has no place in God's church.

In terms of central theological convictions, the New Divinity disciples embraced certain Calvinist tenets such as the supremacy of God, man's personal responsibility for sin, and the pursuit of personal piety. New Divinity men, like Edwards, embraced the notion of loving God because of who God is.[23] They believed genuine religion is one recognizing the supreme greatness of God and loving God above all things.[24] As E. Brooks Holifield states, "The New Divinity allowed no middle ground between sinners and saints. One either loved God above self or one loved self above God."[25] Because one is either an unbelieving sinner or saved saint, the need for salvation and consequent piety was stressed. And because of man's freedom, the will gave man the opportunity to repent from sin.[26] This idea, Guelzo argues, was consistent with "Edwards's moral absolutism. The New Divinity had already established that, so long as men had wills, there was no natural reason for their not repenting, and likewise no excuse for not doing so at once."[27] Likewise Holifield explains, "the Edwardeans claimed that everyone had a natural ability to repent. Everyone who understood the law had a natural ability to accept it."[28]

This New Divinity understanding of natural necessity versus moral necessity was indebted to Edwards's treatise on the will. In fact, "issues of sovereignty, responsibility, grace, and depravity all found their critical substantive locus in the question of the will's freedom—the most important recurring theme in the literature."[29] Specifically, what Edwards meant by natural necessity is that which involves external force. Edwards explains, "By 'natural necessity,' as applied to men, I mean such necessity as men are under through the force of natural causes; as distinguished from what are

conception of the church – and they normally disregarded any requirement for a narration of conversion as a prelude to membership." Holifield, *Theology in America*, 150.

[22]Holifield, *Theology in America*, 127.

[23]Holifield, *Theology in America*, 137.

[24]Holifield, *Theology in America*, 140.

[25]Holifield, *Theology in America*, 140.

[26]Allen C. Guelzo, *Edwards on the Will: A Century of American Theological Debate* (Middletown, CT: Wesleyan University Press, 1989), 113.

[27]Guelzo, *Edwards on the Will*, 113.

[28]Holifield, *Theology in America*, 142–43.

[29]Kuklick, *Churchmen and Philosophers*, 44.

called moral causes, such as habits and dispositions of the heart, and moral motives and inducements."[30] Edwards goes on to explain that, in distinction to moral necessity, natural necessity does not involve one's choosing, but rather what is naturally experienced as a result of external force, such as the sensation of pain when hurt or sight of an object when in view.[31] Contrarily, moral necessity involves moral choice, making the creature culpable for his actions.[32] The distinction between the two necessities becomes key to recognize that which makes man responsible. Sweeney and Guelzo explain,

> No one under the force of natural necessity can be held morally accountable for what he or she does. But the necessity that arises from people's own inclinations is *moral necessity*. Since no one is actually using force in moral necessity, such people can be held responsible for their actions; in fact, the *greater* the force of an evil inclination on their actions, the *more* accountable they are, precisely because they have all the natural, physical power they need to do otherwise.[33]

Natural and moral necessity, then, leads to Edwards's understanding of natural ability and moral inability. The two distinct positions "was taken up and developed systematically by his immediate disciples, Joseph Bellamy and Samuel Hopkins."[34] Like natural and moral necessity, natural ability is outside one's control due to external realities being forced on the individual whereas moral inability involves personal responsibility. Edwards notes, "We are said to be *naturally* unable to do a thing, when we can't do it if we will, because what is most commonly called nature don't allow of it, or because of some impeding defect or obstacle that is extrinsic to the will; either in the faculty of understanding, constitution of body, or external objects."[35] Moral inability has to do with "the want of inclination; or the strength of a contrary inclination; or the want of sufficient motives in view, to induce or excite the act of the will, or the strength of apparent motives to the contrary."[36]

[30]Jonathan Edwards, *Freedom of the Will*, ed. Paul Ramsey, vol. 1, *The Works of Jonathan Edwards* (New Haven, CT: Yale University Press, 2009), 156–57.

[31]*WJE*, 1:157–58.

[32]Sweeney and Guelzo, "Introduction," 16.

[33]Sweeney and Guelzo, "Introduction," 15–16.

[34]Crisp and Sweeney, "Introduction," 2.

[35]*WJE*, 1:159.

[36]*WJE*, 1:159.

The New Divinity disciples embraced this understanding of natural and moral necessity and natural ability versus moral inability, recognizing man as culpable for his own sin.[37] As Bruce Kuklick notes, "A person indisposed to change a wicked temper was accountable precisely for that reason."[38] One may be unable morally to do the right thing due to a depraved nature, but able naturally to do it, thus being culpable for sins.[39]

The Edwardsean understanding of sin for the New Divinity disciples then encouraged concern for personal holiness and activism.[40] The embrace of revivalism and ensuing potential for salvation pressed the need to live a life of love for God and others, recognizing the Spirit's indwelling and transforming presence. Honoring God by obeying the divine or moral law became a key aspect of the movement and along with it, the need to address societal concerns. Antislavery sentiment grew and abolitionism was embraced. And underlying the need to engage "social and moral reform" was the idea of "disinterested benevolence" and the consequent need to "sacrifice their own interests for the common good."[41]

Samuel Hopkins

Hopkins was a direct descendent of this Edwardsean theological tradition. Like Edwards, the ministry was something that was encouraged early in Hopkins's life.[42] Pushed by his family to choose a career in ministry, Hopkins fulfilled their desires and began preparations by beginning his college education at Yale in 1737.[43] Upon completion of his studies, Edwards delivered the commencement address at the college.[44] Moved from hearing Edwards

[37]Kuklick, *Churchmen and Philosophers*, 55.

[38]Kuklick, *Churchmen and Philosophers*, 55.

[39]Crisp and Sweeney, "Introduction," 2. Edwards's understanding of moral agency and the role of man's will in light of divine sovereignty were foundational for his New Divinity heirs. Breitenbach explains, "Edwards's distinction between natural and moral inability taught Hopkinsians how to reconcile determinism with moral accountability. The advocacy of his theory of moral agency was undoubtedly the most important mark of the New Divinity. These divines invariably insisted that the only barrier to holiness was the sinner's voluntary disinclination to be holy." Breitenbach, "The Consistent Calvinism of the New Divinity Movement," 257.

[40]Guelzo, *Edwards on the Will*, 115.

[41]Mark Valeri, *Law and Providence in Joseph Bellamy's New England: The Origins of the New Divinity in Revolutionary America* (New York: Oxford University Press, 1994), 163.

[42]Conforti, *Samuel Hopkins and the New Divinity Movement*, 20.

[43]Conforti, *Samuel Hopkins and the New Divinity Movement*, 20–21.

[44]Conforti, *Samuel Hopkins and the New Divinity Movement*, 28–29.

preach, Hopkins made a decision to study under Edwards.[45] Thus, in December 1741, Hopkins arrived at the Edwards's residence while Edwards was away "on a preaching tour," being welcomed by Edwards's wife Sarah.[46]

Upon her husband's death from smallpox inoculation in March of 1758, Hopkins received the rest of Edwards's "manuscripts and library" from Sarah according to Edwards's request.[47] Hopkins explains, "Upon the death of Mr. Edwards, Mrs. Edwards, in consequence of verbal directions given to her by Mr. Edwards in his life time, put all his manuscripts and his library into my hands, and care: His manuscripts to be disposed of by me, and two other ministers."[48] Hopkins became familiar with Edwards's writings, making them a central component of his disciplined study. It is not surprising, then, that Edwards's theology would be instrumental for the development of Hopkins's theology, namely his doctrine of disinterested benevolence. According to Hopkins, "As these manuscripts were in my hands a number of years, I paid my chief attention to them, until I had read them all, which consisted of a great number of volumes," committing himself to understanding Edwards's thought.[49] Hopkins continues, "In doing this I had much pleasure and profit. My mind became more engaged in study, rising, great part of my time, at four o'clock in the morning to pursue my study, in which I took great pleasure."[50]

The doctrine of benevolence played a central and extensive role in Hopkins's theology. Jauhiainen views Hopkins's understanding of disinterested

[45]In the midst of the Great Awakening, Hopkins had earlier decided to study under Gilbert Tennent, "the most popular itinerant among Yale students," who ended up preaching "seventeen times at New Haven and raised the extravagances of the revival to new heights." After hearing Edwards's commencement address, Hopkins decided not to study under Tennent but rather to study under Edwards. Conforti, *Samuel Hopkins and the New Divinity Movement*, 26, 29.

[46]Kling, *A Field of Divine Wonders*, 30.

[47]Jauhiainen, "An Enlightenment Calvinist," 6.

[48]West, *Sketches of the Life of the Late, Rev. Samuel Hopkins, D.D., Pastor of the First Congregational Church in Newport, Written by Himself; Interspersed with Notes Extracted from His Private Diary*, 57. The insights of this paragraph on Edwards's death and the primary source reference of Hopkins's subsequent reception of Edwards's manuscripts are a result of reading Jauhianen's brief description of the subject matter discussed. See Jauhiainen, "An Enlightenment Calvinist," 6.

[49]West, *Sketches of the Life of the Late, Rev. Samuel Hopkins, D.D., Pastor of the First Congregational Church in Newport, Written by Himself; Interspersed with Notes Extracted from His Private Diary*, 58.

[50]West, *Sketches of the Life of the Late, Rev. Samuel Hopkins, D.D., Pastor of the First Congregational Church in Newport, Written by Himself; Interspersed with Notes Extracted from His Private Diary*, 58.

benevolence as a uniting element for other areas of his theology. Jauhiainen argues, the "notion of 'disinterested benevolence' was the linchpin of his theology, linking together the other parts of his system. It was central to his understanding of God, providence, sin, grace, holiness, and eschatology, and provided a powerful catalyst for social reform in the latter part of his clerical career."[51] Especially important for Hopkins was a selfless and sacrificial love that extended itself to meet the needs of the marginalized. As a result of his doctrine of disinterested benevolence, Hopkins's "theological concerns became focused on social reform" during the latter years of his life when pastoring the "First Congregational Church of Newport, Rhode Island."[52] In Newport Hopkins experienced firsthand the cruel nature of the slave trade and began to develop his fervent abolitionism.

Scholars continue to portray a divergence or betrayal thesis of Hopkins from Edwards. Yet recent revisionist accounts have concluded otherwise. For example, Jauhianen asserts how Hopkins in his theology "simply repeated or drew out the implications of ideas already present in Edwards's theology and the Reformed tradition."[53] A mapping of the scholarly context shows the need for additional revisionist work. Mark Noll perpetuates a classic view of Hopkinsian activism and Edwardsean aesthetics by claiming difference via Hopkins's social concern and Edwards's lack thereof.[54] David Kling, like Noll, claims Hopkins differed from Edwards's "aesthetic concept" of benevolence.[55] Yet a broader understanding of Edwards's doctrine of benevolence clearly indicates activist stimuli. Likewise, Holifield asserts that Hopkins "departed from Edwards by linking love and law in the fashion of Bellamy and by defining all sin as selfishness. His argument was that both reason and revelation defined holiness as disinterested benevolence."[56] While it is true that Hopkins united selfless love to the divine or moral law, Edwards

[51]Jauhiainen, "An Enlightenment Calvinist," 4.

[52]Joseph A. Conforti, "Samuel Hopkins and the New Divinity: Theology, Ethics, and Social Reform in Eighteenth-Century New England," *William and Mary Quarterly* 34, no. 4 (1977): 572–73.

[53]Jauhiainen, "An Enlightenment Calvinist," 7.

[54]Mark A. Noll, *America's God: From Jonathan Edwards to Abraham Lincoln* (New York: Oxford University Press, 2002), 271, 274.

[55]Kling, *A Field of Divine Wonders*, 26.

[56]Holifield, *Theology in America*, 140.

similarly pointed to the moral law as exemplifying disinterested love. Again, an expanded view of Edwards's doctrine of benevolence is needed.[57]

Primary Sources

The Works of Samuel Hopkins contains the material for Hopkins's theology.[58] This three-volume work includes Hopkins's *System of Doctrines* (1793) along with a number of discourses, sermons, letters, and biography of Hopkins by Edwards Amasa Park.[59] Hopkins's systematic work is recognized as "the most influential eighteenth-century American system of theology."[60] So influential was Hopkins's work that many viewed the New Divinity as promoting "Hopkinsianism."[61] Specifically, *System of Doctrines* is a work dependent on Edwards's theology and foundational for New Divinity theology.[62] Therefore, probing Hopkins's ethical thought delineates his application of Edwards's ethical theology, providing evidence of congruence.

[57]This section is not meant to elucidate key points of each work but to provide the reader with a general understanding of key arguments in preparation for chapters 4-5. Specifically, the intention is to provide an overview of why the specific primary works are significant for the study at hand, the scholarly context/discussion of views promoting Hopkins's departure from Edwards, and recent revisionist accounts of each figure.

[58]Samuel Hopkins, *The Works of Samuel Hopkins, D.D.*, 3 vols. (Boston: Doctrinal Tract and Book Society, 1854).

[59]William Breitenbach, "Piety and Moralism: Edwards and the New Divinity," in *Jonathan Edwards and the American Experience*, ed. Nathan O. Hatch and Harry S. Stout (New York: Oxford University Press, 1988), 190–95.

[60]Jauhiainen, "An Enlightenment Calvinist," 6.

[61]Holifield, *Theology in America*, 136.

[62]Noll, *America's God*, 269–70. In discussing the impact of Hopkins's *System of Doctrines*, Jauhiainen notes, "Hopkins's monumental, eleven-hundred page *System of Doctrines*, published in 1793, codified New Divinity teachings . . . His *System* provided the foundation for the theological training of future Edwardsian ministers and set the intellectual agenda for 'almost all theological development in New England for more than half a century.' " Peter Dan Jauhiainen, "Samuel Hopkins and Hopkinsianism," in *After Jonathan Edwards: The Courses of the New England Theology*, ed. Oliver Crisp and Douglas A. Sweeney (New York: Oxford University Press, 2012), 107.

For Edwards, a number of works are relevant for the topic of this study.[63] In particular, *Ethical Writings* deals directly with Edwards's ethics.[64] The volume contains three works: a sermon series *CF*, and two dissertations titled *CEW* and *TV*. In *CF*, Edwards discusses the nature of Christian love and the results of genuine religion. In *CEW*, Edwards establishes God as the original and most excellent being and source of true piety. And in *TV*, Edwards discusses the essence of genuine virtue along with his concept of "benevolence to Being in general." Collectively, the three works are representative of Edwards's ethical theology.[65] *CF* is a key resource to better understand Edwards's meaning of charity or benevolence, expanding the definition often given by scholars when analyzing Edwards's doctrine of benevolence to Being in general in *TV*. As far as the *Two Dissertations*,

[63]Jonathan Edwards, *Freedom of the Will*, ed. Paul Ramsey, vol. 1, *The Works of Jonathan Edwards* (New Haven, CT: Yale University Press, 2009); Jonathan Edwards, *Religious Affections*, ed. John E. Smith, vol. 2, *The Works of Jonathan Edwards* (New Haven, CT: Yale University Press, 2009); Jonathan Edwards, *Original Sin*, ed. Clyde A. Holbrook, vol. 3, *The Works of Jonathan Edwards* (New Haven, CT: Yale University Press, 1970); Jonathan Edwards, *The Great Awakening*, ed. C. C. Goen, vol. 4, *The Works of Jonathan Edwards* (New Haven, CT: Yale University Press, 2009); Jonathan Edwards, *Ethical Writings*, ed. Paul Ramsey, vol. 8, *The Works of Jonathan Edwards* (New Haven, CT: Yale University Press, 1989); Jonathan Edwards, *Sermons and Discourses, 1720–1723*, ed. Wilson H. Kimnach, vol. 10, *The Works of Jonathan Edwards* (New Haven, CT: Yale University Press, 1992); Jonathan Edwards, *Sermons and Discourses, 1723–1729*, ed. Kenneth P. Minkema, vol. 14, *The Works of Jonathan Edwards* (New Haven, CT: Yale University Press, 1997); Jonathan Edwards, *Sermons and Discourses, 1730–1733*, ed. Mark Valeri, vol. 17, *The Works of Jonathan Edwards* (New Haven, CT: Yale University Press, 1999); Jonathan Edwards, *Sermons and Discourses, 1734–1738*, ed. M. X. Lesser, vol. 19, *The Works of Jonathan Edwards* (New Haven, CT: Yale University Press, 2001); Jonathan Edwards, *Sermons and Discourses, 1739–1742*, ed. John E. Smith, vol. 22, *The Works of Jonathan Edwards* (New Haven, CT: Yale University Press, 2003); Jonathan Edwards, *Sermons and Discourses, 1743–1758*, ed. Wilson H. Kimnach, vol. 25, *The Works of Jonathan Edwards* (New Haven, CT: Yale University Press, 2006); Jonathan Edwards, *The "Miscellanies," a-500*, ed. Thomas A. Schafer, vol. 13, *The Works of Jonathan Edwards* (New Haven, CT: Yale University Press, 1994); Jonathan Edwards, *The "Miscellanies," 501-832*, ed. Ava Chamberlain, vol. 18, *The Works of Jonathan Edwards* (New Haven, CT: Yale University Press, 2000); Jonathan Edwards, *The "Miscellanies," 833-1152*, ed. Amy Plantinga Pauw, vol. 20, *The Works of Jonathan Edwards* (New Haven, CT: Yale University Press, 2002); Jonathan Edwards, *The "Miscellanies," 1153-1360*, ed. Douglas A. Sweeney, vol. 23, *The Works of Jonathan Edwards* (New Haven, CT: Yale University Press, 2004)

[64]As Smith notes, *Ethical Writings* contains the three essential works on "Edwards's views concerning the nature of divine love or charity and his conception of a virtuous or holy life," thus being representative of Edwards's ethical theology. John E. Smith, *Jonathan Edwards: Puritan, Preacher, Philosopher* (Notre Dame: University of Notre Dame Press, 1992), 100.

[65]This is the case given that the *CF* sermons expand the definition of benevolence found in the *Two Dissertations*. Of course, additional sermons and miscellany entries that discuss various aspects of Christian love help provide a more robust account of Edwards's doctrine of benevolence.

Edwards's intention was for them to be read together, as "one is the mirror image of the other; the 'end' for which God created the world must be the 'end' of a truly virtuous and holy life."[66]

Religious Affections is another key source for understanding Edwards's ethical thought. In light of the eighteenth century revivals in New England, Edwards sets out to distinguish true from false religion.[67] He asserts, "True religion, in great part, consists in holy affections."[68] Specifically, Edwards's goal is to argue for the revivals as "a genuine work of the divine Spirit."[69] Therefore it is imperative that affections are present in order to validate that it is truly the work of the Spirit.[70] The presence of affections was important for Edwards because he believed there were aspects of both good and evil in the revivals.[71] John E. Smith notes, "In the *Affections* he was anxious to center attention on the gracious activity of the Spirit in the *individual* soul."[72] Love plays a foundational role in understanding the nature of genuine religion. Edwards explains, "The essence of all true religion lies in holy love; and that in this divine affection, and an habitual disposition to it, and that light which is the foundation of it, and those things which are the fruits of it, consists the whole of religion."[73] Edwards goes on to state that love "is the first and chief of the affections, and the fountain of all the affections."[74] Because the ability to love both God and neighbor requires the work of the Spirit, an internal change is required.[75] Only then will genuine religion be present and express itself "in the affections and in the fruits of the Spirit," the chief of which is practice.[76]

[66]Paul Ramsey, "Editor's Introduction," in *Ethical Writings*, vol. 8, *The Works of Jonathan Edwards* (New Haven, CT: Yale University Press, 1989), 5.

[67]John E. Smith, "Editor's Introduction," in *A Treatise Concerning Religious Affections*, vol. 2, *The Works of Jonathan Edwards* (New Haven, CT: Yale University Press, 1959), 1.

[68]*WJE,* 2:95.

[69]*WJE*, 2:5.

[70]*WJE*, 2:8.

[71]*WJE*, 2:10.

[72]*WJE*, 2:11.

[73]*WJE,* 2:107.

[74]*WJE,* 2:108.

[75]*WJE*, 2:51.

[76]*WJE*, 2:51–52.

Works on Edwards's Ethics

The different interpretations of Edwards's virtue theory show the diversity of emphases scholars have placed on his ethical writings, such as beauty, philosophy, and implications for contemporary ethical concerns.[77] William J. Danaher helpfully points out how Perry Miller in *Jonathan Edwards* (1949) viewed *TV* as a source that recapitulated "his earlier writings."[78] Following Miller's lead, many scholars have viewed *TV* as an interpretive key for understanding Edwards's ethics holistically. Danaher explains, "With some modification, recent commentators concur with this assessment and confer upon *True Virtue* the status of paradigm text, treating it as a Rosetta stone that renders Edwards's theological ethics comprehensible."[79] As a result, scholars have incorrectly viewed *TV* as a complete representation of Edwards's ethical thought. Paul Ramsey highlights the problem, asserting that interpretations of *TV* stemming from an isolated reading "have fostered inadequate and even quite mistaken understandings of his ethical writings."[80]

For Miller, *TV* contained not merely "a reasoning about virtue but a beholding of it."[81] He seems to view *TV* as the primary text for properly understanding Edwards's ethical theology. Danaher, discussing Miller's view, explains how the *Two Dissertations* are foundational from which "one must fit Edwards's other moral writings."[82] He refers to Miller's understanding of what would have been Edwards's magnum opus had he lived to complete it. Regarding that great work, the *Two Dissertations* according to Miller, contains

[77]I have been guided to resources on Edwards's ethics by the secondary source references given in particular by Danaher, Wilson, and Ramsey. See William J. Danaher, "Beauty, Benevolence, and Virtue in Jonathan Edwards's The Nature of True Virtue," *Journal of Religion* 87, no. 3 (2007): 386–87; Stephen A. Wilson, *Virtue Reformed: Rereading Jonathan Edwards's Ethics* (Boston: Brill, 2005), 1–12; *WJE*, 8:6, n. 5.

[78]Danaher, "Beauty, Benevolence, and Virtue in Jonathan Edwards's *The Nature of True Virtue*," 386. The impact of Miller's influence for Edwardsean scholarship is significant. He is recognized as one who restored Edwards and his writings as important areas of scholarly inquiry. Jensen explains, "It was Perry Miller's virtuosic *Jonathan Edwards* which in 1949 inspired the contemporary rediscovery of Edwards." Robert W. Jenson, *America's Theologian: A Recommendation of Jonathan Edwards* (New York: Oxford University Press, 1992), vii.

[79]Danaher, "Beauty, Benevolence, and Virtue in Jonathan Edwards's *The Nature of True Virtue*," 386.

[80]*WJE*, 8:6.

[81]Perry Miller, *Jonathan Edwards* (1949; repr., Lincoln, NE: Bison Books, 2005), 286.

[82]William J. Danaher, *The Trinitarian Ethics of Jonathan Edwards* (Louisville, KY: Westminster John Knox, 2004), 218.

"the heart of it," though in condensed form.[83] Ramsey notes that Miller treats the *Two Dissertations* independently, subordinating *CEW* to *TV*.[84] Ramsey explains that in the end, Miller "fails to acknowledge that the treatises were complementary elements of a larger, unified theological-ethical reflection."[85] Given the aesthetic motif and lack of scriptural interaction in *TV*, Miller indeed seems to place priority on *TV* as he believes, for Edwards, "the definition of the ethical is beauty."[86] Thus, what is emphasized is the notion of Edwards's ethics as philosophically oriented.

William Clebsch claims that in *TV* Edwards was non-theological and non-scriptural in his understanding of ethics. Rather his interpretation was aesthetic in nature.[87] He goes on to assert how Edwards translates "the language of religion" to "the language of morality," pointing again to a departure of theology towards aesthetics.[88] It is an example of an errant interpretation of Edwards's virtue theory due to interpreting *TV* independently. Ramsey makes the point, helpfully indicating how Clebsch "mentions *End of Creation* only once, in a listing of the topics to which JE turned his attention in Stockbridge."[89]

While Roland Delattre, aligning himself with Ramsey, views the *Two Dissertations* along with the *CF* sermons as the most important texts for understanding Edwards's theological ethics, he seems to place priority on the *Two Dissertations* by emphasizing the role of aesthetics in Edwards's virtue theory.[90] Specifically for Delattre, the role of beauty is key in order to understand not only Edwards's ethics rightly, but his theology overall. Delattre explains, "Edwards was convinced that beauty is the reality in terms of which the Divine Being and the moral and religious life of human beings as well as the order of the universal system of being, both moral and natural,

[83]Miller, *Jonathan Edwards*, 285.

[84]*WJE*, 8:6, n. 5.

[85]*WJE*, 8:6, n. 5.

[86]Miller, *Jonathan Edwards*, 290.

[87]William A. Clebsch, *American Religious Thought: A History* (Chicago: University of Chicago Press, 1973), 49–50.

[88]Clebsch, *American Religious Thought*, 50.

[89]*WJE*, 8:6, n. 5.

[90]Roland A. Delattre, "The Theological Ethics of Jonathan Edwards: An Homage to Paul Ramsey," *Journal of Religious Ethics* 19, no. 2 (1991): 72.

can best be understood."[91] Moreover, beauty is the most important of all the perfections or attributes of God.[92] It is "by his beauty that he is primarily distinguished as God."[93] Everything "is to be loved in proportion to its being and beauty, i.e., according to its relationship to God."[94] Hence recognition of divine beauty is foundational for genuine virtue, for one participates in the very beauty of God and his activity in the world as he is united to God in fellowship.[95] This participation in God and his ongoing activity in the world is only possible by man responding to God's beauty, establishing the theocentric character of Edwards's virtue theory.[96]

Spohn, like Delattre, highlights aesthetics as a major theme in Edwards's ethics, yet emphasizes as well the role of love and integration of morality and religion. One lives morally as he loves God and participates in God's beauty.[97] Spohn views the *Two Dissertations* as integral components, together providing both the philosophical and theological foundations for Edwards's "metaethical reflections on the nature of beauty, its foundation in God, and its comprehensive ordering of the moral life towards consent to God."[98] Thus, Spohn affirms the need to read the *Two Dissertations* together, viewing them "as parts of a single argument which holds that the love of God is the necessary context for all truly moral acts and that morality finds its proper ground and fulfillment in authentic religion."[99] By reading the *Two Dissertations* as complementary, Spohn disagrees with past claims that view Edwards as retreating from theology in his ethics based upon independent

[91]Roland A. Delattre, *Beauty and Sensibility in the Thought of Jonathan Edwards: An Essay in Aesthetics and Theological Ethics* (New Haven, CT: Yale University Press, 1968), 1.

[92]Roland A. Delattre, "Beauty and Theology: A Reappraisal of Jonathan Edwards," *Soundings: An Interdisciplinary Journal* 51, no. 1 (1968): 67.

[93]Delattre, "Beauty and Theology," 67. Delattre states, "It was Edwards's view that fullness of being and beauty is what most distinguishes God from everything and everyone else, and that the beauty of God consists in the fullness of God's love and joy, or holiness and delight." Roland A. Delattre, "Religious Ethics Today: Jonathan Edwards, H. Richard Niebuhr, and Beyond," in *Edwards in Our Time: Jonathan Edwards and the Shaping of American Religion* (Grand Rapids: Eerdmans, 1999), 71.

[94]Delattre, "Religious Ethics Today," 70.

[95]Delattre, "Religious Ethics Today," 69.

[96]Roland A. Delattre, "Aesthetics and Ethics: Jonathan Edwards and the Recovery of Aesthetics for Religious Ethics," *Journal of Religious Ethics* 31, no. 2 (2003): 278–79.

[97]William C. Spohn, "Sovereign Beauty: Jonathan Edwards and the Nature of True Virtue," *Theological Studies* 42, no. 3 (1981): 399, 401, 409.

[98]Spohn, "Sovereign Beauty," 401.

[99]Spohn, "Sovereign Beauty," 395.

interpretations of *TV*. Yet what is missing for Spohn is interaction with Edwards's broader corpus beyond the *CF* sermons, which deals intentionally with Edwards's understanding of benevolence.[100]

Holbrook contrasts theological objectivism from subjectivism; man finding moral potentiality in God for the former and moral potentiality in himself for the latter.[101] Edwards's theocentric foundation clearly places him in the objectivist camp according to Holbrook's scheme. Like Delattre and Spohn, Holbrook views Edwards's understanding of beauty as directly related to genuine virtue, which finds its origin in God himself.[102] While Holbrook does treat the practical outworking of Edwards's ethics, *TV* is the seminal text he uses in order to exposit Edwards's virtue theory, particularly as it relates to Edwards's aesthetic reflection.

Norman Fiering analyzes Edwards's interaction with eighteenth century British moral philosophers and the ensuing impact on his moral thought. He views *TV* as Edwards's "most comprehensive statement on ethics," recognizing in it both "synthetic" and "critical" ethics.[103] Danaher claims that Fiering uses *TV* "as an independent work of moral philosophy."[104] Similarly, Ramsey comments that "Fiering's book concentrates on Edwards' moral philosophy," separating it from his moral theology.[105] This is made clear by recognizing one of Fiering's goals in writing the book: to avoid Edwards's "theological views" in order to "read Edwards in the context of British and Continental moral philosophy" with the goal to "trace his thought developmentally."[106] Moreover, Fiering claims, "Edwards's dissertation on *The Nature of True Virtue* is about God to be sure, but it is an extraordinary fact that Scripture is never cited in the work, nor does Edwards draw on the theological tradition

[100] See also William C. Spohn, "Union and Consent with the Great Whole: Jonathan Edwards on True Virtue," *Annual of the Society of Christian Ethics* 5 (1985): 19–32.

[101] Clyde A. Holbrook, *The Ethics of Jonathan Edwards: Morality and Aesthetics* (Ann Arbor: University of Michigan Press, 1973), 3.

[102] Holbrook, *The Ethics of Jonathan Edwards*, 97–160.

[103] Norman Fiering, *Jonathan Edwards's Moral Thought and Its British Context* (Chapel Hill: University of North Carolina Press, 1981), 322.

[104] Danaher, "Beauty, Benevolence, and Virtue in Jonathan Edwards's *The Nature of True Virtue*," 386.

[105] *WJE*, 8:6, n. 5.

[106] Fiering, *Jonathan Edwards's Moral Thought and Its British Context*, 11, 12.

for support."[107] Because the scriptural and theological support are found in *CEW*, Fiering shows that he is reading *TV* independently.[108]

Fiering's priority on Edwards's understanding of metaphysics seems to validate the claim. In referring to *TV*, Fiering notes, "With scarcely a reference to the Gospel or to any conventional religious authority, Edwards attempted through force of metaphysical reasoning alone to shift the whole scale of moral valuation that had become established in his day."[109] He goes on to mention that "the combination of a rationally derived metaphysics of morals and an acute critique of the presumptions of natural morality" are what gives *TV* "its permanent stature."[110] Yet by separating Edwards's philosophy from his theology, Fiering "tends to obscure JE's extraordinary confidence that the truths of faith and of reason are *one*."[111]

Stephen Wilson examines the diverse influences upon Edwards's ethical thought. He identifies historic Calvinism and the moral sense philosophy with which Edwards disagreed as significant areas.[112] Specifically, Wilson sees a clear "Edwardsean balance of Calvinism and the moral sense," indicating an embrace of both theocentrism and philosophy in Edwards's ethical thought.[113] He points to Douglas Elwood's 1960 work on Edwards's philosophical theology as an early revisionist treatment to reunite Edwards the theologian and Edwards the philosopher, a task affirmed by Ramsey, representing a consensus opinion among Edwards scholars today.[114] Both Wilson and Jean Porter believe it can be misguiding to interpret *TV* "in isolation from Edwards's wider corpus, including especially the companion treatise, *The End for Which God Created the World*."[115] Yet they use *TV* as the

[107] Fiering, *Jonathan Edwards's Moral Thought and Its British Context*, 9. This quote was identified in Ramsey's introduction. See Ramsey, "Editor's Introduction," 6, n. 5.

[108] *WJE*, 8:6, n. 5.

[109] Fiering, *Jonathan Edwards's Moral Thought and Its British Context*, 361.

[110] Fiering, *Jonathan Edwards's Moral Thought and Its British Context*, 361.

[111] *WJE*, 8:6, n. 5.

[112] Stephen A. Wilson, "Jonathan Edwards's Virtue: Diverse Sources, Multiple Meanings, and the Lessons of History for Ethics," *Journal of Religious Ethics* 31, no. 2 (2003): 201.

[113] Wilson, "Jonathan Edwards's Virtue," 222.

[114] Wilson, "Jonathan Edwards's Virtue," 201; Douglas J. Elwood, *The Philosophical Theology of Jonathan Edwards* (New York: Columbia University Press, 1960), 3; Ramsey, "Editor's Introduction," 11.

[115] Stephen A. Wilson and Jean Porter, "Taking the Measure of Jonathan Edwards for Contemporary Religious Ethics," *Journal of Religious Ethics* 31, no. 2 (2003): 185.

primary text to delimit Edwards's understanding of aesthetics, benevolence, and overall virtue theory.[116]

Michael McClymond similarly sees the integration of moral sense philosophy and Calvinism in Edwards's ethics. Discussing the area of spiritual perception in Edwards's thought, McClymond seeks to show how Edwards synthesized Puritan and Enlightenment thought.[117] Regarding the impact of eighteenth century moral sense philosophy, McClymond asserts that Edwards "assimilated key elements of the new thought and yet preserved much of the Puritan legacy."[118] He views the *Two Dissertations* as "the most important study of ethics" within the Edwardsean corpus, pointing out the scholarly tendency to elevate *TV* while overlooking *CEW*.[119] This is unfortunate in light of the *Two Dissertations* together being "part of an apologetic effort in response to eighteenth-century moral philosophy."[120] Because Edwards used the *Two Dissertations* in order to defend Calvinist views of God from growing natural moralistic sentiment, he intentionally used anthropomorphic language to accomplish his ends.[121] As McClymond puts it, "The only way for Edwards to vindicate God as ethical in the eighteenth-century context was to portray God as more human and more humane than his Puritan predecessors had done."[122] By focusing on the apologetic concerns that Edwards had while opposing the growing humanistic ethics of his day, McClymond concentrates solely on the *Two Dissertations* in discussing Edwards's ethical thought, in particular *CEW*. Moreover, McClymond says, "Edwards's ethics in the *Two Dissertations* is based on ontology," thus viewing the nature of Edwards's ethics as primarily philosophical as Edwards interacted with philosophes such as Shaftesbury and Hutcheson.[123] Consequently, the role of benevolence in Edwards's ethics is sparsely treated by McClymond.

[116]Wilson and Porter, "Taking the Measure of Jonathan Edwards for Contemporary Religious Ethics," 185–90; Jean Porter, "Virtue Ethics," in *The Cambridge Companion to Christian Ethics*, ed. Robin Gill (Cambridge: Cambridge University Press, 2001), 104.

[117]Michael J. McClymond, *Encounters with God: An Approach to the Theology of Jonathan Edwards* (New York: Oxford University Press, 1998), 4.

[118]McClymond, *Encounters with God*, 51.

[119]McClymond, *Encounters with God*, 51–52.

[120]McClymond, *Encounters with God*, 52.

[121]McClymond, *Encounters with God*, 52, 58–59.

[122]McClymond, *Encounters with God*, 58.

[123]McClymond, *Encounters with God*, 54.

Bruce Davidson interprets Edwards's ethics as "radically theocentric," which he believes had a profound affect on Edwards's understanding of self-love.[124] Edwards viewed divine self-love as supreme compared to "all other loves."[125] Moreover, Davidson points out how for Edwards, love corresponds with holiness. Specifically, genuine Christian love includes holiness, as God is the origin of love.[126] Hence, holy love will naturally include "moral purity."[127] Given the divine origin of love, while the believer is to love both God and man, Davidson perpetuates the claim of Edwards's lack of social concern because of his theocentric commitments.[128] Davidson states, "The heavenly-mindedness of holy love would appear to imply limited concern for promoting this-worldly social justice schemes."[129] He additionally says, "Edwards defined love more as the experience of communion with others than as self-sacrifice and self-giving."[130] Consequently, Davidson's statement about the lack of Christian love in the world makes sense: "Edwards reminds us that the world is not the place to find a viable model of Christian love."[131] While Davidson looks beyond *TV* in order to comprehend Edwards's virtue theory, he portrays an Edwards who lacked activism in his ethics.[132]

Danaher not only affirms the need to read *TV* within Edwards's broader ethical corpus, but also identifies the need to probe Edwards's understanding of benevolence. He argues, "The *Two Dissertations* are best viewed as an apologetical effort" as opposed to views which promote the works as "a comprehensive account of Edwards's theological ethics."[133] Specifically, Danaher recognizes clear theocentrism in Edwards's ethics by analyzing

[124]Bruce W. Davidson, "The Four Faces of Self-Love in the Theology of Jonathan Edwards," *Journal of the Evangelical Theological Society* 51, no. 1 (2008): 88.

[125]Davidson, "The Four Faces of Self-Love in the Theology of Jonathan Edwards," 89.

[126]Bruce W. Davidson, "Not from Ourselves: Holy Love in the Theology of Jonathan Edwards," *Journal of the Evangelical Theological Society* 59, no. 3 (2016): 572, 576.

[127]Davidson, "Not from Ourselves," 578, 581.

[128]Davidson, "Not from Ourselves," 575.

[129]Davidson, "Not from Ourselves," 577.

[130]Davidson, "The Four Faces of Self-Love in the Theology of Jonathan Edwards," 91.

[131]Davidson, "Not from Ourselves," 584.

[132]In regards to looking beyond *TV*, Davidson interacts with the concept of love in the *CF* sermons. Davidson, "Not from Ourselves: Holy Love in the Theology of Jonathan Edwards," 575. He also views *TV* as a "companion piece" to *CEW*. Davidson, "The Four Faces of Self-Love in the Theology of Jonathan Edwards," 91.

[133]Danaher, *The Trinitarian Ethics of Jonathan Edwards*, 219.

how "Edwards's Trinitarian thought is indispensible for understanding the ethics of love he articulates in the *Two Dissertations*."[134] Danaher elaborates, "We can only appreciate the compelling nature of Edwards's ethics of love once we are cognizant of the Trinitarianism from which it derives."[135] Given that Edwards was responding to proponents of British moral sense philosophy, Danaher asserts, "Edwards underplays his Trinitarian commitments and develops arguments that operate from common philosophical assumptions."[136] As a result, for Danaher, the philosophical nature of the works due to Edwards's polemic against British moral sense philosophy cancels the *Two Dissertations* as a full representation of Edwards's ethical thought.[137] What is needed is a more thorough account of Edwards's understanding of benevolence, particularly as it relates to his Trinitarian thought.

Elizabeth Cochran identifies several aspects of Edwards's ethics that find their center in God. By identifying "creaturely virtues" in Edwards's ethics, Cochran recognizes humility as a "creaturely excellence" that finds its meaning in a Christological framework for Edwards's virtue theory.[138] The incarnation plays a key role as Christ exemplifies both creaturely humility and divine benevolence.[139] The unity "between love and humility" found in Christ is expressed in "Edwards's account of condescension, a divine virtue that functions as a counterpart to humility in humans."[140] Therefore, humility, as Edwards understands it, "can be understood as an image or type of divine mercy."[141] Cochran also identifies a number of Stoic motifs in Edwards's ethics. She recognizes three specific elements that shed light on parallels with Stoic thought: An "equating of virtue with consent to a benevolent providence, a conception of virtue as a singular and transformative good, and a notion of moral formation as a receptive process."[142] As a result, Cochran argues that Stoic thought can be a useful area of study for moral

[134]Danaher, *The Trinitarian Ethics of Jonathan Edwards*, 201.

[135]Danaher, *The Trinitarian Ethics of Jonathan Edwards*, 202.

[136]Danaher, *The Trinitarian Ethics of Jonathan Edwards*, 219.

[137]Danaher, *The Trinitarian Ethics of Jonathan Edwards*, 219–20.

[138]Elizabeth A. Cochran, "Creaturely Virtues in Jonathan Edwards: The Significance of Christology for the Moral Life," *Journal of the Society of Christian Ethics* 27, no. 2 (2007): 73.

[139]Cochran, "Creaturely Virtues in Jonathan Edwards," 74.

[140]Cochran, "Creaturely Virtues in Jonathan Edwards," 74.

[141]Cochran, "Creaturely Virtues in Jonathan Edwards," 74.

[142]Elizabeth A. Cochran, "Consent, Conversion, and Moral Formation: Stoic Elements in Jonathan Edwards's Ethics," *Journal of Religious Ethics* 39, no. 4 (2011): 624.

insights in line with Edwards's theological heritage.[143] Cochran further expounds on the idea of received virtues by identifying God as foundational for properly interpreting Edwards's virtue theory.[144] Specifically, "Humans receive the virtues only through participation in the being of a God who is inherently good."[145] This participation in God both highlights a dependence on God for virtue while also maintaining human responsibility as morally responsible creatures.[146]

Ki Joo Choi aims to reevaluate Edwards's virtue theory in light of what he refers to as "the motif of vision or perception."[147] In light of treating the first dissertation as a "theological prerequisite to *True Virtue*," Choi argues that genuine virtue for Edwards calls for a simultaneous love for God and neighbor rather than a "sequential ordering of loves."[148] Because the indwelling work of the Spirit is the basis for a person's "thinking and doing," the creature has divine love within and consequently, directs his love to God and his neighbor at the same time.[149] This is possible because one is given a "spiritual sense" or perception by the work of the Holy Spirit within the individual.[150] Without this new perception as a "moral prerequisite," love for one's neighbor will be natural at best.[151]

Given that the "theological outline of *End of Creation* underwrites *True Virtue's* basic claim that Christian virtue consists in love to God and love to neighbor in strict unity," the *Two Dissertations* need to be read together.[152] Choi aligns with Danaher's argument that the *Two Dissertations* cannot be representative of Edwards's ethics due to the philosophical nature of both works as Edwards was refuting "Hutchesons's account of naturalized

[143] Cochran, "Consent, Conversion, and Moral Formation," 624.

[144] Cochran, *Receptive Human Virtues: A New Reading of Jonathan Edwards's Ethics* (University Park, PA: Penn State University Press, 2011), 2.

[145] Cochran, *Receptive Human Virtues*, 8.

[146] Cochran, *Receptive Human Virtues*, 11–12.

[147] Ki Joo Choi, "The Role of Perception in Jonathan Edwards's Moral Thought: The Nature of True Virtue Reconsidered," *Journal of Religious Ethics* 38, no. 2 (2010): 269.

[148] Choi, "The Role of Perception in Jonathan Edwards's Moral Thought," 270.

[149] Choi, "The Role of Perception in Jonathan Edwards's Moral Thought," 277, 272.

[150] Choi, "The Role of Perception in Jonathan Edwards's Moral Thought," 276.

[151] Choi, "The Role of Perception in Jonathan Edwards's Moral Thought," 291.

[152] Choi, "The Role of Perception in Jonathan Edwards's Moral Thought," 272.

ethics."[153] If read as a complete representation of Edwards's ethics, Edwards's ethical theology is in danger of being misrepresented.[154] What is needed is interaction with additional works that supplement the *Two Dissertations*, such as writings that discuss the role of the mind in Edwards's virtue theory.[155]

Conclusion to Works on Edwards's Ethics

In the end, the need for a more comprehensive understanding of Edwards's ethics is made clear due to the narrow, philosophical nature of *TV*. Given Elwood's contribution (1960) of rejoining Edwards's theology with his philosophy from the rehabilitating work by Miller (1949) who portrayed Edwards as a modern philosopher, the scholarly consensus is to keep Edwards's theological convictions with his philosophical thought.[156] Ramsey puts it well when he explains how "it is a grave error, now or ever, to separate Edwards' philosophy from his theology, or his moral philosophy from his theological ethics."[157] Instead what is needed is to "comprehend Edwards' ethics whole and entire and appreciate the integrity of internally related concepts," which also includes works that expand Edwards's concept of benevolence, such as the *CF* sermons.[158] Yet as surveyed, recognizing the conviction to hold Edwards's theology and philosophy together, scholars have historically treated the *Two Dissertations*, *TV* in particular, as representative of Edwards's ethics as a whole. As a result, more attention is needed on the virtue and role of benevolence in Edwards's ethical thought beyond the philosophical nature

[153]Choi, "The Role of Perception in Jonathan Edwards's Moral Thought," 273.

[154]Choi explains that "relying singularly on the *Two Dissertations* for a systematic account of Edwards's ethics can too easily lead to a distorted or incomplete view of his notion of virtue. Inasmuch as the *Two Dissertations* is perhaps the most familiar of Edwards's ethical writings (Ramsey 1989, 5-6), it is appropriate that we begin our inquiry with this work. However, claims to it as Edwards's most comprehensive statement on ethics need qualification as attested by the question of moral agency this text raises (see also Danaher 2007)." Choi, "The Role of Perception in Jonathan Edwards's Moral Thought," 273, n. 2.

[155]Choi, "The Role of Perception in Jonathan Edwards's Moral Thought," 273–75.

[156]In noting Miller's portrayal of Edwards, McClymond and McDermott state, "Perry Miller's Edwards was a naturalist masquerading as a theologian and moving beyond the Calvinist tradition." Michael J. McClymond and Gerald R. McDermott, *The Theology of Jonathan Edwards* (New York: Oxford University Press, 2012), 8.

[157]*WJE*, 8:11.

[158]*WJE*, 8:12.

of the *Two Dissertations*.[159] Benevolence is the most important virtue in Edwards's virtue theory and thus plays a crucial role in developing a comprehensive understanding of Edwards's ethics. Given the narrow depictions of benevolence in the *Two Dissertations*, a holistic understanding of Edwards's ethics is achieved by interacting with his broader corpus.[160] This will result in a portrait of an Edwards who, out of a God-centered foundation, indeed valued activism and societal concern in his virtue theory.

Works that Claim Divergence

A survey of important sources claiming Hopkins's departure from Edwards provides representative perspectives of Hopkins's seeming disregard of all self-love and Edwards's philosophical bent in their respective virtue theories. Thus, interpretations of Hopkins's pragmatism and Edwards's lack of activism are made clear. Consequently, the need for revisionist perspectives that provide a more holistic understanding of their respective ethics is established.

Haroutunian established the classic betrayal thesis of Hopkins and the New Divinity disciples from Edwards's theology; a thesis still perpetuated by some in current scholarship, albeit in nuanced versions.[161] Haroutunian bemoans the decline of Calvinist theology in the modern period, claiming the infection of humanistic morality, and praising Edwards for revitalizing "religion for at least a part of New England."[162] For Edwards, according to Haroutunian, "religion was independent of the problems of social morality and civil government. He ignored the social principles in the Calvinistic idea of theocracy, and made Calvinistic piety a matter which concerned primarily the relation to the individual soul to God."[163] Haroutunian pits Edwards's "theocentric piety" against the New England Theology's "humanitarian morality," asserting that the New Divinity men neglected Edwards's

[159]As highlighted, scholars such as Danaher, Cochran, and Choi have provided recent scholarship on the need to engage Edwards's broader corpus to accurately delineate his ethical thought.

[160]For an excellent discussion on this topic, see Danaher, "Beauty, Benevolence, and Virtue in Jonathan Edwards's *The Nature of True Virtue*," 386–410.

[161]Douglas A Sweeney, "Edwards and His Mantle: The Historiography of the New England Theology," *New England Quarterly* 71, no. 1 (1998): 108, 112.

[162]Joseph Haroutunian, *Piety Versus Moralism: The Passing of the New England Theology* (New York: H. Holt, 1932), xi, xix, xxi.

[163]Haroutunian, *Piety Versus Moralism*, xxi.

"supreme regard for the glory of God and His sovereignty over man" for specific social concerns arising in the eighteenth century.[164]

Hopkins was not spared in Haroutunian's scheme. He viewed Hopkins, like the rest of the New Divinity men, as lacking both Edwards's piety and intellectual acumen, thus altering Edwards's thought.[165] In particular for the study at hand, Haroutunian claims a complete departure by Hopkins from Edwards's virtue theory. He asserts that Hopkins changed the "metaphysical counterpart of benevolence" from Edward's doctrine of benevolence to Being in general by equating "Being in general" to God and humanity.[166] While Hopkins defended Edwards's theory of benevolence to Being in general from William Hart's assertion of Edwards's aestheticism at the expense of practical morality, Haroutunian believes Hopkins moralized and legalized Edwards's theory with his focus on the need to obey the divine law.[167] Thus, according to Haroutunian, Hopkins, like the rest of the New Divinity men, changed Edwards's ethical theology into a humanistic one, neglecting key Calvinist tenets such as divine sovereignty and glory.[168]

Haroutunian's betrayal thesis for the New England Theology and consequently, Hopkins, was the consensus view up until Conforti's work on Hopkins in 1981.[169] Conforti depicts the New Divinity men and their theology favorably overall, recognizing key theological and social contributions, such as addressing social needs and encouraging piety. Furthermore, he acknowledges parallels between Hopkins and Edwards while also affirming distinctions. According to Conforti, while Hopkins "liberalized major aspects

[164] Haroutunian, *Piety Versus Moralism*, xxiv, xxii.

[165] Haroutunian, *Piety Versus Moralism*, 82.

[166] Haroutunian, *Piety Versus Moralism*, 78, 82.

[167] Haroutunian, *Piety Versus Moralism*, 89; For William Hart, see William Hart, *Brief Remarks on a Number of False Propositions, and Dangerous Errors, Which Are Spreading in the Country; Collected out of Sundry Discourses Lately Publish'd, Wrote by Dr. Whitaker and Mr. Hopkins* (New London: T. and S. Green, 1769); William Hart, *A Sermon of a New Kind, Never Preached, nor Ever Will Be; Containing a Collection of Doctrines, Belonging to the Hopkintonian Scheme of Orthodoxy* (New Haven, CT: T. and S. Green, 1769); William Hart, *Remarks on President Edwards's Dissertations Concerning the Nature of True Virtue: Shewing That He Has given a Wrong Idea, and Definition of Virtue, and Is Inconsistent with Himself* (New Haven, CT: T. and S. Green, 1771).

[168] Haroutunian, *Piety Versus Moralism*, 87.

[169] Sweeney explains, "A number of fine studies on individual Edwardsians has appeared since the mid-1960s, but only since Joseph Conforti's study of Samuel Hopkins and the New Divinity (1981) have scholars really begun to escape the force of Haroutunian's paradigm," thus providing a helpful corrective to Haroutunian's view of Hopkins's full betrayal of Edwards's thought. Sweeney, "Edwards and His Mantle," 113–14.

of Edwardsianism," Hopkins, in contrast to Haroutunian's view, "stopped far short of transforming Calvinist piety into Christian moralism."[170] Thus Conforti represents a mediating position between views of Hopkins's full-fledged betrayal of Edwards and revisionist portrayals of Hopkins's overall faithfulness to Edwards's thought. Yet Conforti makes clear his position that Hopkins altered key tenets of Edwards's theology; in particular Edwards's understanding of benevolence to Being in general. In doing so, Conforti perpetuates a classic thesis of Edwards's philosophical and aesthetic bent and Hopkins's stress on pragmatic activism in their respective virtue theories. As Conforti explains, "Whereas Edwards had located true virtue in exalted consciousness, Hopkins placed it in elevated social behavior. Consequently, evangelical activism superseded mystical quietism."[171] Conforti's belief in Hopkins's reshaping of Edwards's ethical theology continues to hold influence in current scholarship, inadvertently pointing to past claims of betrayal.[172]

Post analyzes the ethics of Edwards and Hopkins, "who differed markedly on the question of whether all self-love is prohibited from Christian ethics."[173] This addresses the broader goal of Post's work, which seeks to discover the amount of self-love, if any, one can have in order to love God.[174] According to Post, though Edwards affirmed an amount of self-love in his virtue theory, Hopkins rejected this notion and instead advocated a self-denial that had no end in sight.[175] As a result, "Hopkins built his ethic, then, on careful revisions of his mentor Edwards' thought."[176] Hence Hopkins's extreme view of self-denial is one Edwards would not recognize. Post seems to point to views of Hopkins's activist inclination and Edwards's lack thereof, noting how "Edwards' insistence on proper consent to oneself may not have allowed

[170]Conforti, *Samuel Hopkins and the New Divinity Movement*, 192.

[171]Conforti, *Samuel Hopkins and the New Divinity Movement*, 117.

[172]For example, in discussing Hopkins's difference from Edwards's virtue theory, Noll argues that "Edwards's conception of virtue as affectional love to Being in general proved too impractical for Hopkins. His 1773 essay *An Inquiry into the Nature of True Holiness* made ethics more concrete by defining it as benevolence 'to God and our neighbors . . . or friendly affection to all intelligent beings.' " Noll, *America's God*, 135.

[173]Stephen Garrard Post, *Christian Love and Self-Denial: An Historical and Normative Study of Jonathan Edwards, Samuel Hopkins, and American Theological Ethics* (Lanham: University Press of America, 1987), vii.

[174]Post, *Christian Love and Self-Denial*, 1.

[175]Post, *Christian Love and Self-Denial*, 67.

[176]Post, *Christian Love and Self-Denial*, 68.

for the radically self-denying idealism helpful in this inspiration of serious social activism."[177] Thus, Post helps preserve assertions of Hopkins's extreme pragmatism at the expense of a theocentric commitment and Edwards's lack of activist stimuli in his ethical theory.

Lovejoy believes Hopkins's understanding of disinterested love places more emphasis on man than God compared to Edwards's view. Consequently, Lovejoy believes Edwards would not recognize the amount of disinterestedness or "selflessness" in Hopkins's view.[178] Hopkins's understanding of selfless service was so extreme, according to Lovejoy, that one could destroy his own self if carried to its extreme.[179] This selfless service, then, should lead one to embrace the oppressed, such as those enslaved.[180] For Hopkins, it was the enslaved Africans that needed Christian benevolence the most.[181] He viewed the slaves as "neighbors" who deserved to be treated with the same respect as whites.[182] As a result, from Hopkins's perspective stemming from his theology, he "came to two conclusions: slavery was contrary to God's will and therefore sinful, and Negroes and whites were equal as members of the human race."[183] Lovejoy believes Hopkins diverged from Edwards's understanding of benevolence by stating that Hopkins "first twisted the doctrine of benevolence as it was earlier understood and stretched it to include Negroes who most needed universal goodwill."[184]

Oliver Elsbree interprets Hopkins's desire to improve on Edwards's thought as one of departure, "especially in the field of human relations."[185] He espouses a classic interpretation of Hopkins's understanding of self-damnation as self-neglecting in nature. Elsbree notes, Hopkins "was destined to develop a theory of disinterestedness so extreme that it actually required a man not to concern himself about his own salvation."[186] Although Ed-

[177]Post, *Christian Love and Self-Denial*, 68.

[178]David S. Lovejoy, "Samuel Hopkins: Religion, Slavery, and the Revolution," *New England Quarterly* 40, no. 2 (1967): 233.

[179]Lovejoy, "Samuel Hopkins," 233.

[180]Lovejoy, "Samuel Hopkins," 233.

[181]Lovejoy, "Samuel Hopkins," 233–34.

[182]Lovejoy, "Samuel Hopkins," 234.

[183]Lovejoy, "Samuel Hopkins," 234.

[184]Lovejoy, "Samuel Hopkins," 242.

[185]Oliver Wendell Elsbree, "Samuel Hopkins and His Doctrine of Benevolence," *New England Quarterly* 8, no. 4 (1935): 535.

[186]Elsbree, "Samuel Hopkins and His Doctrine of Benevolence," 536.

wards was influential for Hopkins's thought, Hopkins, according to Elsbree, clearly diverged from Edwards's theory; in particular in "the theories of the atonement and of the nature of true holiness."[187] For atonement, Elsbree believes Hopkins disagreed with the doctrine of election and "that man is not punished for the sin of Adam but for his own sinful disposition."[188] On the nature of holiness, Hopkins "went beyond Edwards in his theological exposition of the relation between the divine being and true holiness."[189] According to Elsbree, Edwards believed divine benevolence centered on the attributes of God while Hopkins believed God was the very essence of benevolence.[190] Specifically, disinterested benevolence, for Hopkins, "is the sum of all holiness" and consequently, selfishness is the opposite and "sum of all sin."[191] The degree of disinterestedness in their understanding of benevolence is a key difference between the two figures.

Conclusion to Works that Claim Divergence

Scholars have given several reasons why they believe Hopkins departed from Edwards's ethical thought. Haroutunian claims Hopkins lacked Edwards's Calvinistic commitment to a God-centered theology, altering Edwards's understanding of benevolence to mere human-centered morality. While not going as far as Haroutunian, Conforti does portray a pragmatic activism in Hopkins's doctrine of disinterested benevolence, thus diverging from Edwards's more philosophical concept of benevolence to Being in general. Post espouses a classic thesis of Hopkins's extreme self-denial stemming from his doctrine of damnation for the glory of God and Edwards's lack of activism. Similarly, for Lovejoy, Edwards would not recognize such a degree of selflessness. Edwards would also not acknowledge Hopkins's alteration of his doctrine of benevolence by including those enslaved in his definition. And Elsbree believes the degree of disinterestedness in Hopkins's doctrine of benevolence differs significantly from that of Edwards's. Given that the betrayal or divergence theses have long been established, recent revisionist works contrarily evidence strong social concern and activism in Edwards's ethical thought. For Hopkins, evidence of a theocentric foundation and

[187]Elsbree, "Samuel Hopkins and His Doctrine of Benevolence," 536.

[188]Elsbree, "Samuel Hopkins and His Doctrine of Benevolence," 539.

[189]Elsbree, "Samuel Hopkins and His Doctrine of Benevolence," 540.

[190]Elsbree, "Samuel Hopkins and His Doctrine of Benevolence," 540.

[191]Elsbree, "Samuel Hopkins and His Doctrine of Benevolence," 541.

self-regard in his ethical thought have been brought to light. The revisionist works are discussed next.

Revisionist Works

A survey of works evidencing social concern in Edwards's ethical theology provides a portrait of an Edwards who valued activism in his ethical theory. Likewise, a survey of works dealing with Hopkins's theocentric commitments and self-regard in his ethical thought helps correct past depictions of extreme pragmatism and disregard for self. This will show Hopkins's overall faithfulness to Edwards's virtue theory and thus, provide potential for the claim of Hopkins's agreement with Edwards's doctrine of benevolence.

Revisionist Works on Edwards

Edwards has been portrayed as a figure that did not concern himself with the needs of society.[192] More specifically, the focus on God limited his perspective of needed social activism. Perry Miller famously claimed that, "In Edwards, social theory seems conspicuous by its absence."[193] Miller goes on to assert that, "Edwards' attitude toward society, it has been generally concluded, was detachment or downright indifference."[194] Robert Westbrook argues that Edwards did indeed have "an imposing social vision," but that his social vision was rooted in God's work of redemption and millennial society to come.[195] Herbert Schneider asserts that for Edwards, "religion was essentially a kind of private experience" that had to do more with one's

[192] I have been guided to resources by McDermott for the following discussion on Edwards's seeming lack of social concern. Gerald R. McDermott, *One Holy and Happy Society: The Public Theology of Jonathan Edwards* (University Park, PA: Penn State University Press, 1992), 94, n. 8.

[193] Perry Miller, "Jonathan Edwards' Sociology of the Great Awakening," *New England Quarterly* 21, no. 1 (1948): 51.

[194] Miller, "Jonathan Edwards' Sociology of the Great Awakening," 51–52.

[195] Robert B. Westbrook, "Social Criticism and the Heavenly City of Jonathan Edwards," *Soundings: An Interdisciplinary Journal* 59, no. 4 (1976): 396–97. In discussing Edwards's focus on the world to come rather than on the temporal needs of a broken society, Westbrook explains, "Edwards turned his eyes from what is to what should and, according to God's will, shall be. Just as the regenerate saint dissented from the lack of beauty in the sinners around him, so Edwards turned away from the tarnished City of Man and fixed his gaze on the City of God that lay over the horizon." Westbrook, "Social Criticism and the Heavenly City of Jonathan Edwards," 397.

personal spirituality.[196] Similarly, Haroutunian claimed Edwards limited piety to a relationship between an individual and God. Edwards, according to Haroutunian, "ignored the social principles in the Calvinistic idea of theocracy, and made Calvinistic piety a matter which concerned primarily the relation of the individual soul to God."[197] In other words, piety is experiential in nature as one personally relates to God.[198] Likewise, Fiering notes that for Edwards, it was more a matter of one's virtuous state than one's actions.[199] In discussing the Great Awakening and its emphasis on individual salvation, John Corrigan argues that Edwards and other revivalists were unable to give account of practical ramifications of salvation.[200] Once one is saved, the resultant fruit of one's life should naturally follow.[201] Finally, William McGloughlin notes that for Edwards, "there is scarcely a word in all his writings to justify social reform, and nothing on politics."[202]

[196]Herbert W. Schneider, *The Puritan Mind* (Ann Arbor, MI: University of Michigan Press, 1958), 106. Examining the social nature of religion in New England in comparison to Edwards's view, Schneider explains, "For in New England, ever since the defeat of the familists, religion had been an objective social institution, preoccupied with public concerns; Edwards, however, transformed it into an inner discipline of emotions. The gospel of the divine sovereignty, of election, of predestination, and of the Covenant of Grace, which the New England Puritans had constructed into a social and political philosophy, was now transferred to the inner life of the soul." Schneider, *The Puritan Mind*, 106.

[197]Haroutunian, *Piety Versus Moralism*, xxi.

[198]Haroutunian, *Piety Versus Moralism*, xxi. Haroutunian continues, "Edwards put the theology of Calvinism upon the basis of an empirical piety, and defended its doctrines philosophically and rationally. He reinterpreted Calvinism as a religious philosophy of nature, and reasserted its doctrines in view of the facts of life as well as on scriptural foundations. Calvinistic theology was thus separated from its temporary social and political aspects, and restated as a religion of permanent human significance." Haroutunian, *Piety Versus Moralism*, xxi.

[199]Fiering asserts that for Edwards, "Being good was for him distinguishable from doing good in any conventional sense. He was more on the side of Mary than Martha." Fiering, *Jonathan Edwards's Moral Thought and Its British Context*, 349.

[200]John Corrigan, *The Hidden Balance: Religion and the Social Theories of Charles Chauncy and Jonathan Mayhew* (Cambridge: Cambridge University Press, 1987), 2.

[201]Corrigan explains his understanding of the priority for conversion and assumption of subsequent activism in Edwards and other revivalist contemporaries: "They instead proposed that Christian virtue, faithfully practiced by converted individuals, would almost mystically lead to a social order that was family-like in character. In short, supporters of the revival, in their thinking about the relationship between the individual and the Christian society, found themselves stressing both the essential primacy of individual experience and the indistinguishability of the individual from the social body." Corrigan, *The Hidden Balance*, 2.

[202]William G. McLoughlin, *Revivals, Awakenings, and Reform: An Essay on Religion and Social Change in America, 1607–1977* (Chicago: University of Chicago Press, 1978), 71. McLoughlin's comment is in large part due to many of Edwards's sermons dealing with his treatment of pertinent themes not having been published at the time.

In light of past claims of Edwards's lack of social theory and activism in his writings, revisionist accounts arguing for the latter are needed. The following is a discussion on recent sources that argue for evidences of social concern and activism in Edwards's virtue theory.

Because scholars have ignored certain Northampton texts, Richard Hall argues that their "chronic neglect of a significant portion of the Edwards corpus has led scholars to seriously misconstrue him either by utterly misconceiving his social-political philosophy or, more commonly, by denying that he had any such thing—indeed, that he had nothing at all worth saying about society or politics."[203] Arguing against the portrayal of a philosophically immersed Edwards due to preferential selections of Edwards's philosophical writings by earlier scholars, Hall believes "that there is indeed a social-political philosophy implicit in Edwards' thought—one that is articulate, sophisticated, suggestive and contrary to the socio-political theory regnant in his day."[204] The four texts Hall focuses on were written during the latter years of Edwards's Northampton pastorate: *An Humble Attempt*, *The Life of David Brainerd*, *An Humble Inquiry*, and *A Farewell-Sermon*. What arises from an analysis of these four works, according to Hall, is a clear theme of what genuine virtue entails.[205] Moreover, a moral, social, and political dynamic arises from a reading of the four texts.

Hall identifies in Edwards's writings "not only a social and political philosophy but also a philosophical sociology."[206] In *Humble Attempt*, Hall distills millennial implications from Edwards's understanding of a pious society, pro-

[203] Richard A. S. Hall, *The Neglected Northampton Texts of Jonathan Edwards: Edwards on Society and Politics* (Lewiston, NY: E. Mellen Press, 1990), 45–46. Hall sums up why he believes scholars have tended to neglect some of Edwards's Northampton texts: "The unconscionable neglect by Edwards scholars of some of his Northampton texts is explicable by the occasional character of the texts themselves and their ostensible lack of philosophical or theological interest; and by the traditionally narrow focus of most Edwards scholarship on his 'Natural Philosophy' and 'The Mind' because of the antitheological bias of the pioneers in the field, their predilection for Edwards' philosophical works, and their view of Edwards' private notebooks as epitomizing his thought." Hall, *The Neglected Northampton Texts of Jonathan Edwards*, 45.

[204] Hall, *The Neglected Northampton Texts of Jonathan Edwards*, 47.

[205] In discussing the theme of true virtue located in the four texts he's chosen to focus on, Hall explains: "Though these four works of Edwards from the last three years of his Northampton pastorate have not received the scholarly attention they deserve, they are by no means negligible or peripheral. These texts are linked by theme and aim to two of Edwards' major and most acclaimed texts, viz. *Religious Affections* and *True Virtue*, and are profoundly concerned with one of the persistent themes of Edwards' life and thought—namely, the nature of true piety or virtue." Hall, *The Neglected Northampton Texts of Jonathan Edwards*, 57–58.

[206] Hall, *The Neglected Northampton Texts of Jonathan Edwards*, 59.

moting unity through the activity of prayer.[207] Both social and pious union in society is likened to beauty, promoting harmony and agreement.[208] In *The Life of David Brainerd*, Edwards identifies in Brainerd a life that exuded genuine religion and virtue, modeling well Christian benevolence.[209] As a result, Hall argues for both a socio-political philosophy and "philosophical sociology" in Edwards's thought.[210] Both the pious and civil societies promote unity as distinct norms are employed, citizens are to show love, concern, and care for others, embrace community, pursue personal holiness, and activism.[211]

Gerald McDermott identifies in Edwards's thought a legitimate "public theology," which he describes as Edwards's "understanding of civil community and the Christian's responsibility to it."[212] More specifically, McDermott contends "Edwards's public theology does indeed encompass social and political theory, and that in fact it is at least as fully developed as the most prominent liberal social theories of his day."[213] He elucidates both the philosophical and theological aspects of Edwards's ethical thought.[214] Specifically, he recognizes two sources from which Edwards's social ethic is derived: ontology and Christian benevolence or love.[215]

While much attention has been given to Edwards's ontology from *TV*, understanding Edwards's "philosophy of being" is indeed necessary because

[207]Hall, *The Neglected Northampton Texts of Jonathan Edwards*, 104–5.

[208]Hall, *The Neglected Northampton Texts of Jonathan Edwards*, 106–8.

[209]Hall, *The Neglected Northampton Texts of Jonathan Edwards*, 155–74.

[210]Hall, *The Neglected Northampton Texts of Jonathan Edwards*, 309.

[211]Hall, *The Neglected Northampton Texts of Jonathan Edwards*, 313–30.

[212]McDermott, *One Holy and Happy Society*, 5.

[213]McDermott, *One Holy and Happy Society*, 96.

[214]The philosophical aspect of Edwards's ethical thought deals primarily with the ontological aspect of benevolence to God or Being. The social aspect, then, deals more explicitly with Edwards's understanding of love and how love is expressed. Both are distinct yet necessary in order to properly understand Edwards's ethics. McDermott explains: "The relationship between Edwards's ontology and social ethic may be better understood by distinguishing them in two ways. First, they have different functions. Edwards's ontology, like all ontologies, explicates the 'is' of reality, whereas his ethic moves from what is to what ought to be. His ethic, naturally, is explicitly moral, but his ontology is not. Second, each describes a different aspect of the system of being. The ontology, as we have seen, is an analysis of the *nature* of being. The Edwardsean social ethic, on the other hand, appeals to the *structure* of being." McDermott, *One Holy and Happy Society*, 101.

[215]McDermott, *One Holy and Happy Society*, 101.

there are implications for his social and political thought.[216] Human beings are "active, propensive, and directed toward other beings" as God continues to extend himself in the world "by creating, and then relating to, other beings."[217] In fact, there is a relational dynamic that pushes one to be united with other beings.[218] As a relational God communicates himself to his creatures, creatures in turn reach out relationally to others, thus making up a relational system of intelligent beings.[219] By actively engaging in genuine benevolence, one loves God first and foremost as the greatest being.[220] All creatures are dependent on God and will naturally love other creatures and seek their good.[221]

For a comprehensive account of Edwards's understanding of Christian benevolence or love, McDermott not only mines various published works such as the *CF* sermons, but also what were at the time Edwards's unpublished sermons. This is important because Edwards "also made use of his theological principles to ground a specifically Christian ethic of public responsibility."[222] The believer reaching out towards other creatures expresses Christian benevolence for Edwards.[223] Specifically, it causes a "reorientation of concern from self to neighbor" as one, having God's love, actively lives out Christian love to all humanity.[224] This will result in the believer meeting both the spiritual and material needs of others.[225] Faith plays a key role in Christian benevolence for Edwards as love "belongs to the very nature

[216]McDermott, *One Holy and Happy Society*, 97.

[217]McDermott, *One Holy and Happy Society*, 97. McDermott continues: "So God created beings to whom he could communicate good, the essential nature of which is God's own being. God is in a never-ending process of enlarging his own being by creating new relationships. Hence created existence is the spatiotemporal repetition of God's inner-trinitarian fullness, a process that will be everlasting in duration." McDermott, *One Holy and Happy Society*, 98.

[218]McDermott, *One Holy and Happy Society*, 99. In describing the directional process of "being" uniting to other beings, McDermott notes, "Being is continually in the process of moving from 'virtuality' to full actuality, which is achieved for intelligent beings by a union of mutual consent." McDermott, *One Holy and Happy Society*, 99.

[219]McDermott, *One Holy and Happy Society*, 100.

[220]McDermott, *One Holy and Happy Society*, 102.

[221]McDermott, *One Holy and Happy Society*, 101–2.

[222]McDermott, *One Holy and Happy Society*, 107.

[223]McDermott, *One Holy and Happy Society*, 107.

[224]McDermott, *One Holy and Happy Society*, 107–8.

[225]McDermott, *One Holy and Happy Society*, 109.

and essence of true faith."[226] Because love is active, it will naturally lead the believer to practice, which, for Edwards, was key in pointing to genuine conversion.[227]

For McDermott and Ronald Story, the common portrayals of Edwards as a preacher of damnation and wrath are inaccurate. While Edwards certainly preached on the realities of divine judgment, he also had much to say on the topics of "love, justice, and society."[228] For example, Edwards not only evidenced social concern in his writings, but in fact taught the inseparability of genuine religion and social activism.[229] Specifically for Edwards, "religious sensibility was never to be divorced from its social expression. Inner spiritual experience and outward social action were movements of the same soul with true affections, pieces of the same cloth."[230] In short, the Spirit-indwelt Christian will bear fruit as he extends benevolence. Because genuine love is a result of a regenerated heart, it moves beyond self and extends towards the betterment of neighbor and society.[231] This is made clear due to the foundational nature of Christian benevolence for Edwards's "social vision."[232] Thus, genuine benevolence will naturally express itself through a believer's activism. He is to fight for the marginalized and outcast of society.[233]

Story embarks on a "lengthy personal effort to discover the real Jonathan Edwards."[234] Having contributed to the hell, fire, and brimstone preacher caricature in his 1984 work *A More Perfect Union: Documents in U.S. History*, Story sets out to correct "an unfair and misleading stereotype of a

[226]McDermott, *One Holy and Happy Society*, 112.

[227]McDermott, *One Holy and Happy Society*, 112. The twelfth and most important sign of "gracious affections" is practice. See Edwards, *RA*, 383–461.

[228]Gerald R. McDermott and Ronald Story, "Introduction," in *The Other Jonathan Edwards: Selected Writings on Society, Love, and Justice* (Amherst: University of Massachusetts Press, 2015), 1.

[229]McDermott and Story explain: "Edwards was convinced that religion cannot be understood apart from its social manifestations. True religion, he preached and wrote, necessarily has social expression. It is concerned for the good of others and the world. Religion without social concern is therefore false." "Introduction," 16.

[230]McDermott and Story, "Introduction," 17.

[231]McDermott and Story, "Introduction," 17.

[232]McDermott and Story, "Introduction," 18.

[233]McDermott and Story, "Introduction," 19.

[234]Ronald Story, *Jonathan Edwards and the Gospel of Love* (Amherst: University of Massachusetts Press, 2012), ix.

remarkable man whose lessons on charity, community, and love we need now more than ever."[235] Drawing largely from Edwards's sermons, Story gives a picture of an Edwards who was deeply concerned with the expression of Christian benevolence and consequent activism in the lives of believers. Charity is "the inevitable corollary and consequence of genuine love to God that flows from and demonstrates the gift of grace, the true hallmark of the sanctified life."[236] The way Edwards uses the word "charity" is key, denoting a generous spirit, love for God and men, and Christian practice.[237] Especially important to Edwards is the need to care for and serve the poor.[238] Edwards also championed the importance of Christian community. Aspects of Christian unity were certainly important in light of benevolence.[239] Finally, the theme of Christian love "pervades Jonathan Edwards's ministry and writings, a point often overlooked given his lingering reputation as a preacher of damnation."[240] Love permeates Edwards's writings and points to what Edwards considers genuine religion.[241]

In *Edwards on the Christian Life*, Dane Ortlund writes on Edwards's view of the Christian life and how it is relevant for Christian living today. Ortlund establishes Edwards's understanding of divine beauty as central for the Christian life. Beauty is, for Ortlund, the "organizing theme of Edwards's theology of the Christian life."[242] Specifically, the Christian life "is to enjoy and reflect the beauty of God. Everything Edwards wrote on Christian living funnels down into this."[243] It is dynamic and multifaceted.

[235] Story, *Jonathan Edwards and the Gospel of Love*, xi. The fiery damnation preacher caricature is in large part due to the portrayal given by scholars stemming from Edwards's famous sermon delivered in 1741 to his Northampton congregation, "Sinners in the Hands of an Angry God." See Edwards, *Sermons and Discourses, 1739–1742*, 404–35.

[236] Story, *Jonathan Edwards and the Gospel of Love*, 54.

[237] Story, *Jonathan Edwards and the Gospel of Love*, 54–55.

[238] Story, *Jonathan Edwards and the Gospel of Love*, 55–65.

[239] Story explains, "The notion of togetherness—social peace, amiableness, unity, harmony, collective worship, conversation, friendship, neighborliness, holy community, the oneness of mankind—was a major Edwardsian theme, important for its earthly significance, for its relation to salvation and holiness, and for the way it foreshadows the realm of Heavenly love, the glorious culmination, in Edwards's view, of the whole of history." Story, *Jonathan Edwards and the Gospel of Love*, 75.

[240] Story, *Jonathan Edwards and the Gospel of Love*, 98.

[241] Story, *Jonathan Edwards and the Gospel of Love*, 98–99.

[242] Dane C. Ortlund, *Edwards on the Christian Life: Alive to the Beauty of God* (Wheaton, IL: Crossway, 2014), 23.

[243] Ortlund, *Edwards on the Christian Life*, 16.

God himself is beauty and thus: his holiness is beauty, man's happiness is a result of seeing God's beauty, and Christ himself reflects God's beauty as does his creation, especially believers as they participate "in the unceasing explosion of delighted intratrinitarian joy and love."[244] As one is gifted new birth, he is able to see the beauty of God and live a God honoring life. For Edwards, "regeneration implants within the believer a new inclination toward holiness."[245] Regeneration, then, leads to a life of love.[246] Stemming from the "intratrinitarian love" of God, the Spirit is gifted to believers, giving believers the ability to love God and others.[247] As Ortlund notes, "True love to God will always be accompanied by love to people; true love to people will always be accompanied by love to God."[248] Love for Edwards, according to Ortlund, is a "life of love. Believers delight in the well-being and joy of others. It is who they are."[249]

In an earlier work, Ortlund discusses what Edwards "has to say on the subject of Christian motivation."[250] Like his more recent work, *Edwards on the Christian Life*, a major goal for Ortlund is to give the contemporary church an opportunity to listen to Edwards's theology.[251] Specifically, motivation to live the Christian life begins with God, for there is no holiness "*apart from the grace of God.* God is the source of the moral life. Only by sovereignly imported power does true obedience–obedience from the heart– blossom."[252] Thus motivation to live morally unto God was key for Edwards. Themes of holy inclinations, selfless love, holiness, and giving charitably to those in need are only several areas of what Edwards wanted his parishioners to live out, motivated and changed by the Spirit of God.[253]

[244]Ortlund, *Edwards on the Christian Life*, 23–37.

[245]Ortlund, *Edwards on the Christian Life*, 42.

[246]Ortlund observes, "If there is one mark of the Christian life to which Edwards returns more than any other, it is love." Ortlund, *Edwards on the Christian Life*, 55.

[247]Ortlund, *Edwards on the Christian Life*, 56.

[248]Ortlund, *Edwards on the Christian Life*, 55–59.

[249]Ortlund, *Edwards on the Christian Life*, 59.

[250]Dane C. Ortlund, *A New Inner Relish: Christian Motivation in the Thought of Jonathan Edwards* (Fearn, UK: Christian Focus, 2008), 19.

[251]Ortlund, *A New Inner Relish*, 10–11.

[252]Ortlund, *A New Inner Relish*, 89.

[253]Ortlund, *A New Inner Relish*, 37–86.

Similar to Ortlund, Sean Lucas presents Edwards primarily as a "theologian of the Christian life."[254] As a pastor, according to Lucas, Edwards spent the majority of his time reflecting on the Christian life for himself and for the people under his care.[255] His understanding of the Christian life was foundationally theological as man is to seek to glorify God.[256] Lucas identifies two levels of this "theological vision" for the life of the believer: the first is cosmic, dealing with Edwards's understanding of redemption history, and the second is personal; God changing the believer to live a life that glorifies him.[257] It was God centered as "Edwards rooted his understanding of the Christian life in the cosmic purpose of God himself—namely, for God to glorify himself and enjoy himself forever."[258] God does this by drawing his "redeemed creation into the Trinitarian life that they might participate and communicate in the eternal happiness of God."[259] More specifically, it is the Spirit that God uses to communicate himself to the believer's soul, thus giving the believer knowledge of himself, divine love, and producing holiness.[260] In the end, believers are to model genuine virtue, consisting in selfless love first and foremost to God and then to men.[261] The believer living a holy life and embracing community will then express this Christian benevolence.[262]

Ramsey's introduction to volume 8 of the Yale *Works of Jonathan Edwards* series is highly regarded amongst scholars as a seminal contribution to scholarship on Edwards's ethics.[263] Ramsey recognizes writings such as *RA* and the sermon series *CF* as accounts of Edwards's "moral theology"

[254]Sean Michael Lucas, *God's Grand Design: The Theological Vision of Jonathan Edwards* (Wheaton, IL: Crossway, 2011), 11.

[255]Lucas, *God's Grand Design*, 12.

[256]In discussing God's purpose in glorifying himself, Lucas explains: "By rooting his understanding of God's purposes in his own Trinitarian being, and especially God's passion to glorify himself by communicating his glory in creation and redemption and receiving back his glory in love and praise, Edwards set forth a vision of the Christian life that was deeply *theological*." Lucas, *God's Grand Design*, 13.

[257]Lucas, *God's Grand Design*, 13–14.

[258]Lucas, *God's Grand Design*, 23.

[259]Lucas, *God's Grand Design*, 27.

[260]Lucas, *God's Grand Design*, 87–88.

[261]Lucas, *God's Grand Design*, 122.

[262]Lucas, *God's Grand Design*, 123–27.

[263]For example, Wilson views Ramsey's "scholarly introduction" as "comprising the fourth of the major studies of Edwards's ethics" due to "the extensive analysis, comprehensive scope,

or of "the Christian moral life."[264] It begins with God as the creature is given "divine love" in order to love God and others.[265] In *TV*, Edwards explains that the believer is to live a life of selfless benevolence, loving others first and even placing "his own happiness in the other's happiness," looking on the "other's happiness as his own."[266] This is possible because the believer exercising genuine benevolence is united to the one he loves.[267] This aspect of Christian love is dealt with in detail in *CF*. The union between a believer and God and consequently, between a believer and his neighbor is possible because of the Spirit influencing one to love God and others.[268] Consequently, the presence of God's love in the heart of the believer changes him and leads him to live a life of holiness.[269]

Revisionist Works on Hopkins

In light of theses claiming the New Divinity men betrayed Edwards, Breitenbach argues against the classic piety versus moralism paradigm, believing that "the leading tendencies of Edwards's system can be discovered by tracing the trajectory of his ideas in the theology of his New Divinity successors."[270] Edwards's fight against Antinomian and Arminian tendencies pushed him to embrace both piety and moralism in his theology.[271] Likewise, Edwards's New Divinity heirs followed suit and stayed faithful to him while

and unified interpretation offered by these remarks," considering Ramsey's introduction as a seminal source for understanding Edwards's ethical thought. Wilson, *Virtue Reformed*, 9.

[264] *WJE*, 8:2. Discussing the moral nature of the two works, Ramsey explains the priority of the *CF* sermons compared to *RA*, stating that *RA* is "the finest fruit of the revival controversy" and "generally regarded as a major work in the psychology of religion. *Affections* can also be read as moral theology; and when so read, *Charity* is clearly superior to it." *WJE*, 8:2.

[265] *WJE*, 8:21–23.

[266] *WJE*, 8:18.

[267] Ramsey explains, "How can we creatures, who are on earth and not in heaven, place our happiness in God's glory and look on another person's happiness as our very own? Only if, in truth, we are first made one with them in 'pure' or 'absolute' benevolence, Edwards answers." *WJE*, 8:19.

[268] *WJE*, 8:59.

[269] *WJE*, 8:83–86.

[270] William Breitenbach, "Piety and Moralism: Edwards and the New Divinity," in *Jonathan Edwards and the American Experience*, ed. Nathan O. Hatch and Harry S. Stout (New York: Oxford University Press, 1988), 178. Breitenbach argues that the "*dominant* New England theological tradition, the clerical orthodoxy, was one of piety *and* moralism." Breitenbach, "Piety and Moralism," 179.

[271] Breitenbach, "Piety and Moralism," 190–91.

applying the principles of his thought to address contemporary issues.[272] Specifically, William Breitenbach views Hopkins as a genuine Edwardsean who like Edwards, embraced the notion of disinterested love.[273] Furthermore, Hopkins like Edwards according to Breitenbach, believed that only regenerated believers could truly live a life of genuine virtue.[274] In the end Hopkins and the New Divinity men "believed that they alone could preach a consistent Calvinism, balancing grace and law, piety and moralism."[275] From Breitenbach's perspective, the New Divinity movement arose from Edwards himself.[276]

Jauhiainen investigates how Hopkins appropriated modern Enlightenment thought with Reformed theology.[277] In doing so, he argues that Hopkins "adapted" Edwards's "teaching to suit better the conditions of a new generation . . . and that his doctrinal formulations were largely faithful to the substance of Edwards's work."[278] Importantly, Jauhiainen argues that Hopkins was consistent with Edwards's doctrine of benevolence to Being in general. The differences between Hopkins and Edwards "was not so much substantive but a matter of *emphasis*."[279] Both Edwards and Hopkins af-

[272]Breitenbach notes, "When Joseph Bellamy and Samuel Hopkins assumed the leadership of the Edwardsian party in the 1760s, they remained true to Edwards's principles. The New Divinity was Edwardsianism responding to new challenges." Breitenbach, "Piety and Moralism," 191.

[273]Breitenbach, "Piety and Moralism," 193. In discussing Edwards's *TV*, Breitenbach explains how Edwards defined genuine virtue "as disinterested love to being, so that only the holiness of regenerated saints can be said to be truly virtuous." This type of love is not selfish in any way, but rather "disinterested love to being in general." Breitenbach, "Piety and Moralism," 188.

[274]Breitenbach, "Piety and Moralism," 193–94, 203, n. 40. In discussing Hopkins's view of the moral strivings of the unregenerate, Breitenbach says that "before regeneration everything done by a sinner was totally wicked and unacceptable to God." William Breitenbach, "Unregenerate Doings: Selflessness and Selfishness in New Divinity Theology," *American Quarterly* 34, no. 5 (1982): 481–82.

[275]Breitenbach, "Piety and Moralism," 195.

[276]Breitenbach, "Piety and Moralism," 195.

[277]Jauhiainen, "An Enlightenment Calvinist," 3.

[278]Jauhiainen, "An Enlightenment Calvinist," 6. Jauhiainen continues, "Thus I hope to provide a corrective to past interpretations of Hopkins and his allegedly 'new' doctrines. The charge of newness stemmed from his forceful restatement of certain Reformed doctrines." Jauhiainen, "An Enlightenment Calvinist," 7. I interpret Jauhiainen to mean here that Hopkins did not invent new teachings out of Edwards's thought but rather used different language. This makes sense since Hopkins was, "Inspired by the work of Jonathan Edwards," and since the New Divinity disciples "reconfigured Reformed doctrine to address the challenges of Enlightenment rationalism with the New England churches." Jauhiainen, "An Enlightenment Calvinist," 1.

[279]Jauhiainen, "An Enlightenment Calvinist," 236.

firmed an amount of self-regard as well as an understanding of self-love that primarily meant selfishness.[280] Specifically for Hopkins, since "disinterested benevolence was exercised toward the good of the whole, it necessarily included the love of self. The self was properly loved as part of the entire system of existence, as an object included in being in general."[281] This idea of a "system of existence" is in harmony with Edwards's understanding of genuine virtue as benevolence to Being in general.[282] Furthermore, this love for God and others required that one be regenerated by God, for there is no true virtue otherwise.[283]

Both Edwards and Hopkins believed natural morality was insufficient, for any "virtue that was generated from principles inherent to human nature was woefully deficient, falling infinitely short of universal or disinterested benevolence."[284] Thus, for genuine holiness to be a reality, both Edwards and Hopkins believed that creaturely participation with God was necessary.[285] In the end, according to Jauhiainen, Hopkins did not change Edwards's views on true virtue but tried to make Edwards's teaching more clear.[286]

Conclusion of the Revisionist Works

By engaging Edwards's broader corpus, recent scholars have evidenced a strong social vision and activist commitment in Edwards's ethical thought. For Hopkins, the revisionist work is extremely limited. Breitenbach has argued for both theocentrism and practical moral engagement for the New Divinity disciples and consequently, Hopkins as well. Jauhiainen has argued that Hopkins was faithful overall to Edwards's virtue theory, developing his doctrine of disinterested benevolence from Edwards's doctrine of benevolence to Being in general. As a result, recent revisionist perspectives claiming congruence challenge past theses that argue for Edwards's ethics as primarily philosophical and aesthetic and Hopkins's ethics as purely pragmatic.

[280] Jauhiainen, "An Enlightenment Calvinist," 236, 266.

[281] Jauhiainen, "An Enlightenment Calvinist," 263.

[282] Jauhiainen, "An Enlightenment Calvinist," 249–50.

[283] Jauhiainen, "An Enlightenment Calvinist," 245.

[284] Jauhiainen, "An Enlightenment Calvinist," 256–57.

[285] Jauhiainen, "An Enlightenment Calvinist," 262.

[286] Jauhiainen, "An Enlightenment Calvinist," 257–58.

Conclusion

Hopkins was part of a theological tradition that applied Edwards's theology to address the needs of a changing social and political climate arising from the growing republican ethos of Revolutionary America. In particular, the abolition of both the slave trade and institutionalized slavery was a major priority for Hopkins. Given the scholarly tendency to view differences between Edwards and Hopkins, not only in regards to the slavery issue but in their ethics, recent revisionist accounts help correct exaggerated claims of Edwards's philosophically oriented ethics and Hopkins's anthropocentric ethics. In order to gain a more holistic understanding of their respective virtue theories, it is important to understand the times they lived in, for their social, cultural, and intellectual environment certainly shaped their ethics and the differences of opinion regarding institutionalized slavery. The character of Edwards's prerevolutionary Puritan America and Hopkins's Revolutionary America will be discussed next to understand the social, intellectual, and cultural influences upon both figures that helped shape their respective ethics and differences of opinion on slavery.

CHAPTER 3: HISTORICAL CONTEXT

THE GOAL OF THIS CHAPTER is to identify social and cultural influences that likely impacted Edwards's agreement with slave owning and Hopkins's opposition to it.[1] Thus, I survey the time periods of Edwards and Hopkins in order to situate each figure in their respective historical context. This will be accomplished by providing a general narrative of each time period. Furthermore, the purpose of this chapter is preparatory in nature for chapters four and five, which will discuss Edwards's and Hopkins's personal views on slavery and the slave trade.

Eighteenth-Century Pre-Revolutionary America (Puritan America)

Jonathan Edwards lived in a time and place rooted in Puritan ideals.[2] While the Enlightenment was growing in Europe during Edwards's lifetime,

[1] Considering the transition from prerevolutionary to Revolutionary America, it is important to note that culture is neither monolithic nor static but rather evolves as time progresses. Because the focus is on the social and cultural influences that impacted Edwards's proslavery stance and Hopkins's abolitionism, there are a number of issues that fall beyond the scope of this study.

[2] As Noll states, "The story of religion in the American colonies is the story of Puritanism." Mark A. Noll, *Christians in the American Revolution* (Grand Rapids: Christian University Press, 1977), 29. For a discussion on whether Edwards embraced or rejected the "national covenant" rooted in Puritanism, see Harry S. Stout, "The Puritans and Edwards," in *The Princeton Companion to Jonathan Edwards*, ed. Sang Hyun Lee (Princeton, NJ: Princeton University Press, 2005), 274–88.

Enlightenment sentiment was in its infancy in the British colonies.[3] He grew up approximately a century after the first Puritans arrived to the colonies, "but he died before there was an inkling of the American Revolution," though "many of the potentialities were there."[4] As a result, Edwards should be viewed as an "English colonial loyal to the British crown" as he lived in a distinctly British, Protestant world.[5] More specifically, according to Marsden, Edwards can be understood best "if we think of him as living near the intersection of three competing civilizations: British Protestant, French Catholic, and Indian."[6] All were, at the time, fighting to gain control of North America.[7] Thus, Edwards found himself living in the midst of a wartime situation for the duration of his life.

Puritanism

As a Puritan, "Edwards was loyal to the theology inherited from the seventeenth-century Puritans and their continental 'Reformed,' or Calvinistic, counterparts."[8] According to Marsden, Edwards viewed divine sovereignty as the "central principle" of his thought.[9] Puritanism comes from the Calvinist tradition stemming from the sixteenth century Reformation.[10] The tradition encouraged one to view life holistically, considering the social, ecclesial, and

[3]George M. Marsden, "Biography," in *The Cambridge Companion to Jonathan Edwards*, ed. Stephen J. Stein (New York: Cambridge University Press, 2007), 19.

[4]Marsden, "Biography," 19; George M. Marsden, *Jonathan Edwards: A Life* (New Haven, CT: Yale University Press, 2003), 2.

[5]Marsden, "Biography," 19–20.

[6]Marsden, "Biography," 20. Marsden continues: "British Protestants had recently settled western New England, displacing most of the Indians. Many of the displaced Indians were just to the north and to the west, and most of them were allied with the French Catholics not far beyond in Upper Canada. Edwards's lifetime was punctuated by various wars, usually of European origin, that typically pitted New Englanders against the French and Indians." Marsden, "Biography," 20.

[7]Marsden, *Jonathan Edwards*, 3.

[8]Marsden, *Jonathan Edwards*, 4.

[9]Marsden, *Jonathan Edwards*, 4. For an examination of Edwards's Puritan roots, see Richard L. Bushman, "Jonathan Edwards and Puritan Consciousness," in *Puritan New England: Essays on Religion, Society, and Culture*, ed. Francis J. Bremer and Alden T. Vaughan (New York: St. Martin's Press, 1977), 346–62.

[10]Noll, *Christians in the American Revolution*, 31. For resources on the religious and social dimensions of Puritanism, see Gerald R. Cragg, *From Puritanism to the Age of Reason: A Study of Changes in Religious Thought within the Church of England, 1660 to 1700* (Cambridge: Cambridge University Press, 1950); Herbert W. Schneider, *The Puritan Mind* (Ann Arbor, MI: University of Michigan Press, 1958); Edmund S. Morgan, *Visible Saints: The History of a Puritan*

personal spheres of one's life as harmoniously united.[11] The standard for living was the Bible, for God's special revelation provided the instructions for how to live a God honoring life for his glory.[12] It was a shift away from viewing authority as resting primarily in tradition to alignment with scriptural teaching.[13] The authority of Scripture over tradition was evident during the coming revivals.[14]

When the Puritans began to make their way towards the American colonies in the early seventeenth century, groups such as the Pilgrims, Virginians, and Dutchmen were already living there.[15] The Pilgrims came to the

Idea (New York: New York University Press, 1963); Norman Pettit, *The Heart Prepared: Grace and Conversion in Puritan Spiritual Life* (New Haven, CT: Yale University Press, 1966); Richard L. Bushman, *From Puritan to Yankee: Character and the Social Order in Connecticut, 1690–1765* (Cambridge: Harvard University Press, 1967); Edmund S. Morgan, "The Puritan Ethic and the American Revolution," *The William and Mary Quarterly* 24, no. 1 (1967): 4–43; Stephen Foster, *Their Solitary Way: The Puritan Social Ethic in the First Century of Settlement in New England* (New Haven, CT: Yale University Press, 1971); James William Jones, *The Shattered Synthesis: New England Puritanism before the Great Awakening* (New Haven, CT: Yale University Press, 1973); Margo Todd, *Christian Humanism and the Puritan Social Order* (Cambridge: Cambridge University Press, 1987); T. Dwight Bozeman, *To Live Ancient Lives: The Primitivist Dimension in Puritanism* (Chapel Hill: University of North Carolina Press, 1988); Francis J. Bremer, ed., *Puritanism: Transatlantic Perspectives on a Seventeenth-Century Anglo-American Faith* (Boston: Massachusetts Historical Society, 1993); Janice Knight, *Orthodoxies in Massachussetts: Rereading American Puritanism* (Cambridge, MA: Harvard University Press, 1997); Mark A. Peterson, *The Price of Redemption: The Spiritual Economy of Puritan New England* (Stanford, CA: Stanford University Press, 1997); E. Brooks Holifield, *Theology in America: Christian Thought from the Age of the Puritans to the Civil War* (New Haven, CT: Yale University Press, 2003); Harry S. Stout, "The Puritans and Edwards," in *The Princeton Companion to Jonathan Edwards*, ed. Sang Hyun Lee (Princeton, NJ: Princeton University Press, 2005); Francis J. Bremer and Tom Webster, eds., *Puritans and Puritanism in Europe and America: A Comprehensive Encyclopedia*, 2 vols. (Santa Barbara, CA: ABC-CLIO, 2006).

[11]Noll, *Christians in the American Revolution*, 30.

[12]Noll, *Christians in the American Revolution*, 30–31.

[13]William G. McLoughlin, *Revivals, Awakenings, and Reform: An Essay on Religion and Social Change in America, 1607–1977* (University of Chicago Press, 1978), 31.

[14]McLoughlin explains the impact the revivals had on the Puritans in the British colonies and their separation from England: "During the generation in which this revitalization movement worked itself out, the colonists came to see that acculturation to the New World had opened an enormous gap between them and the mother country. They felt a new and semiautonomous identity as a people; and when the king, their royal father, refused to acknowledge this, they turned against him as a wicked, unnatural parent, unwilling to grant freedom to his mature and self-reliant sons of liberty. However, during that awakening generation, an immense amount of new experience and new ideas had to be accommodated to the new world view in order to give it shape and coherence." McLoughlin, *Revivals, Awakenings, and Reform*, 59. More on the importance of revivals/awakenings will be discussed in the next section.

[15]Cedric B. Cowing, *The Great Awakening and the American Revolution: Colonial Thought in the 18th Century* (Chicago: Rand McNally, 1971), 8. The Pilgrims arrived earlier in 1620

colonies seeking spiritual autonomy while maintaining their cultural identity as a British people.[16] They, according to Cedric B. Cowing, embraced "a vague Calvinistic evangelism coupled with a renewal of the congregational form and a vigorous re-assertion of 'soul liberty,' namely the importance of individual consent to an idea or program."[17] The Pilgrims wanted to break away from the "Church of England," which they did not view as a "true church."[18]

The Puritans, on the other hand, came to the colonies with a stronger religious agenda. Unlike the separatist mentality of the Pilgrims, the Puritans sought to purify the English church.[19] What they had in common with the Pilgrims was their ecclesial governance as they were both Congregationalist and not Episcopalian in polity.[20] A key difference, then, is that the Puritans recognized the English Church as a legitimate church, believing they had enough of a Congregationalist foundation.[21] As a result, the Puritans "could profess communion with the Church of England," thereby setting up "an autonomous congregational model of what the Church should be and hope their brethren at home would follow it in attempting to reform the Church of England."[22] The heart behind the desire to reform the church was to purge the church of what they deemed as Roman Catholic corruption.[23] Furthermore, the Puritans wanted a more basic church polity rather than the

(Plymouth) while the Puritans arrived in 1629 (Cape Ann). Robert H. Romer, *Slavery in the Connecticut Valley of Massachusetts* (Florence, MA: Levellers Press, 2009), 8.

[16]As Cowing explains, "What they sought was livelihood in a place where they could retain their simple amorphous faith and sectarian ways in isolation and peace yet remain under the British flag." Cowing, *The Great Awakening and the American Revolution*, 6.

[17]Cowing, *The Great Awakening and the American Revolution*, 6.

[18]Cowing, *The Great Awakening and the American Revolution*, 5.

[19]Cowing, *The Great Awakening and the American Revolution*, 8. Discussing the idea of Puritanism and the desire to reform the church, Marsden explains, "Puritanism was part of an international Calvinistic movement to *reform* Christendom, not to destroy it. Its goal had been to establish one pure church supported by each Christian state." Marsden, *Jonathan Edwards*, 7. For a discussion on the different approaches scholars have taken to define Puritanism, see Peter Lake, "Defining Puritanism-Again?," in *Puritanism: Transatlantic Perspective on a Seventeenth-Century Anglo-American Faith*, ed. Francis J. Bremer (Boston: Massachusetts Historical Society, 1993), 3–29.

[20]Cowing, *The Great Awakening and the American Revolution*, 8.

[21]Cowing, *The Great Awakening and the American Revolution*, 8.

[22]Cowing, *The Great Awakening and the American Revolution*, 8–9.

[23]According to Todd, the Puritans "were a self-conscious community of protestant zealots committed to purging the Church of England from within of its remaining Roman 'superstitions,' ceremonies, vestments and liturgy, and to establishing a biblical discipline on the larger society,

clerical hierarchy and ritualism of Catholicism, desiring to pattern church life after New Testament teaching.[24] The Puritan priority of Scripture over tradition was significant in governing such decisions.

Another unique aspect of the Puritans is that they had "a clear and characteristic vision of godly social reform," desiring for society to reflect the kingdom of God.[25] Avihu Zakai argues that the Puritans understood their arrival to New England through "*ecclesiastical history*," viewing themselves as part of "the unfolding story of God's plan of salvation and redemption."[26] It was to be a "sacred" and "redemptive" place where the Gospel would extend to the unreached places of the world.[27] Moreover, because, like the Israelites, they believed they "enjoyed a special covenant relationship with God," the Puritans felt a responsibility to reflect the realities of the

primarily through the preached word." Todd, *Christian Humanism and the Puritan Social Order*, 14.

[24]Thomas S. Kidd, *God of Liberty: A Religious History of the American Revolution* (New York: Basic Books, 2010), 20.

[25]Todd, *Christian Humanism and the Puritan Social Order*, 16. Todd argues that the Puritan social vision was largely informed by Erasmian humanism. Todd explains that the "conditioning influence, in the sixteenth and early seventeenth centuries, was Christian humanism, and that one of the defining characteristics of puritan social thought in the seventeenth century was its maintenance of Erasmian ideals and methods in the face of growing conservatism and authoritarianism on the part of its enemies. The importance of puritans as social thinkers lies in the fact that they contributed heavily to the propagation of a belief in social reform, which they, along with contemporaries both protestant and Catholic, had derived from the Renaissance and its classical sources." Todd, *Christian Humanism and the Puritan Social Order*, 17. Moreover, for Todd, the Puritan's social outlook was largely influenced by the marriage between humanism and their commitment to scriptural authority. Todd notes, "While internal contradictions are to be expected from an intellectual milieu which in England combined humanist optimism with the Calvinist doctrine of human depravity, it was the activism and the reformist ethic of Christian humanism which proved most formative for protestant social theory. It was Christian humanism which determined how protestants would apply their biblicism and their theological grounding in their day-to-day conduct in the family, in the market-place, in Parliament." Todd, *Christian Humanism and the Puritan Social Order*, 18. Another aspect of societal reform for the Puritans was through one's vocation. Morgan coined the phrase "Puritan Ethic" to illustrate the Puritan understanding of serving God and society through one's vocational calling. Morgan writes: "God, the Puritans believed, called every man to serve Him by serving society and himself in some useful, productive occupation." Morgan, "The Puritan Ethic and the American Revolution," 4. One needed to be productive in order to benefit society, staying away from material prosperity and ease due to the danger of idleness, desiring instead to live with frugality and adversity to keep one in obedience to God. Morgan, "The Puritan Ethic and the American Revolution," 5–7.

[26]Avihu Zakai, *Exile and Kingdom: History and Apocalypse in the Puritan Migration to America* (Cambridge: Cambridge University Press, 1991), 1.

[27]Zakai, *Exile and Kingdom*, 2, 10.

coming kingdom in their present world.[28] They believed themselves to be a shining example of God's righteousness; a bright city on a hill for the world to marvel at.[29]

Identifying with Israel as a divinely chosen people, the logic was blessing for obedience and discipline for disobedience.[30] As a result, if there was sincere repentance, earthly success, such as in the case of wars with the French and Indians, was guaranteed whereas continued sin would bring hardship.[31] In fact, "American success in the French and Indian Wars gave further proof that God might have predestined the rising glory of America."[32] And in order for New England to fulfill its God-given mission, it needed to defend its liberties against its enemies. As Harry S. Stout notes, "All believed that, as God's covenant people, New Englanders had a glorious mission to fulfill in the world, and that mission required the preservation of their liberties against external enemies."[33] Furthermore, "Civil and religious liberties were interconnected in New Englanders' minds, and both were

[28] Stout, "The Puritans and Edwards," 276. Marsden highlights the dual concerns both Edwards and the Puritans had, wanting to purify the church and develop a God-honoring society. Marsden explains, "Edwards was impaled on the horns of a dilemma inherited from his tradition. Puritanism and its Reformed-pietist successors constantly vacillated between whether they were rebuilding Christendom by making towns and eventually nations into virtually Christian societies, or whether they were advocating a pure, called-out church. Edwards had strong commitments to both ideals. Heir to the Puritan establishment and part of a powerful ruling clan, he was jealous of the privileges of ministerial prestige in town and province. He looked forward to a worldwide Reformed Christendom as the millennium approached." Marsden, *Jonathan Edwards*, 350.

[29] Stout, "The Puritans and Edwards," 288. Personal piety was a crucial distinctive for the Puritans, for they believed personal godliness results in a pious society. Brauer discusses the Puritan understanding of piety, explaining, "Piety as understood by the Puritans was a person's essential religiousness which underlies all religious obedience, actions, and virtues. It was the source for the way one worshipped, for the style and content of one's actions—both private and public. It was the ground from which group life emerged and embodied itself, and it was the fundamental experience that one sought to explore through rational categories. Piety was the root of everything for the Puritan." Jerald C. Brauer, "Types of Puritan Piety," *Church History* 56, no. 1 (1987): 39.

[30] Stout, "The Puritans and Edwards," 277.

[31] Stout, "The Puritans and Edwards," 276–80. Kidd explains the idea of divine aid to ensure colonial victories in wars, supporting the notion of the British colonists being God's chosen people. "American colonists saw the series of wars from the 1740s to the 1770s, leading up to the American Revolution, as divinely designed to vindicate both liberty and Protestantism. They perceived God's power behind every success and puzzled at God's mysterious purposes behind every failure." Kidd, *God of Liberty*, 25–26. It was believed that God was working providentially through wars by providing victory for his people against their enemies. Kidd, *God of Liberty*, 27.

[32] McLoughlin, *Revivals, Awakenings, and Reform*, 77.

[33] Stout, "The Puritans and Edwards," 285.

essential to their corporate identity as the New Israel."[34] This is why New Englanders valued societal reform, engaging in a "Puritan synthesis" where they melded individual or personal religion with a desire to reform society for the glory of God.[35] In fact, awakenings or revivals emphasized both grace and individual holiness with the need to make a difference in society.[36]

Revivals/Awakenings

A direct connection to the desire for a godly society was the desire for revivals to spur spiritual awakening. Due to growing immorality in the late seventeenth century, Thomas S. Kidd writes, "Puritan leaders began calling for an outpouring of the Holy Spirit to revive their languishing churches, and some also began experimenting with new measures that raised the possibility of corporate renewal of individual churches and towns."[37] In fact, a number of Puritan clergy believed that revivals alone "could deliver the churches from their sins, and that the advent of great new awakenings might herald the last days."[38] A wartime setting increased the people's desire for God to move greatly in their midst.[39] Hence it is safe to assume that heightened danger by constant threats of war encouraged a life of dependence on God. By the early eighteenth century, clergy were specifically praying for a great work of the Spirit that would bring a wave of salvation and new spiritual life.[40]

Noll highlights two main parts of what he calls the "Puritan synthesis."[41] The primary emphasis was on personal religion, for "societal good was a function of personal virtue, personal godliness, and personal deeds manifesting the goodness of God."[42] Noll explains that the awakeners believed that society "must indeed be transformed by the gospel, but this transformation had to proceed from the supernatural act of God in renewing the individ-

[34]Stout, "The Puritans and Edwards," 285.

[35]Noll, *Christians in the American Revolution*, 39.

[36]Noll, *Christians in the American Revolution*, 41.

[37]Thomas S. Kidd, *The Great Awakening: The Roots of Evangelical Christianity in Colonial America* (New Haven, CT: Yale University Press, 2007), 1.

[38]Kidd, *The Great Awakening*, 12.

[39]Kidd, *God of Liberty*, 20–21.

[40]Kidd, *God of Liberty*, 21.

[41]Noll, *Christians in the American Revolution*, 39.

[42]Noll, *Christians in the American Revolution*, 39.

ual."[43] In other words, a divine work transforming a believer preceded the transformation of society. The agent of societal transformation was the Christian changed and used by God. Thus, the priority of preaching the Gospel was of paramount importance. In fact, for the Puritans, it was the preaching of Scripture that would eventually bring salvation to the world.[44]

For Edwards, awakenings were a means in which God worked through the Spirit throughout history.[45] Marsden observes, "Edwards viewed himself as part of an international Reformed evangelical movement that saw awakenings as God's greatest works in the current age."[46] Marsden also notes that revivals were such a great work of God in Edwards's mind that he believed they could possibly usher in the millennial age.[47] The awakening in the Connecticut River Valley would take on such a characteristic. When Edwards moved from assistant to head minister in his grandfather Solomon Stoddard's church in Northampton after Stoddard's passing, there was a state of spiritual lethargy not only in the church but in Northampton overall.[48] That changed during the Connecticut River Valley revivals between

[43]Noll, *Christians in the American Revolution*, 39.

[44]McLoughlin, *Revivals, Awakenings, and Reform*, 3.

[45]Marsden, *Jonathan Edwards*, 236.

[46]Marsden, *Jonathan Edwards*, 201.

[47]Marsden, *Jonathan Edwards*, 211. It is important to note that Edwards established the year A.D. 2000 for when the millennium would commence. Glenn R. Kreider, *Jonathan Edwards's Interpretation of Revelation 4:1–8:1* (Lanham, MD: University Press of America), 173–74. For an example of Edwards's comments on the timing of the millennium, see Jonathan Edwards, "An Humble Attempt," in *Apocalyptic Writings*, ed. Stephen J. Stein, vol. 5, *The Works of Jonathan Edwards* (New Haven, CT: Yale University Press, 1977), 410–11. I am indebted to Glenn R. Kreider for pointing me to this primary source reference. In light of Edwards's comments on the commencement of the millennium in *An Humble Attempt*, Kreider notes: "Edwards's evaluation of the spiritual state of the church is such that she was in need of revival in order to prepare her for the coming of the kingdom. Even if God were to pour out his Spirit immediately, there would still be the need for a miraculous work of God to accomplish the establishment of this glorious state of the church prior to 2000. In short, Edwards's conviction now seems to be that it would take about 150 years to prepare the church for her millennium." Kreider, *Jonathan Edwards's Interpretation of Revelation 4:1–8:1*, 174. As a result, Kreider argues, "This sounds like a much more subdued and pessimistic Edwards than during the revivals in New England. This seems to lend support to the view that his 'misunderstood' comments in 'Some Thoughts on the Revival' were written in the euphoria of the moment, which, upon reflection, Edwards rejected and returned to his conviction that the millennium was yet several centuries in the future." Kreider, *Jonathan Edwards's Interpretation of Revelation 4:1–8:1*, 174. Thus, it is important to understand Edwards's posture towards the timing of the millennium during the Connecticut River Valley revivals and the Great Awakening versus after the Awakening.

[48]Cowing, *The Great Awakening and the American Revolution*, 47.

the years of 1734–1735.[49] There was rising spiritual excitement, a growing desire for piety, and scores of people experiencing salvation in Christ.[50] The revival spread throughout the area and Edwards believed many of the new awakenings were a direct result of the awakening occurring in Northampton.[51] C. C. Goen notes how the revivals of 1734–1735 were something entirely new, that "nothing like it had ever occurred before in New England, where previous revivals were largely sporadic and isolated instances," this awakening was spreading.[52] Unfortunately, in large part due to Edwards's Uncle Joseph Hawley's suicide, the awakening cooled off and ended.[53]

In 1740, a greater awakening than the Connecticut River Valley awakening was on the horizon.[54] Marsden explains three key differences between the two revivals:

> First, it seemed to radiate out from Boston to include the entire region. The earlier awakening (and its smaller New England predecessors) had arisen in the hinterlands and never penetrated the

[49]Edwards describes the Connecticut River Valley revivals in a letter to Benjamin Colman, a pastor in Boston (Brattle Street Church). See Jonathan Edwards, "A Faithful Narrative," in *The Great Awakening*, ed. C. C. Goen, vol. 4, *The Works of Jonathan Edwards* (New Haven, CT: Yale University Press, 2009), 128–211.

[50]Discussing the connection between revivalism and personal piety, Goen writes that "all pietists agreed that true Christianity has its main locus in a meaningful relationship of the individual to God. For this reason they stressed personal repentance and faith, warm devotion, and assurance that they were in truth the children of God. Always strongly biblical and intensely missionary, pietism encouraged lively preaching to persuade unbelievers and complacent church members to commit themselves cordially to the obedience of faith. In short, the character of pietism required it to be aggressively conversionist." Also important is the fact that revivals were a vehicle for "mass evangelism" and conversions. C. C. Goen, "Editor's Introduction," in *The Great Awakening*, vol. 4, *The Works of Jonathan Edwards* (New Haven, CT: Yale University Press, 2009), 1, 3.

[51]Marsden, *Jonathan Edwards*, 162.

[52]*WJE*, 4:25.

[53]*WJE*, 4:46; Marsden, *Jonathan Edwards*, 163–69.

[54]For general sources on the Great Awakening, see Charles Hartshorn Maxson, *The Great Awakening in the Middle Colonies* (Chicago: University of Chicago Press, 1920); Perry Miller, "Jonathan Edwards' Sociology of the Great Awakening," *The New England Quarterly* 21, no. 1 (1948): 50–77; Edwin S. Gaustad, *The Great Awakening in New England* (New York: Harper, 1957); Alan Heimert, *Religion and the American Mind: From the Great Awakening to the Revolution* (Cambridge: Harvard University Press, 1966); Cowing, *The Great Awakening and the American Revolution*; Harry S. Stout, "The Great Awakening in New England Reconsidered: The New England Clergy," *Journal of Social History* 8, no. 1 (1974): 21–47; J. M. Bumsted, *What Must I Do to Be Saved? The Great Awakening in Colonial America* (Hinsdale, IL: Dryden Press, 1976); Susan O'Brien, "A Transatlantic Community of Saints: The Great Awakening and the First Evangelical Network, 1735–1755," *American Historical Review* 91, no. 4 (1986): 811–32.

> cultural capital. Second, Whitefield's itinerancy connected the New England events directly to both an intercolonial awakening and an international movement. Third, Whitefield's spectacular successes suggested that awakenings were more likely to be generated by itinerants or visiting preachers than under the strict guidance of local clergy.[55]

George Whitefield would be instrumental in the birthing of the Great Awakening.[56] A celebrity in his own right, Whitefield's preaching of new birth in Christ, along with Edwards, would usher in the Great Awakening.[57] Both Whitefield and Edwards "were passionate about the same concern: true Gospel preaching that God would use to save souls and to bring in his kingdom."[58] Following the excitement generated by Whitefield, Edwards defended both the conversions in the Great Awakening as legitimate and the Awakening itself as a genuine work of God.[59]

Deism and Arminianism

Edwards was adamantly opposed to early sentiments of Enlightenment religion, particularly Deism and Arminianism. On Deism, Zakai notes: "It signified the crisis of Christian culture during the age of Enlightenment, as manifested in the fracturing of doctrinal orthodoxy through attacks on established theological culture and authority, such as the authority of the

[55]Marsden, *Jonathan Edwards*, 214–15.

[56]For examples of primary and secondary sources on Whitefield, see George Whitefield, *The Sermons of George Whitefield*, ed. Lee Gatiss, vol. 1 (Wheaton, IL: Crossway, 2012); George Whitefield, *The Sermons of George Whitefield*, ed. Lee Gatiss, vol. 2 (Wheaton, IL: Crossway, 2012); George Whitefield, J. C. Ryle, and Richard Elliot, *Select Sermons of George Whitefield* (London: Banner of Truth Trust, 1958); Geordan Hammond and David Ceri Jones, *George Whitefield: Life, Context, and Legacy* (Oxford: Oxford University Press, 2016); Thomas S. Kidd, *George Whitefield: America's Spiritual Founding Father* (New Haven, CT: Yale University Press, 2014); Stuart C. Henry, *George Whitefield: Wayfaring Witness* (New York: Abingdon Press, 1957); Arnold A. Dallimore, *George Whitefield: The Life and Times of the Great Evangelist of the Eighteenth-Century Revival* (London: Banner of Truth Trust, 1970).

[57]Marsden, *Jonathan Edwards*, 205; Kidd, *God of Liberty*, 21.

[58]Marsden, *Jonathan Edwards*, 206.

[59]Cowing, *The Great Awakening and the American Revolution*, 64–65. For Edwards's thoughts on the Great Awakening of 1740–1743, see Jonathan Edwards, "The Distinguishing Marks," in *The Great Awakening*, ed. C. C. Goen, vol. 4, *The Works of Jonathan Edwards* (New Haven, CT: Yale University Press, 2009), 213–88; Jonathan Edwards, "Some Thoughts Concerning the Revival," in *The Great Awakening*, ed. C. C. Goen, vol. 4, *The Works of Jonathan Edwards* (New Haven, CT: Yale University Press, 2009), 289–530.

Bible, the integrity and validity of revelation, the credibility of Old Testament prophecies, and the reliability of New Testament miracles."[60] Revelation was rejected and autonomous human reason was elevated in order to understand who God is.[61] Consequently, ethical implications are made evident as "reason should be the basis of belief and that it is essential in making moral decisions" instead of divine revelation.[62] This made sense to the Deist mindset since Deists, in light of natural "moral sense," believed that "human beings can know from within themselves, without reliance on traditional sources of religious authority, what God intends and expects of them as moral creatures."[63] In other words, an innate sense of morality exists within each individual, thus canceling the need of any external source to inform one of virtue, such as Scripture.

Edwards vehemently rejected this Enlightenment mindset and considered Deism, according to McDermott, as "the gravest threat facing Christian faith."[64] The reason for taking such a threat so seriously, according to McDermott, was due to Edwards's belief that if "Christian thinking seriously entertained the most elemental deist presumptions, the Reformed faith would collapse."[65] Affirming man's corruption of nature, Edwards rejected

[60]Avihu Zakai, "The Age of Enlightenment," in *The Cambridge Companion to Jonathan Edwards*, ed. Stephen J. Stein (New York: Cambridge University Press, 2007), 82. For sources on Deism, see for example Peter Gay, *Deism: An Anthology* (Princeton, NJ: Van Nostrand, 1968); Kerry S. Walters, *The American Deists: Voices of Reason and Dissent in the Early Republic* (Lawrence, KS: University Press of Kansas, 1992); Kerry S. Walters, *Rational Infidels: The American Deists* (Durango, CO: Longwood Academic, 1992); Peter Dan Jauhiainen, " 'Reasoning Out of the Scriptures': Samuel Hopkins, the Theological Enterprise, and the Deist Threat," *Journal of Presbyterian History* 79, no. 2 (June 1, 2001): 119–33.

[61]Zakai, "The Age of Enlightenment," 82.

[62]Zakai, "The Age of Enlightenment," 82.

[63]Zakai, "The Age of Enlightenment," 91. McDermott discusses the central role of morality for Deism, noting that the Deist's "purpose of religion is morality. Not only is the function of true religion moral and social—that is, its role is to show the way to a good society—but in its very essence religion is morality. Some denied the validity, others just the importance, of what might be called the doxological character of religion, or its capacity for worship of the divine, and for that matter its mystical dimension as well." Gerald R. McDermott, *Jonathan Edwards Confronts the Gods: Christian Theology, Enlightenment Religion, and Non-Christian Faiths* (New York: Oxford University Press, 2000), 21. While "religion is static and moralistic" for the Deist, for Edwards, "religion is dynamic and draws the believer into mystical participation in the divine." McDermott, *Jonathan Edwards Confronts the Gods*, 8.

[64]McDermott, *Jonathan Edwards Confronts the Gods*, 5. Also see McDermott, *Jonathan Edwards Confronts the Gods*, 18–19. Contrarily, many scholars like Marsden point to Arminianism as Calvinism's most important threat. See Marsden, *Jonathan Edwards*, 138.

[65]McDermott, *Jonathan Edwards Confronts the Gods*, 34. For a good, concise discussion on the two Deists whom Edwards knew well, Thomas Chubb and Mathew Tindal, see McDermott,

Deism's optimism of human reason to attain knowledge of true religion and stressed the necessity of revelation.[66] It is by way of revelation that man gains the knowledge of how to live a virtuous life.[67]

Edwards and the Puritans viewed Arminianism as a serious threat to Calvinist religion.[68] A key concern had to do with how salvation should be understood. For Edwards, human inability due to man's depraved nature and consequent need for divine grace went against the Arminian understanding of necessary human effort in order to procure salvation.[69] Regarding creaturely dependence on God for salvation, Edwards writes: "Man's redemption is often spoken of as a work of wonderful power as well as grace. The great power of God appears in bringing a sinner from his low state, from the depths of sin and misery, to such an exalted state of holiness and happiness."[70] Because of man's moral and salvific inability due to sin, divine grace is necessary. On the other hand, Arminians, notes Clebsch, "made man God's partner in producing true saints," recognizing the necessity of human

Jonathan Edwards Confronts the Gods, 35–37. For an overview of Edwards's writings dealing with Deism, see McDermott, *Jonathan Edwards Confronts the Gods*, 38–50.

[66]Zakai, "The Age of Enlightenment," 84.

[67]Zakai, "The Age of Enlightenment," 84. Edwards's opposition to proponents of natural religion and its consequent humanistic morality led to his use of particular philosophical language in *CEW* and *TV*.

[68]For primary works dealing with Edwards's opposition to Arminian thought, see for example, Jonathan Edwards, *Freedom of the Will*, ed. Paul Ramsey, vol. 1, *The Works of Jonathan Edwards* (New Haven, CT: Yale University Press, 2009); Jonathan Edwards, *Original Sin*, ed. Clyde A. Holbrook, vol. 3, *The Works of Jonathan Edwards* (New Haven, CT: Yale University Press, 1970); Jonathan Edwards, "God Glorified in Man's Dependence," in *Sermons and Discourses, 1730–1733*, ed. Mark Valeri, vol. 17, *The Works of Jonathan Edwards* (New Haven, CT: Yale University Press, 1999), 200–16. For sources on Arminianism, see Jacobus Arminius, *The Writings of James Arminius*, trans. James Nichols and W. R. Bagnall, 3 vols. (Grand Rapids: Baker, 1977); Jacobus Arminius, *Arminius Speaks: Essential Writings on Predestination, Free Will, and the Nature of God*, ed. John D. Wagner (Eugene, OR: Wipf & Stock, 2011); Nicholas Tyacke, *Anti-Calvinists: The Rise of English Arminianism, c. 1590–1640* (Oxford: Clarendon Press, 1987); Ava Chamberlain, "The Theology of Cruelty: A New Look at the Rise of Arminianism in Eighteenth-Century New England," *Harvard Theological Review* 85, no. 3 (1992): 335–56.

[69]Marsden notes: "Although Arminians affirmed that God's grace was essential to salvation, they also believed that people retained some natural ability to choose God's grace or to resist it. Salvation was not simply the result of God's sovereign decree from eternity to save some and not others." Marsden, *Jonathan Edwards*, 86.

[70]Edwards, "God Glorified in Man's Dependence," 205. McClymond and McDermott note that "God Glorified in Man's Dependence" was "Edwards's first publication" and that it "offered a strong anti-Arminian argument." Michael J. McClymond and Gerald R. McDermott, *The Theology of Jonathan Edwards* (New York: Oxford University Press, 2012), 57.

choice.[71] Because the Arminian understanding undermines the doctrine of divine sovereignty, it is not surprising that Edwards viewed Arminianism as a threat to genuine religion.[72]

Social Tensions

In terms of the social climate, hierarchal and patriarchal assumptions were normative.[73] It was a result of the migration from England to the colonies and consequently, the cultural continuity with Britain. Leaving behind the familiar monarchical and aristocratic world of England to living life on the frontier range, the colonists were unable to sever themselves from their own native culture.[74] Michal Rozbicki writes, "The necessity of adjusting to their new, often disorded, experience brought a typical reaction by the colonists of strongly asserting their Englishness. Such self-assertion was a shield against both the instability of their new environment and contempt from the English, who often treated the colonists with disdain as inferior citizens."[75] It seems that by asserting their own British culture in the colonies, the colonists were able to cope with the challenges of a new environment. What was unfamiliar needed to become familiar. Yet at the same time the social influences of the new world on the colonists were significant. As Rozbicki explains, the combination of the new influences along with the "new, colonial forms

[71]William A. Clebsch, *American Religious Thought: A History* (Chicago: University of Chicago Press, 1973), 13.

[72]Several years prior to the Great Awakening, Edwards writes: "About this time, began the great noise that was in this part of the country about Arminianism, which seemed to appear with a very threatening aspect upon the interest of religion here." *WJE*, 4:148. For a discussion on the context of this quote in relation to the Robert Breck affair, see McClymond and McDermott, *The Theology of Jonathan Edwards*, 57.

[73]For a good, concise discussion on Edwards's understanding of the Great Chain of Being and consequently, his "notion of a hierarchically ordered universe," see Avihu Zakai, *Jonathan Edwards's Philosophy of Nature: The Reenchantment of the World in the Age of Scientific Reasoning* (New York: T & T Clark, 2010), 27–30. Viner puts it this way: "The doctrine of the Great Chain of Being maintains that the universe was so designed as to comprise a complete scale of beings from the lowest to the highest, and a complete range of beings of every possible species, so that it would possess to the utmost possible extent the characteristics of gradation, variety, and continuity." Jacob Viner, *The Role of Providence in the Social Order: An Essay in Intellectual History* (Princeton, NJ: Princeton University Press, 1972), 90. A consequence of the Great Chain of Being is accepted social inequality; a necessary reality in order to promote the good of the whole.

[74]Michal J. Rozbicki, "The Cultural Development of the Colonies," in *The Blackwell Encyclopedia of the American Revolution*, ed. Jack P. Greene and J. R. Pole (Cambridge, MA: Blackwell Reference, 1991), 82.

[75]Rozbicki, "The Cultural Development of the Colonies," 82.

of economic organization," brought forward societal characteristics such as "intense individualism, practicality, and orientation towards economic achievement, which clearly emerged in the colonial period as the central values of British-American culture."[76]

Patricia Tracy likens the changing social environment in Northampton by the 1740s, regardless of the recent awakenings, as "more worldly and contentious," looking like any other town in the eighteenth century.[77] Consequently, a once united society began to break down and manifest individual competition, the distancing of church and state relations, and an isolation of piety in daily life.[78] What remained permanent during the changing social environment of the British colonies was the hierarchical nature of society. Edwards certainly embodied this hierarchical reality as he embraced his elite social status. This in large part allowed him to condone institutionalized slavery, which Hopkins ended up vehemently denouncing.

Understanding the British, colonial world Edwards lived in during the early to mid-eighteenth century is key to understanding his proslavery stance. The social sphere Edwards found himself in was ordered by way of one's social status. As a result, a patriarchal authoritarianism was assumed, spanning professional and family life.[79] A lengthy quote by Marsden is helpful in grasping the implications of such views in society:

> Eighteenth-century British-American society depended on patriarchy. One's most significant relationships were likely to be vertical rather than horizontal. Fathers had authority over families and households, the cornerstones of good order. Women, children, hired servants, indentures, and African slaves were all dependent on persons directly above them. Society was conceived of as an extended household. In this arrangement paternalism was a virtue, not a term of opprobrium. Although British people spoke much of "liberty," few had personal freedom in a modern sense. Gentlemen ruled largely through a hierarchical system of patronage extending from the king down. Good

[76]Rozbicki, "The Cultural Development of the Colonies," 83.

[77]Patricia J. Tracy, *Jonathan Edwards, Pastor: Religion and Society in Eighteenth-Century Northampton* (New York: Hill and Wang, 1980), 147.

[78]Tracy, *Jonathan Edwards, Pastor*, 147–48.

[79]Marsden, *Jonathan Edwards*, 3.

> order, especially for the lower ranks of society, was enforced by strict surveillance and stern punishments.[80]

People related to each other by a connection that was either subordinate or hierarchical as society was ordered vertically. It was more prevalent for one to look at another as an authority figure or in subordination rather than as a social equal.[81] For the Puritans, it was necessary to submit to all in authoritative positions because of their role in being God's representatives.[82] As a result, "To honor them was to honor God."[83] Correspondingly, the Edwards family valued submission that was patriarchal in nature.[84] The idea of a well-functioning household was crucial for the well ordering of society.[85] Wood describes the centrality of the family structure in relation to societal life:

> The family household was still the place where most of the work in the society was done and where most of the education and training took place. In the absence of all the elaborate institutions of modern society—from hospitals and nursing homes to prisons and asylums—the family remained the primary institution for teaching the young, disciplining the wayward, and caring for the poor and insane. No wonder that the colonists believed that society was little more than a collection of family households, to which all isolated and helpless individuals necessarily had to be attached. Everywhere families reached out and blended almost imperceptibly into the larger community.[86]

The family was the primary place where one found fellowship and immediate hierarchical ordering of life.[87] The Puritans and Edwards "viewed the submission of wives in marriage as a type of the spiritual submission to

[80] Marsden, *Jonathan Edwards*, 3.

[81] Gordon S. Wood, *The Radicalism of the American Revolution* (New York: Vintage, 1993), 23.

[82] Marsden, *Jonathan Edwards*, 12.

[83] Marsden, *Jonathan Edwards*, 12.

[84] Marsden, *Jonathan Edwards*, 247. For a concise discussion on the authoritarian role of the father figure in Puritan New England, see McLoughlin, *Revivals, Awakenings, and Reform*, 47–50.

[85] Wood, *The Radicalism of the American Revolution*, 44.

[86] Wood, *The Radicalism of the American Revolution*, 44.

[87] Wood, *The Radicalism of the American Revolution*, 44.

Christ to which all should aspire."[88] As a result, dependence on the patriarch was key.[89] To the chagrin of colonial women, the subordination was to the point of degradation. Wives were regarded legally and socially similar to the husband's children and in turn treated as such.[90] This type of patriarchal authoritarianism extended its way to the family structure, as fathers were the recognized authority both in position and instruction.[91] Discussing the authoritarian role of the father figure, Wood writes,

> Almost everyone spent some time in his or her life living in an extended household. And everyone in the household was dependent on the will of the father or master (the terms were indistinguishable). The family was, in fact, not simply those living under one roof but all those dependent on the single head. And this head, the patriarch, was the only one who dealt with the larger world.[92]

Monarchical society was largely relationship driven.[93] People recognized their place in the hierarchal order and related to one another accordingly. Interestingly, according to Wood, the reputation of the colonists was that of an "unruly lot, crude if not barbarous, and especially defiant of social and political authority."[94] Certainly the social, political, and military freedoms they experienced living in the British colonies informed their attitudes towards monarchical authority, though the hierarchical subjection to the king was clearly understood.[95] It was a tension that the Puritans felt in light

[88]Marsden, *Jonathan Edwards*, 248.

[89]Wood, *The Radicalism of the American Revolution*, 49.

[90]Wood, *The Radicalism of the American Revolution*, 49. While this is true of the time period, it is difficult to see Edwards as embodying this posture towards his wife. Edwards loved Sarah and appreciated her love for God and piety. This is exemplified in a personal letter he likely gave her during his years at Yale. See Jonathan Edwards, "On Sarah Pierpont," in *Letters and Personal Writings*, ed. George S. Claghorn, vol. 16, *The Works of Jonathan Edwards* (New Haven, CT: Yale University Press, 1998), 789–90. For introductory comments on Edwards's letter to Sarah, see George S. Claghorn, Introduction to "On Sarah Pierpont," in *Letters and Personal Writings*, ed. George S. Claghorn, vol. 16, *The Works of Jonathan Edwards* (New Haven, CT: Yale University Press, 1998), 745–47.

[91]Marsden, *Jonathan Edwards*, 19.

[92]Wood, *The Radicalism of the American Revolution*, 44.

[93]Wood, *The Radicalism of the American Revolution*, 11.

[94]Wood, *The Radicalism of the American Revolution*, 13.

[95]Wood, *The Radicalism of the American Revolution*, 13. In discussing the hierarchical nature of society and the understanding of a monarchical idea of submission to authority, Wood explains

of individual liberty and subservience to authority, a tension for freedom and the need to obey authority.[96] Edwards certainly fit the picture of the era as he embodied an eighteenth-century prerevolutionary understanding of authority.[97]

With a hierarchical ordering of society came clear social inequalities. The majority of colonists agreed that this was not a bad thing.[98] Under the sovereignty of God, each man had his place for the betterment of society.[99] Inequality, in fact, was not only viewed as "natural but beneficial, of value to superior and inferior alike," for his place in the hierarchy of society "served the good of all men," not just of those in authority over him or for individual reasons.[100] This worked its way into ecclesial life as the seating of parishioners was decided by social status.[101] Likewise the economy was driven "in

how the "theoretical underpinnings" of the colonist's "social thought still remained largely monarchical. They may not have known much of real kings and courts, but they knew very well the social hierarchy that the subjection and subordination of monarchy necessarily implied. Monarchy presumed what Hume called 'a long train of dependence,' a gradation of degrees of freedom and servility that linked everyone from the king at the top down to the bonded laborers and black slaves at the bottom." Wood, *The Radicalism of the American Revolution*, 18–19.

[96]McLoughlin, *Revivals, Awakenings, and Reform*, 35.

[97]Marsden, *Jonathan Edwards*, 259. This understanding of authority for Edwards was not only earthly but also cosmic. Marsden notes, "He viewed the universe and this world as hierarchical and assumed that social relationships should be governed by respect for divinely instituted authority." Marsden, *Jonathan Edwards*, 259. An example of Edwards's prerevolutionary understanding of authority is when Edwards defends the slave-owning right of a fellow pastor when parishioners began voicing concern about his slave-owning practices. By "casting such reproaches on their pastor," they do so "to the great wounding of religion." Jonathan Edwards, "Draft Letter on Slavery," in *Letters and Personal Writings*, ed. George S. Claghorn, vol. 16, *The Works of Jonathan Edwards* (New Haven, CT: Yale University Press, 1998), 73. Edwards's understanding of slavery and the slave trade will be detailed in chapter four.

[98]Foster, *Their Solitary Way*, 15.

[99]Foster, *Their Solitary Way*, 15.

[100]Foster, *Their Solitary Way*, 15.

[101]Kidd, *God of Liberty*, 21; McLoughlin, *Revivals, Awakenings, and Reform*, 35. In describing the role one's social status had on church seating in Edwards's Northampton environment, Tracy writes, "Almost all New England Congregationalists before the Revolution assigned meetinghouse seats to all adults on the basis of age and social rank, and in many towns the process of determining the correct order of precedence occasioned significant disturbances of the Christian community. Northampton escaped these troubles until the 1730s. Ever since the building of the second meetinghouse in 1664, a committee of church officers (after 1700 including the pastor) and leading laymen had assigned seats according to a person's age, estate, and 'usefulness' (community service, military rank, or other secular distinctions.)." Tracy, *Jonathan Edwards, Pastor*, 125. Specifically for enslaved Africans as Greene notes, because they "were considered lowest in the economic and social order, the lowliest place in the meeting

accordance with the organic social hierarchy—everything in its proper and needed place—became the key to proper political management."[102] As a result of the rapid growth of the economy during the late seventeenth to early eighteenth century, colonial society changed with it, reflecting more of an environment rich with commerce as compared to the traditional old-world order.[103] With the growing economy came behavior contrary to traditional Puritan values. For example, the desire for individual wealth became more important than benefiting the public good.[104] This also impacted social attitudes as middle and lower class individuals recognized their place of subservience and aimed to foster appropriate attitudes and qualities.[105] Despite the growing desire for individual economic growth, a key function of the economy was to care for the greater public by the emphasis placed on land productivity and protection.[106]

A cause of friction was the population of Native Americans and Africans.[107] Non-European culture was viewed as uncivilized compared to European standards and thus, the colonists viewed their own identity "in categories of superiority."[108] As the colonists moved forward with the acquisition of land

house would probably have been assigned to them, irrespective of their color. . . . Generally however, there was an 'African corner,' where Negroes either stood in the rear of the church or sat upon benches. Sometimes they sat on the stairs." Lorenzo J. Greene, *The Negro in Colonial New England: 1620–1776* (1942; repr., Eastford, CT: Martino, 2016), 283.

[102]Wood, *The Radicalism of the American Revolution*, 64.

[103]Jack P. Greene, "Search for Identity: An Interpretation of the Meaning of Selected Patterns of Social Response in Eighteenth-Century America," *Journal of Social History* 3, no. 3 (1969): 195. Greene explains, "The rapid economic and demographic growth of the colonies after 1680 and more especially after 1713 opened up vast new economic opportunities in land, trade, and services and greatly accelerated the transformation of the colonies from the largely traditional and relatively static societies most of them had been throughout much of the seventeenth century into the market-oriented, rapidly changing societies most of them would become by the middle of the eighteenth century." Greene, "Search for Identity," 195.

[104]Greene, "Search for Identity," 197.

[105]Greene, "Search for Identity," 197–98.

[106]Mark Valeri, *Law and Providence in Joseph Bellamy's New England: The Origins of the New Divinity in Revolutionary America* (New York: Oxford University Press, 1994), 77–78.

[107]In the conquest for land, new Protestants failed to consider the rights and religious realities of those that were already occupying the colonies. As Marty explains, "Almost never did it occur to them that these people, misnamed *Indians* by Christopher Columbus, had values—including religious systems—which needed to be understood." Martin E. Marty, *Protestantism in the United States: Righteous Empire*, 2nd ed. (New York: Scribner's, 1986), 13.

[108]Rozbicki, "The Cultural Development of the Colonies," 73. For a concise discussion on the foundational aspect of European culture and identity on American cultural and religious life, see Winthrop S. Hudson, *Religion in America*, 3rd ed. (New York: Scribner's, 1981), 3–5.

in the seventeenth century, Native Americans were primarily viewed as both "unattractive and threatening," a people that needed to be removed from their land.[109] Thus the British colonial reaction to the different cultures populating the colonies was a desire to convert others into their own cultural image.[110] Conflicts would naturally transpire. In discussing the contention with Native Americans, Kidd explains that conflict "with Native Americans started almost as soon as the first colonies were settled. At various times, it threatened to wipe out entire Native American groups, the English colonists, or both."[111] While the Puritans originally had intentions of sharing the Gospel with Native Americans in New England, they, according to Kidd, "tended more often to provoke and bully the Indians over land rights and other issues."[112] It was believed that God had providentially delivered Native Americans into the control of the colonists.[113] Wars ensued. Often captured Native Americans were exchanged for enslaved Africans in the

[109]Marty, *Protestantism in the United States*, 14. A number of Native Americans forced into slavery was also an issue in colonial New England. Richard A. Bailey, *Race and Redemption in Puritan New England* (New York: Oxford University Press, 2011), 33. Discussing the civilizing process by Protestant and Catholic missionaries to Native Americans, Axtell notes: "At its most extreme, the civilization process entailed the wholesale substitution of a European lifestyle for the natives' own, beginning with material artifacts—clothing, weapons, tools—and ending with deeply engrained habits of thought and feeling." James Axtell, *The Invasion Within: The Contest of Cultures in Colonial North America* (New York: Oxford University Press, 1985), 4.

[110]As Rozbicki puts it, "The colonists had to build the Indian, and later the African, into their notions of world order. In both cases it resulted in the emergence of separatist and exclusionist attitudes towards non-Europeans." Rozbicki, "The Cultural Development of the Colonies," 74. Skin color played a key role in the denigration of Native Americans and Africans. Robinson states that by "European standards, Indians were dark-complexioned, heathen, savage folk." Donald L. Robinson, *Slavery in the Structure of American Politics, 1765–1820* (New York: W. W. Norton, 1979), 14. Likewise for those of African descent, Robinson explains how in light of the negative connotation associated with the color black in the sixteenth century, British colonists, who "adopted the Spanish term 'Negro,' meaning 'black,' " used it as reason to show prejudice. Robinson, *Slavery in the Structure of American Politics, 1765–1820*, 14. Discussing the response by the first settlers to non-Europeans, Stewart asserts: "The Africans' blackness, symbolizing sin, affirmed by visual contrast the English colonists' sanctified self-image as 'white' people. Soon a cycle of debasement and exploitation took hold." James Brewer Stewart, *Holy Warriors: The Abolitionists and American Slavery*, rev. ed. (New York: Hill and Wang, 1997), 6.

[111]Kidd, *God of Liberty*, 20.

[112]Kidd, *The Great Awakening*, 6. Kidd also highlights the reality of patriarchal authority and dependency, stating, "Land-owning white men ruled over their families, social inferiors, servants, and slaves. The elites integrated all these people into a vast system of dependencies." Kidd, *The Great Awakening*, xv.

[113]Lorenzo J. Greene, "Slave-Holding New England and Its Awakening," *Journal of Negro History* 13, no. 4 (1928): 493.

West Indies.[114] For example, after the Pequot War (1636–1637), "numerous captured Pequots were sold into slavery in the Indies" by New England colonists.[115] And after King Philip's War (1675–1676), Native American indentured servitude and slavery became prominent in Massachusetts.[116] Consequently, Native Americans were the first slaves in New England.[117]

Similarly, the African slave experience was arduous in light of colonial slave owning. Franklin argues that "the Renaissance and the Commercial Revolution" were the reasons why institutionalized slavery and the slave trade became a reality.[118] The Renaissance provided one the freedom to pursue what was personally beneficial, even if it meant taking the freedom of another while commerce and the pursuit of material wealth provided "new techniques of exploitation," encouraging slavery and the slave trade.[119] In New England, as the African slave population grew gradually during the seventeenth century, the eighteenth century "saw the rise of the New England colonies as the greatest slave-carriers of America."[120] While England dominated the slave trade to the Americas in the first half of the eighteenth century, New England slave traders were encouraged by the motherland to participate in light of the abundance of slaves available.[121] Thus, New

[114]Romer, *Slavery in the Connecticut Valley of Massachusetts*, 14.

[115]Romer, *Slavery in the Connecticut Valley of Massachusetts*, 14–15.

[116]Romer, *Slavery in the Connecticut Valley of Massachusetts*, 17–18.

[117]Greene, "Slave-Holding New England and Its Awakening," 493. Greene continues, stating how "Indian slavery was, however, soon to be supplemented by Negro servitude, for the redskin was considered lazy, intractable, vindictive, and inclined to run away." Greene, "Slave-Holding New England and Its Awakening," 494. African slavery would become the dominant form of slavery up to the American Revolution. Generally speaking, the subjugation during colonial American times included African slavery, Native American slavery, periodic white slavery, along with African American, Native American, and white indentured servitude. Greene, *The Negro in Colonial New England*, 18–19.

[118]John Hope Franklin, *From Slavery to Freedom: A History of Negro Americans*, 4th ed. (New York: Knopf, 1974), 31.

[119]Franklin, *From Slavery to Freedom*, 31–32.

[120]Greene, "Slave-Holding New England and Its Awakening," 496. Greene highlights the proportionate growth of slaves in light of increasing wealth: "In 1735, there were 2,600 Negroes in Massachusetts; in 1764 the number had increased to 5,779. In 1742, Boston alone had 1,514 slaves and free Negroes, the number having almost quadrupled in about forty years." Greene, "Slave-Holding New England and Its Awakening," 496–97.

[121]Franklin, *From Slavery to Freedom*, 65.

England slave trading grew tremendously from the early to mid eighteenth century.[122]

Those of African descent in prerevolutionary America were recognized as slaves upon arriving to the colonies.[123] David Brion Davis points out in general, "it has been said that the slave has three defining characteristics: his person is the property of another man, his will is subject to his owner's authority, and his labor or services are obtained through coercion."[124] A slave was involuntarily owned and thus, was at the service of his owner at all times. Specifically, slaves were the chattel or possession of their owner. It makes sense, then, that slave owners "in colonial New England liked to think of slavery as essentially private—as were domestic affairs generally. What they did to their slaves, they hoped, was of no concern to anyone else."[125] Enslavers felt the freedom to do as they pleased. Viewed and treated as property by their owners, slaves, as Romer notes, were sold and taxed in the same manner as livestock and other possessions owned by the owner.[126] Romer continues, arguing for actual slave practices in the North against claims questioning whether slavery was truly slavery in the North compared to the harsher slave realities of the South. He highlights how children and spouses were often taken from their families when sold and how children obtained the slave status of their parents.[127] Moreover, a slave's "status does not depend on his relation to a particular owner, and is not limited by

[122]Franklin, *From Slavery to Freedom*, 65.

[123]Edmund S. Morgan, "Slavery and Freedom: The American Paradox," *Journal of American History* 59, no. 1 (1972): 17. Because institutionalized slavery did not technically exist when the colonies were beginning, there was little to no difference "between Negro slavery and indentured servitude." Greene, *The Negro in Colonial New England*, 125. Massachusetts would be the first to legalize institutionalized slavery in the colonies. Greene, *The Negro in Colonial New England*, 125. Furthermore, during the sixteenth to eighteenth centuries of the slave trade, there were "at least fifteen million" enslaved Africans brought to "the New World." David Brion Davis, *The Problem of Slavery in Western Culture* (Ithaca, NY: Cornell University Press, 1966), 9.

[124]Davis, *The Problem of Slavery in Western Culture*, 31.

[125]John W. Sweet, *Bodies Politic: Negotiating Race in the American North, 1730–1830* (Philadelphia: University of Pennsylvania Press, 2006), 9.

[126]Romer, *Slavery in the Connecticut Valley of Massachusetts*, 23. For examples of bills of sale by owners selling enslaved Africans, see Romer, *Slavery in the Connecticut Valley of Massachusetts*, 33–44.

[127]Romer, *Slavery in the Connecticut Valley of Massachusetts*, 31, 44. The enslaver often separated family members when deciding to sell. Zilversmit notes: "Contemporary advertisements show that in some instances masters sold husbands, wives, and children separately, and groups of slaves were frequently offered for sale with no mention of family ties." Arthur Zilversmit, *The First Emancipation: The Abolition of Slavery in the North* (Chicago: University of Chicago Press, 1967), 10.

time or space. His condition is hereditary and ownership in his person is alienable."[128] Strictly speaking, slaves were the property of their owners with no rights of their own, able to be sold at any moment.[129] The status as a slave was permanent.

Prior to the Revolution, institutionalized slavery was rarely questioned and was universally accepted in the colonies.[130] As Gordon S. Wood says, "By the middle of the eighteenth century black slavery had existed in the colonies for several generations or more without substantial questioning or criticism."[131] Likewise Noll states how slavery in the colonies "came into existence without a great deal of conscious reflection."[132] In fact, even during the spiritual euphoria of the Great Awakening, the vast majority of church leaders never criticized institutionalized slavery.[133] Instead, the focus was

[128]Davis, *The Problem of Slavery in Western Culture*, 32.

[129]Bonwick explains the nature of a slave's lack of rights and status of being owned: "Slaves were a form of property. They were bound for life, subject to the will of their owners and could be bought and sold; their condition was transmitted to succeeding generations through the female line. The law offered limited protection against maltreatment but no rights. Race provided the crucial determinant of status. Colin Bonwick, *The American Revolution* (Charlottesville, VA: University Press of Virginia, 1991), 33. To further underscore the idea of enslaved Africans as property, slave owners who lacked work for their slaves often times placed them on loan to those who needed labor in order to gain financial compensation for what they viewed as a personal investment. Greene, *The Negro in Colonial New England*, 120.

[130]Sylvia R. Frey, "Slavery and Anti-Slavery," in *The Blackwell Encyclopedia of the American Revolution*, ed. Jack P. Greene and J. R. Pole (Cambridge, MA: Blackwell Reference, 1991), 385. While Quakers voiced their displeasure against slavery, they were very much the minority voice compared to the majority that condoned institutionalized slavery. Wood, *The Radicalism of the American Revolution*, 54. For Quaker opposition to slavery, also see Cowing, *The Great Awakening and the American Revolution*, 101–2; Kidd, *God of Liberty*, 133–34.

[131]Wood, *The Radicalism of the American Revolution*, 54. Marsden notes that when enslavers in New England did recognize the injustices of institutionalized slavery, "their most common way of dealing with the subject was to avoid it; so the topic received little more public discussion until the era of the American Revolution." Marsden, *Jonathan Edwards*, 20. An exception is Sewall's *The Selling of Joseph*. Originally published in 1700, it provides a clear condemnation of both slavery and the slave trade in Massachusetts. See Samuel Sewall, *The Selling of Joseph: A Memorial*, ed. Sidney Kaplan (Amherst: University of Massachusetts Press, 1969). It was New England's first "antislavery tract." Mark Valeri, *Heavenly Merchandize: How Religion Shaped Commerce in Puritan America* (Princeton, NJ: Princeton University Press, 2010), 170. According to Valeri, for Sewall, "No biblical exegesis or design to evangelize captured Africans . . . justified the vice and inhumanity of the slave trade. The Middle Passage began with outright theft, severed families, and ended with 'Murder.' Fornication and violence spread through the whole trade." Valeri, *Heavenly Merchandize*, 170.

[132]Mark A. Noll, *The Old Religion in a New World: The History of North American Christianity* (Grand Rapids: Eerdmans, 2002), 55.

[133]James D. Essig, *The Bonds of Wickedness: American Evangelicals Against Slavery, 1770–1808* (Philadelphia: Temple University Press, 1982), 14.

on the needed salvation of the lost.[134] Thus slavery was justified not only for spiritual reasons, but also for economic and legal reasons.[135] In fact, the personal "economic and social" benefits that slaves brought to New England slave owners outweighed any moral concerns about institutionalized slavery or the slave trade discussed by the few.[136] For enslavers, slave labor meant personal economic growth and independence.[137] Furthermore, as the economy grew in New England, the need for labor grew.[138] The enslavement and/or servitude of whites and Native Americans were insufficient to keep up with labor demands.[139] Thus, enslaved Africans were viewed as the answer to the shortage of labor.[140] In the end, slavery was an inherent reality of the American colonies from the very beginning; a major aspect of the New World's birth and development.[141]

White servitude was also widespread, further highlighting the hierarchical nature of colonial society. Like African slavery, forced dependence was a reality with white servitude. This gave enslaving colonists reason to view both types of servitude similarly:

> Under such circumstances it was often difficult for the colonists to perceive the distinctive peculiarity of black slavery. Slavery often seemed to be just another degree of servitude, another degree of labor, more severe and more abject, to be sure, but not in the eyes of most colonists all that different from white servitude and white labor. Both kinds of servants shared the necessity of laboring and the contempt in which manual labor was traditionally held, and both were plainly dependent in a world that valued only independence. Slaves, like servants,

[134]The Puritan understanding of the Old Testament and thus, God instituting slavery, along with viewing themselves as God's chosen people, allowed slavery to be viewed as something given by God according to his providence. Furthermore, any suffering the slave may experience on earth was inconsequential compared to the eternal salvation granted to them while in their state of subjugation. Hence, the Puritan conscience was at peace with the reality of slavery. Greene, *The Negro in Colonial New England*, 61–62.

[135]Greene, *The Negro in Colonial New England*, 60.

[136]Franklin, *From Slavery to Freedom*, 67.

[137]Zilversmit, *The First Emancipation*, 33.

[138]Greene, *The Negro in Colonial New England*, 60.

[139]Greene, *The Negro in Colonial New England*, 60.

[140]Greene, *The Negro in Colonial New England*, 60.

[141]Davis, *The Problem of Slavery in Western Culture*, 24.

were often described simply as another kind of dependent in the patriarchal family.[142]

While the oppression placed on white servants was not to the extent of that placed on enslaved Africans, it was harsh nonetheless.[143] Key differences are that white servitude was typically temporal and usually for young people.[144]

Cultural and religious priorities for enslaved Africans were ignored as they were forced to depart from their native land.[145] In colonial America, the bright, God-ordained future of Puritan America did not apply to Native Americans and Africans. While the colonists exuded spiritual concern for both Native Americans and enslaved Africans, the desire to fulfill God's will as his special people was the priority. In light of slavery, the extension of Christian society from the colonies was expected to have a European, colonial character to it.

Churches embraced what they viewed as God's work in America as "the source of much of their restless energy as they sought to keep abreast of the western tide of migration and to make sure that the United States would fulfill its calling as a godly nation."[146] As a result, "Indians were treated as an alien presence to be pushed back beyond the forward-moving edge of 'civilization' " while enslaved Africans "were outsiders who had little reason to view the future as pregnant with the possibility of all things being made new."[147] Slaves lost their freedom as they were taken from Africa, their rights withheld by colonists as owned slaves, while living in a "Christian society" that did not offer them freedom or rights.[148] The brutal conditions of colonial servitude blighted the will of slaves to pursue freedom as personal

[142]Wood, *The Radicalism of the American Revolution*, 54.

[143]Wood, *The Radicalism of the American Revolution*, 54.

[144]Wood, *The Radicalism of the American Revolution*, 56. Marsden notes, "White servants, most indentured for a period of years, were treated much like slaves. They were thoroughly dependent on the patriarchal authority of their masters. They needed permission to marry, buy or sell property, or leave the premises. They could be bought or sold, seized to pay debts, or willed to heirs. The vast differences, of course, were that African slavery was always involuntary and usually perpetual." Marsden, *Jonathan Edwards*, 256.

[145]Marty, *Protestantism in the United States*, 31.

[146]Hudson, *Religion in America*, 21–22.

[147]Hudson, *Religion in America*, 22.

[148]Morgan, "Slavery and Freedom," 26.

resolve often waned as a result.[149] Nevertheless, there were consistent attempts by enslaved Africans to pursue freedom from their bondage in light of the unhappiness of their condition.[150] Such an experience would be cause for a bleak outlook of the future.

British colonists understood forced dependency as a normative aspect of society.[151] Discussing the Puritan understanding of slavery in light of God's sovereign favor upon them as divinely chosen people, Greene explains:

> But the Puritans based their right to human chattel upon the highest spiritual grounds. God had given the heathen Indians and the Negroes to them as part of their inheritance. Were not the Puritans, even as the Israelites, God's chosen people? Slavery was a sacred privilege the Almighty was pleased to grant His Elect, and they quoted extensively from the Bible in support of their position.[152]

Larry E. Tise argues that European cultural identity and history provided the colonists with a familiarity of "human bondage and with forms of thought that urged its perpetuation."[153] A view of European civil sophistication compared to the uncivilized culture of non-European people groups perpetuated

[149]Bernard Bailyn, *The Ideological Origins of the American Revolution* (Cambridge, MA: Belknap Press of Harvard University Press, 1967), 233–34.

[150]Greene, *The Negro in Colonial New England*, 144, 164. In discussing some of the different ways enslaved Africans reacted to their unhappy conditions, Franklin explains that since "the number of slaves in New England remained relatively small throughout the colonial period, there was little fear of insurrections. Nevertheless, many slaves indicated their dislike of the institution by running away. Others attacked their masters and even murdered them. Still others plotted to rebel. In 1658 some Negroes and Indians in Hartford decided to make a bid for their freedom by destroying several houses of their masters. In the eighteenth century there were a number of conspiracies to rebel in Boston and other towns in Massachusetts." Franklin, *From Slavery to Freedom*, 66. Also contributing to the unhappy condition of slaves were the frustrations directed at them by some "white laborers" who viewed African slave labor as unfair competition. Zilversmit, *The First Emancipation*, 46–47.

[151]Wood explains, "By modern standards it was a cruel and brutal age, and the life of the lowly seemed cheap. Slavery could be regarded, therefore, as merely the most base and degraded status in a society of several degrees of unfreedom, and most colonists felt little need as yet either to attack or to defend slavery any more than other forms of dependency and debasement." Wood, *The Radicalism of the American Revolution*, 55. Also see Marsden, *Jonathan Edwards*, 256. Of significance was the vertical ordering of society in prerevolutionary America. For the colonists, subservience was expected for slaves.

[152]Greene, "Slave-Holding New England and Its Awakening," 500.

[153]Larry E. Tise, *Proslavery: A History of the Defense of Slavery in America, 1701–1840* (Athens, GA: University of Georgia Press, 1987), 14.

the thought of social hierarchy. The "social habits" of Africans seemed to the colonists, according to Donald L. Robinson, as "not just different, but wild, and distinctly inferior."[154] Thus we may conclude, in the colonist's mind, it was acceptable for non-Europeans to be in subjugation. Consequently, forms of servitude like institutionalized slavery spread across the British colonies without much opposition.[155] And because there was little resistance, there was silence to its defense for African slavery was viewed as normative and socially acceptable.[156]

Because converting African slaves was a priority, the relationship between religious and racial realities became difficult for those enslaved. Martin E. Marty explains the tension African slaves experienced in light of their acceptance of the Gospel from European Protestants:

> The blacks' relation to dominant Protestantism was ambiguous. On one hand, the degree to which they accepted evangelical Christianity, adapted it, and lived by it, was an impressive compliment to its spiritual power. Much in the faith worked well and rang true for them. On the other hand, every aspect of the black-and-Protestant bond was conditioned by the fact that only parts of the evangelical experience were permitted them. Even these parts were transformed by the white experience. The Jesus around whose name they gathered seemed to be an Anglo-Saxon. The traditions that were parceled out to blacks with such guarded care were white translations of an historical religion that had not been born on Anglo-Saxon, Teutonic, or Caucasian soil.[157]

The perception of slaves upon conversion was also a difficult reality. Though they were now spiritual equals with white colonials, racially they were considered as mere slaves.[158] As far as their humanity and culture,

[154]Robinson, *Slavery in the Structure of American Politics, 1765–1820*, 14–15.

[155]Tise, *Proslavery*, 15.

[156]Tise, *Proslavery*, 15. Tise explains that the scarcity of proslavery literature in the eighteenth century was due to the broad acceptance of slave owning, noting that "the paucity of early American proslavery literature resulted neither from the absence of proslavery notions nor from any indisposition toward upholding slavery. What was missing was the need to defend an institution that nearly everyone took for granted." Tise, *Proslavery*, 16.

[157]Marty, *Protestantism in the United States*, 32–33.

[158]Davis, *The Problem of Slavery in Western Culture*, 165.

according to Davis, they were viewed as pagans who "deserved in some sense to be slaves."[159] Consequently, the given perception of enslaved Africans, whether saved or unsaved, certainly contributed to the Western dehumanizing of Africans and the belief that they were subhuman objects to be owned.[160]

For New England, though it is not certain when enslaved Africans first arrived, the institution of slavery existed prior to the establishment of the Massachusetts Bay Colony in the early seventeenth century.[161] Due to social and economic realities, New England had a smaller slave population compared to colonies in the South.[162] Specifically for New England, the fewer number of slaves was largely due to the more favorable environment of the South in terms of climate and soil conditions.[163] Noting the difference between slaves in the South, "where most slaves lived on large plantations and where there was comparatively little civil infrastructure," slaves in "colonial New England—where farms were smaller and more people lived in commercial seaports" were "intimately intertwined in the tangled web of household and community relations."[164] Slaves in New England were also treated more kindly compared to "plantation colonies" as they were considered for the most part as members of the family.[165] Also unique

[159]Davis, *The Problem of Slavery in Western Culture*, 165.

[160]Davis, *The Problem of Slavery in Western Culture*, 10.

[161]Greene, *The Negro in Colonial New England*, 15–16. Romer notes, "Massachusetts was in fact the very first colony to legalize slavery, in 1641." Romer, *Slavery in the Connecticut Valley of Massachusetts*, 6.

[162]Frey, "Slavery and Anti-Slavery," 384.

[163]Greene notes that in "the South, the mild climate, fertile soil, and the plantation system, rendered the employment of large numbers of slaves profitable. But in the New England colonies, climatic conditions, the barrenness of the soil, the town system, and the general poverty of the inhabitants, all militated against slavery. . . . Slavery was to disappear in New England not because of any exalted moral objection to the holding of human beings as chattel, but because it did not pay. It is safe to assume then, that had physical conditions been as favorable to slavery in the North as in the South, the sentiments of both sections would undoubtedly have been identical. The very nature of the environment prohibited the keeping of slaves in large numbers. Thus, the average number of slaves for each household was two, although a few families owned from five to thirty; but this proved the exception rather than the rule, and obtained only in the Narragansett Country." Greene, "Slave-Holding New England and Its Awakening," 502–3.

[164]Sweet, *Bodies Politic*, 9.

[165]Greene, "Slave-Holding New England and Its Awakening," 510. Discussing the difference of the New England slave experience compared to that of the South, Franklin explains: "Negroes in New England were in a unique position in colonial America. They were not subjected to the harsh codes or the severe treatment that their fellows received in the colonies of the

to New England and the "middle colonies" were educational and church membership opportunities for enslaved Africans.[166]

Edmund S. Morgan describes how the concurrent rise of freedom and equality with institutionalized slavery produced an American societal contradiction: "That two such contradictory developments were taking place simultaneously over a long period of our history, from the seventeenth century to the nineteenth, is the central paradox of American history."[167] Similarly, Bernard Bailyn points to the conflict between the colonial pursuit of freedom and the reality of institutionalized slavery as the American Revolution approached: "It was not grasped by all at once, nor did it become effective evenly through the colonies. But gradually the contradiction between the proclaimed principles of freedom and the facts of life in America became generally recognized."[168] The number of slaves was significant, making up one fifth of the population when the American Revolution was commencing.[169] In New England throughout the colonial period, the African

South. Nevertheless, it is possible to exaggerate the humanitarian aspects of their treatment. Masters in New England held a firm hand on the institution and gave little consideration to the small minority that argued for the freedom of the slaves. Although the New Englander took his religion seriously, he did not permit it to interfere with his appreciation of the profits of slavery and the slave trade. At the same time, he did not glut his home market with slaves and increase the number to the point where he would be fearful for the safety of himself and his family. There seemed to be the characteristic Yankee shrewdness in the New Englander's assessment of the importance of slavery to his economic and social life." Franklin, *From Slavery to Freedom*, 66–67. Discussing the unique status African slaves had in terms of their "legal position" compared to other colonies, Zilversmit explains: "The Puritans' aim of establishing a bible commonwealth led them to grant Negro slaves rights based on the Mosaic laws of bondage, which regarded slavery as a mark of personal misfortune and not as evidence of inherent inferiority. Consequently, New England slaves enjoyed rights that were regarded as incompatible with slavery in other colonies." Zilversmit, *The First Emancipation*, 19. Zilversmit goes on to explain a number of rights enslaved Africans had in New England, such as the right to own property and to exercise personal rights in the court of law. Zilversmit, *The First Emancipation*, 19. While the situation for enslaved Africans in New England was clearly better than in other colonies, it is important to remember, as Franklin highlights, the fact that slaves were owned and subject to the will of their owners. Forced servitude, dependence, and social inequality were always present.

166 Frey, "Slavery and Anti-Slavery," 384–85.

167 Morgan, "Slavery and Freedom," 5–6. Considering the enslaving tendencies of the colonists, the argument of prerevolutionary America presenting "itself as a white nation when it was, and had been from the start, diverse, hybrid, and multiracial" seems to hold merit. Sweet, *Bodies Politic*, 10. As Sweet puts it in regards to the North during "the early years of the Republic," the dilemma was the fact that there was now freedom along with inequality, with America as a whole modeling "universal freedom but racial inequality." Sweet, *Bodies Politic*, 11.

168 Bailyn, *The Ideological Origins of the American Revolution*, 235.

169 Morgan, "Slavery and Freedom," 5, 7.

population grew steadily while the Native American population declined due to the process of colonization and procuring of land.[170] In fact, the decline of the Native American population was a result of the colonists believing it was God's will for them to take control of the colonies in order to establish a Christian society from what was, in their minds, an uncivilized and godless culture.[171] The result of the diversity in population both racially and numerically worsened the "problems and perceived differences" between the colonists and non-Europeans.[172] The racial differences are what Davis coins "racial incompatibility," providing an excuse by the colonists for the allowance of slavery.[173] In describing the tension between a nation ascribing to Christian principles and the acceptance of slavery and the slave trade, Sydney E. Ahlstrom notes:

> That Western Christendom turned Africa into a hunting ground for slaves rather than a field for philanthropic and missionary endeavor is one of the world's great tragedies. That the New World became the chief arena for the European exploitation of slave labor is an extension of the same tragedy. That the United States—the first new nation, the elect nation, the nation with the soul of the church, the great model of modern democracy—moved into the nineteenth century with one of the largest and cruelest of slave systems in its midst with full constitutional protection is surely one of the world's greatest ironies.[174]

The proffering of spiritual freedom to enslaved Africans while denying human freedom from institutionalized slavery created a discordant situation. Where spiritual equality was embraced, the humanity and culture of slaves were denigrated as colonial subjugation was normative. To further complicate matters, the tension between the growing desire for liberation from the motherland and refusal to extend the same pursuit of freedom to slaves would reach an impasse during the Revolutionary years. The fight for the abolition of both institutionalized slavery and the slave trade would become a reality in Revolutionary America. The changing social, political,

[170]Bailey, *Race and Redemption in Puritan New England*, 27–28.

[171]Bailey, *Race and Redemption in Puritan New England*, 29–30.

[172]Bailey, *Race and Redemption in Puritan New England*, 27.

[173]Davis, *The Problem of Slavery in Western Culture*, 23.

[174]Sydney E. Ahlstrom, *A Religious History of the American People*, 2nd ed. (New Haven: Yale University Press, 2004), 635.

and cultural landscape of Revolutionary America towards abolitionism will be discussed next.

Eighteenth-Century Revolutionary America (Enlightened America)

Unlike Edwards, Hopkins lived into the years of the American Revolution, and thus the pinnacle of Enlightenment thought in America. Like Edwards, Hopkins grew concerned over the growing humanist sentiment in religion. The natural religion that was in its infancy in Edwards's day blossomed during the years of the American Revolution. As a consequence of its progression, the Calvinism in prerevolutionary America was no longer universally revered as "the times demanded a theology stressing man's power and freedom, not its inability and sin."[175] Strong emphasis was placed on autonomous reason, leading to a denigration of revelation and thus, making clear the changing religious landscape and Enlightenment ethos in the mid to late eighteenth century. Libertarian ideas grew, especially in the late eighteenth century, leading to societal concerns. Chief social concerns for Hopkins were the slave trade and institutionalized slavery, resulting in his abolitionist stance.

Enlightenment Thought

The Enlightenment stressed humanism, placing man as sovereign while in turn rejecting the idea of subordination underneath a superior deity or religious institution.[176] Specifically, rationalism was emphasized, creating

[175]Robert L. Ferm, *Jonathan Edwards the Younger, 1745–1801: A Colonial Pastor* (Grand Rapids: Eerdmans, 1976), 53. Discussing the religion espoused by the Enlightenment, such as Deism, Schneider asserts: "The success of the American Revolution acted as a seal of divine approval on this liberal theology. During the war the clergy were active in patriotic rhetoric and patriotic service. After the war it was impossible for them to revert to their old themes. The spirit of independence, having won its political success, went on to complete its theological conquest." Schneider, *The Puritan Mind*, 197–98.

[176]For examples of French sources detailing the ideology of Enlightenment thought, see Tzvetan Todorov, *L'Esprit des Lumières* (Paris: Le Livre de Poche, 2007); Paul Hazard, *La pensée européenne au XVIIIe siècle: De Montesquieu à Lessing* (Paris: Hachette Littératures, 2006); Paul Hazard, *La crise de la conscience européenne, 1680–1715* (Paris: Le Livre de Poche, 1994). For examples of German sources detailing the ideology of Enlightenment thought, see Günter Grass, *Der Traum der Vernunft: Vom Elend der Aufklärung* (Darmstadt: Luchterhand, 1985); Johann Christoph Hampe, *Ehre und Elend der Aufklärung gestern wie heute: Ein engagierter Vergleich* (Munich: Kaiser, 1971); Fritz Valjavec, *Geschichte der abendländischen Aufklärung* (Munich: Herold, 1961).

a shift from ecclesiastical authority to autonomous reason. Ernst Cassirer identifies "reason" as "the unifying and central point" of the eighteenth century, the height of Enlightenment thought.[177] Similarly as Gerald R. Cragg highlights, the eighteenth century can be recognized as the "Age of Reason."[178] There was strong confidence in man's intellectual ability and consequently, ability to think and reason as he pursued truth.[179] It was not about accepting truth that was passed down by way of tradition, but rather about "discovery and determination of truth."[180] As a result, the enlightened man was anti-dogmatic, viewing dogma as an enemy of both religion and knowledge due to its sensationalism and ignorance of truth. It was now about the pursuit of truth by way of reason, having confidence in one's own intellectual ability apart from any external authority. In fact, "the authority of reason" in the Enlightenment age was now "regarded as superior to the authority of revelation."[181] As David Hempton explains, if "there is a single thread running through the complexity of Enlightenment thought, it is that human reason and reasonableness offered a better way forward for human flourishing than religious dogma, inherited opinions and ancient habits of intolerance."[182] As a result, there was a move away from religious commitment to a modernist mindset. Furthermore, in both Europe

[177]Ernst Cassirer, *The Philosophy of the Enlightenment* (Princeton, NJ: Princeton University Press, 1951), 5.

[178]Gerald R. Cragg, *Reason and Authority in the Eighteenth Century* (Cambridge: Cambridge University Press, 1964), ix.

[179]Gerald R. Cragg, *The Church and the Age of Reason, 1648–1789* (Grand Rapids: Eerdmans, 1960), 235–36.

[180]Cassirer, *The Philosophy of the Enlightenment*, 13.

[181]Cragg, *The Church and the Age of Reason, 1648–1789*, 280. Discussing the superiority of reason over revelation in the modern period, Cragg writes: "The role of reason was magnified, that of revelation was depressed. The scriptures were subjected to intensive and often to unsympathetic scrutiny. Miracles were challenged. Prophecy was reassessed. Christian thought faced a threat which might have stripped it of all its uniqueness and its authority. In this struggle lies the perennial interest of this period. At the outset the new thought was cordially disposed toward the Christian faith. Gradually the balance shifted from what God has revealed to what man has discovered. In due course the sufficiency of reason was confidently affirmed, and the whole content of Biblical theology was relegated to a marginal status of comparative insignificance." Cragg, *The Church and the Age of Reason, 1648–1789*, 13.

[182]David Hempton, *The Church in the Long Eighteenth Century* (New York: I.B. Tauris, 2011), 109.

and America, societal progress was now sought at the expense of religious commitment, resulting in the "dechristianization of public life."[183]

The commitment to science and consequent rejection of Christianity became indicative of the Enlightenment.[184] Movement away from the mysterious nature of religion toward a commitment to science meant a clear route to discover truth.[185] What was irrational needed to give way to what was reasonable. In other words, as Hempton states, reason informed by science "was thus the antidote to credulous superstition and revelation."[186] Religious beliefs were now subservient to autonomous reason. Consequently, religious beliefs should be open to reform by way of critical reasoning and the use of science.

Hopkins discussed the detrimental impact of Enlightenment thought on Christianity in New England during the eighteenth century and the sustained attacks on special revelation. In his sermon, "A Serious Address to Professing Christians," Hopkins expressed his concern of the "volumes written in Europe by men whose learning, knowledge, and veracity cannot be reasonably questioned," whose aim was to attack Christianity.[187] In Hopkins's mind, this resulted in the spreading of the "principles of infidelity, and the practice of immorality, to a degree never known before since Christianity was received by those nations."[188] Hopkins continues, explaining that this spread of European Enlightenment thought allows the "multitudes of those who do not professedly renounce Christianity embrace those doctrines which are so contrary to the gospel as to lead to infidelity . . . while the multitude of common people are sunk into vice, carelessness about religion, and ignorance of the nature and true doctrines of it."[189] Hopkins notes the

[183]Claude Welch, *Protestant Thought in the Nineteenth Century: 1799–1870*, vol. 1 (New Haven, CT: Yale University Press, 1972), 191.

[184]Peter Gay, *The Enlightenment: An Interpretation*, vol. 1 (New York: Knopf, 1967), 18.

[185]Peter Gay, *The Enlightenment: A Comprehensive Anthology* (New York: Simon & Schuster, 1985), 17.

[186]Hempton, *The Church in the Long Eighteenth Century*, 116.

[187]Samuel Hopkins, "A Serious Address to Professing Christians, in the Name, and from the Words, of Jesus Christ," in *The Works of Samuel Hopkins, D.D.*, vol. 3 (Boston: Doctrinal Tract and Book Society, 1854), 166. This resource was identified by reading Jauhiainen's comments on the Enlightenment. I am indebted to Jauhiainen's thoughts on Hopkins's rejection of Enlightenment religion. See Peter Dan Jauhiainen, "An Enlightenment Calvinist: Samuel Hopkins and the Pursuit of Benevolence" (PhD diss., University of Iowa, 1997), 9.

[188]Hopkins, "A Serious Address to Professing Christians," 166.

[189]Hopkins, "A Serious Address to Professing Christians," 166.

spread of Enlightenment thinking from Europe to America occurred by way of conversations and the disseminating of "books written against divine revelation."[190] Moreover, "a number of books and pamphlets have been published against Christianity, and in favor of Deism and atheism, which are spreading and highly approved by many."[191]

As a pastor committed to the Christian faith in the face of a modernist intellectual revolution, Hopkins denounced the naturalistic religion promoted by Deism. For Hopkins, divine revelation was never meant to be subservient to reason but vice versa. Libertarian opinions also grew as the political landscape began to change due to the coming Revolution. Hopkins found himself in this religious and political milieu as one who remained committed to the Christian faith.[192] He was a progressive as he characterized the growing "connection between religious thinking and socio-political behavior that characterized the entire period," demonstrating his concern for the marginalized and desire to see all people as equals stemming from the growing libertarian ideals of Revolutionary America, which will be discussed next.[193]

Growing Libertarian Sentiment

According to Sweet, "The Founding Fathers liked to think of the Revolution as a new birth," viewing America as having a "clean break with the colonial period, which is in turn defined as a kind of prehistory of political dependency that ended abruptly and forever with the Declaration of Independence."[194] Clearly what was of paramount importance was gaining of national independence from the motherland. This would have implications for the growing antislavery movement. Discussing antislavery motivation for New Divinity men, Saillant notes that "the War of Independence drew from the New Divinity men not only a vigorous endorsement of the republican cause, which many blacks understood as a slaves' cause, but also a statement

[190]Hopkins, "A Serious Address to Professing Christians," 167.

[191]Hopkins, "A Serious Address to Professing Christians," 167.

[192]Hopkins is a prime example of one who maintained "the integrity of religious thought in the face of the Patriotic surge," holding fast to Scripture as divine truth. Noll, *Christians in the American Revolution*, 92.

[193]Noll, *Christians in the American Revolution*, 92.

[194]Sweet, *Bodies Politic*, 2.

about the effect of unfreedom on human life."[195] Truly the pursuit of liberty and commitment to freedom in America became central to the Revolutionary cause.[196] As America headed towards its independence from the monarchical reality of British control, the idea of liberty and power residing in the hands of the people continued to grow. Consequently, the notion of human equality grew as well. In fact, "the principle of equality" is as Wood states, "a principle central to republican thinking," signifying impartiality.[197] This is what it meant to be part of a republic. If, as Noll asserts, "American republican language" involves "fear of abuses from illegitimate power and a nearly messianic belief in the benefits of liberty," the desire for national freedom and individual liberty followed suit.[198] And with the pursuit of individual liberty came a desire for the "private integrity of the individual citizen," thus taking personal responsibility for virtuous living.[199] It makes sense then, as Wood says, that "it was republicanism and republican principles that ultimately destroyed this monarchical society."[200] As a result, obedience to authority was no longer assumed but rather questioned, social distinctions

[195]John Saillant, "African American Engagements with Edwards in the Era of the Slave Trade," in *Jonathan Edwards at 300: Essays on the Tercentenary of His Birth*, ed. Harry S. Stout, Kenneth P. Minkema, and Caleb J. D. Maskell (Lanham, MD: University Press of America, 2005), 144. Similarly, Essig asserts, "Like many Americans of the Revolutionary era, Hopkins embraced republican ideals in response to some unsettling changes which took place in eighteenth-century society," such as the economic industry generated by the slave trade in Newport, RI. Essig, *The Bonds of Wickedness*, 89.

[196]Gordon S. Wood, *The Creation of the American Republic, 1776–1787* (Chapel Hill: University of North Carolina Press, 1998), 129.

[197]Wood, *The Creation of the American Republic, 1776–1787*, 70.

[198]Mark A. Noll, *America's God: From Jonathan Edwards to Abraham Lincoln* (New York: Oxford University Press, 2002), 56.

[199]Bonwick, *The American Revolution*, 52.

[200]Wood, *The Radicalism of the American Revolution*, 95. The replacement of monarchy with a republican government as the American Revolution commenced had far reaching consequences on the social dimensions of both private and public life. Wood explains that republicanism "challenged the primary assumptions and practices of monarchy—its hierarchy, its inequality, its devotion to kinship, its patriarchy, its patronage, and its dependency. It offered new conceptions of the individual, the family, the state, and the individual's relationship to the family, the state, and other individuals. Indeed, republicanism offered nothing less than new ways of organizing society. It defied and dissolved the older monarchical connections and presented people with alternative kinds of attachments, new sorts of social relationships. It transformed monarchical culture and prepared the way for the revolutionary upheavals at the end of the eighteenth century." Wood, *The Radicalism of the American Revolution*, 96–97.

were now viewed as nonessential in light of the denigration of hierarchical ordering, and the power now belonged to the people.[201]

The shift from a prerevolutionary hierarchical understanding of society to a libertarian republican society began to take place around midcentury. It was around this time where the traditionally assumed power of those in authority began to be questioned as those underneath grew more and more disgruntled with their subordinate positions.[202] What was once normative was now being challenged as established "social bonds were coming apart," with those in authority struggling to maintain their traditional social positions as superiors.[203] Keeping in step with Enlightenment ideals, the people now viewed "Monarchy and hereditary aristocracy" as "deviations from nature, the products of oversophistication, of age and decay."[204] Accordingly, the notion of dependent service to an authority figure was now a cause of frustration. By the time America claimed its independence from Britain, "in the eyes of the revolutionaries, all the fine calibrations of rank and degrees of unfreedom of the traditional monarchical society became absurd and degrading. The Revolution became a full-scale assault on dependency."[205] In an Enlightened age, the power of reason was key for the colonists to seek their own liberty and thus, "the continued submission of slaves to their masters became much more difficult to defend on logical grounds."[206] Indeed any form of servitude was now viewed as socially archaic.[207] The Revolutionary man answered to no one and exercised his right to think and act independently. Even the patriarchal authoritarianism of Edwards's day was no longer universally revered as it was viewed with growing suspicion.[208]

[201]Bailyn, *The Ideological Origins of the American Revolution*, 319.

[202]Wood, *The Radicalism of the American Revolution*, 146.

[203]Wood, *The Radicalism of the American Revolution*, 146–47.

[204]Wood, *The Creation of the American Republic, 1776–1787*, 100. Wood explains the need for the colonists to separate from England in order to truly become the people they desired to be: "By 1776 it had become increasingly evident that if they were to remain the kind of people they wanted to be they must become free of Britain. The calls for independence thus took on a tone of imperativeness. Only separating from the British monarchy and instituting republicanism, it seemed, could realize the social image the Enlightenment had drawn of them." Wood, *The Creation of the American Republic, 1776–1787*, 108.

[205]Wood, *The Radicalism of the American Revolution*, 179.

[206]Stewart, *Holy Warriors*, 13.

[207]Wood, *The Radicalism of the American Revolution*, 184.

[208]Patriarchal dependency did not disappear with the coming Revolution but was rather diminished to a significant degree. As Wood explains, it resulted in the notion of dependency in

The attack on forced dependency and the reality of national liberty for the colonies from British control had significant implications for antislavery sentiment starting midcentury.

The Slave Trade

As discussed earlier in this chapter, slavery was considered the main source of labor in colonial America.[209] Institutionalized slavery was both legal and socially acceptable.[210] Intricately tied to the reality of slavery was the slave trade.[211] In Newport, Hopkins was witness to a seaport that depended on commerce and the economic growth that thrived on the shipping and receiving of both material products and human slaves.[212] Crane notes that although we "cannot point to any particular year in which Newport entered its so-called golden era," economic success was flourishing by 1760.[213] The busy seaport and the activity thereof made Newport the "commercial center" of Rhode Island.[214]

Elain Forman Crane highlights how Newport in the 1760s and 1770s was immersed in what is known as the "triangular trade."[215] Crane notes: "In this infamous triangle, Newport merchants sent rum to Africa where it was exchanged for slaves who were sold in the Caribbean for molasses to be returned to Newport for distillation into rum."[216] While tobacco

general to be questioned: "Women and children no doubt remained largely dependent on their husbands and fathers, but the revolutionary attack on patriarchal monarchy made all other dependencies in the society suspect." Wood, *The Radicalism of the American Revolution*, 184.

[209]Davis, *The Problem of Slavery in Western Culture*, 9.

[210]Bonwick, *The American Revolution*, 167. Bonwick notes that free African Americans made up less than one percent of the total population prior to the Revolution. Bonwick, *The American Revolution*, 167.

[211]According to Hempton, "By 1820 nearly 8.7 million slaves had left Africa for the New World and African slaves constituted a staggering 77 per cent of the total population that had sailed towards the Americas." Hempton, *The Church in the Long Eighteenth Century*, 127. This section on the slave trade will center on the slave trade in Newport, RI since that is where Hopkins struggled for the abolitionist cause.

[212]Elaine Forman Crane, *A Dependent People: Newport, Rhode Island in the Revolutionary Era* (New York: Fordham University Press, 1985), 35.

[213]Crane, *A Dependent People*, 3–4.

[214]Crane, *A Dependent People*, 11.

[215]Crane, *A Dependent People*, 9.

[216]Crane, *A Dependent People*, 10. Crane discusses more specifically the products brought from the Caribbean Islands by way of the transatlantic trade: "Sugar, molasses, and rum flowed

was occasionally used, it was rum that acted as the main currency for the purchase of slaves along the coast of Africa.[217] In terms of commercial success, it was the industry of rum, slaves, and molasses that drove the economic wellbeing of the seaport.[218] This is in large part what made the people of Newport dependent on the transatlantic trade itself.[219] Other items were shipped as well. As Crane explains, because of Newport's economic relationship with the trade and being on a seaport, the people were "forced to import the necessities of life" as "Newport became a community completely dependent on the sea for sustenance and livelihood."[220] It was through the trade that the people were able to obtain the products and resources to live.[221]

Slaves were not only sold in the Caribbean but also brought to the colonies to be sold as well.[222] Newport gained a reputation for being the colonial seaport most invested in the slave trade, carrying out over 70% of slave shipping and selling by 1770.[223] It is no surprise then, that Newport "was the center of the slave trade in the North," having "the largest proportion of blacks in New England."[224] In terms of frequency, slave merchants desired efficiency for economic purposes. Quicker trips meant increased profit as more trips would lead to additional commerce.[225] It also raised the chances of healthy slaves arriving to the seaport. Crane observes: "A number of healthy slaves brought quickly to market meant potential profits. Sick, injured, or rebellious slaves simply did not sell."[226]

from the islands to Newport, to the exclusion of nearly everything else. Loaded with these commodities, Newport vessels sped back from the Caribbean to sell the cargoes. Not only did the molasses trade stimulate the rum industry in Newport—as evidenced by the increasing number of distilleries—but the trade between Newport and neighboring colonies expanded as well." Crane, *A Dependent People*, 14.

[217]Crane, *A Dependent People*, 21. Franklin reminds us that slavery in Africa, as in other parts of the world, was active and far-reaching since the earliest accounts of the continent's history. Franklin, *From Slavery to Freedom*, 30.

[218]Crane, *A Dependent People*, 35.

[219]Crane, *A Dependent People*, 35.

[220]Crane, *A Dependent People*, 47.

[221]Crane, *A Dependent People*, 14.

[222]Crane, *A Dependent People*, 16.

[223]Crane, *A Dependent People*, 20.

[224]Crane, *A Dependent People*, 65.

[225]Crane, *A Dependent People*, 33.

[226]Crane, *A Dependent People*, 33.

Like institutionalized slavery, the forced capture, selling, and soon to be reality of slavery in the New World was cause of great anguish for those taken. John Franklin describes the process of captured Africans en route to the New World and the mournful state of Africans forced to leave their homeland:

> The Africans offered stiff resistance to their capture, sale, and transportation to the unknown New World. Fierce wars broke out between tribes when the members of one sought to capture members of another to sell them to traders. Slaves brought to the post for sale were always chained, for the caboceers and slave captains very early learned that without such safeguards the slaves would make their escape. Guards were employed to chaperone the slaves out to the ship and see to it that they were held there until the ship was ready to set sail. . . . At the first opportunity, if indeed it ever presented itself, many would leap off the ship into the mouths of hungry sharks to avoid enslavement in the New World.[227]

The resistance and willingness to choose death rather than enslavement illustrates the depth of the despondency experienced by captured Africans. Forced servitude in a foreign land was not an option for many. Those that were not able to escape or those that accepted their fate were subject to inhumane conditions on the slave ships. Discussing the ships coming from England, Franklin notes a common problem with slave ships in general: "There was hardly standing, lying, or sitting room. Chained together by twos, hands and feet, the slaves had no room in which to move about and no freedom to exercise their bodies even in the slightest."[228] A greater number of slaves meant greater profits and as a result, ships were filled with as many slaves as possible.[229] It is not surprising then, that disease and illness ran

[227]Franklin, *From Slavery to Freedom*, 42. Noting Britain's domination in slave trading, Hempton states that "from the 1660s to 1807 Britain, perhaps the most 'advanced' nation in the world, carried the greatest number of enslaved Africans to the New World." Hempton, *The Church in the Long Eighteenth Century*, 129. It makes sense, then, that Britain was recognized as "the world leaders in the slave trade" prior to the Revolution. Romer, *Slavery in the Connecticut Valley of Massachusetts*, 212.

[228]Franklin, *From Slavery to Freedom*, 42.

[229]Franklin, *From Slavery to Freedom*, 42.

rampant onboard the slave ships.[230] As a result, a high mortality rate was normative.[231]

Opposition to both slave trafficking and slavery would pick up momentum as the years neared the Revolution. Yet the true abolishment of both the slave trade and slavery would be a slow process. The desire for economic growth along with continued proslavery support by supporters of slave trafficking would contribute to the restoration of slave trading during the early years following the Revolutionary War.[232] Elizabeth Donnan explains:

> Not only had the trade continued until the outbreak of the Revolution forced its cessation, but it was revived as soon as peace made possible a general restoration of commerce. Remembering the profits of earlier days, merchants whose fortunes had been shattered by war might well look to the slave traffic to restore their vanished estates. Captains and seamen so habituated to the commerce in blacks that it offered no offence to conscience, were still available. On the surface the attitude of the public toward the trade seemed to have changed slightly. However, the pregnant decade before the Revolution, in which the rights of man had found frequent and eloquent expression, had left its traces. Disapproval of the traffic in slaves found occasional and isolated expression before 1765; after 1783 a small but courageous group adopted the cause of the negro as their own and pushed steadily toward their goal — legislative prohibition of the trade and of slavery.[233]

Rejection of abolitionist thought, especially by states supporting institutionalized slavery, would continue up until the Civil War. Yet the Jeffersonian

[230]Franklin, *From Slavery to Freedom*, 42.

[231]Describing the consequences of such conditions aboard the slave ships, Franklin writes: "The filth and stench caused by close quarters and disease brought on more illness and the mortality rate was increased accordingly. Perhaps not more than half the slaves shipped from Africa ever became effective workers in the New World. Many of those that had not died of disease or committed suicide by jumping overboard were permanently disabled by the ravages of some dread disease or by maiming, which often resulted from the struggle against the chains." Franklin, *From Slavery to Freedom*, 42–43.

[232]Elizabeth Donnan, "The New England Slave Trade after the Revolution," *New England Quarterly* 3, no. 2 (1930): 252. According to Davis, it was not until 1825 that both Britain and America would outlaw "their Atlantic slave trades." David Brion Davis, *Inhuman Bondage: The Rise and Fall of Slavery in the New World* (Oxford: Oxford University Press, 2006), 142.

[233]Donnan, "The New England Slave Trade after the Revolution," 252.

republican understanding of the equality of all people by creation would help establish growing abolitionist belief that began in the mid eighteenth century. What was once unquestioned was now up for debate as the colonies faced a moral dilemma regarding human bondage. Proponents of both the slave trade and slavery had to deal with growing abolitionist sentiment during the Revolutionary years.

Abolitionism

Revolutionary ideology espouses, "a belief in individual freedom and inalienable natural rights."[234] Davis continues and expands on the republican idea of personal liberty and equality in relation to slavery, explaining that "this Revolutionary ideology, epitomized by the opening lines of the Declaration of Independence, showed that the very idea of slavery is a fiction or fraud, since liberty and equality are fundamental rights that no one can legitimately lose."[235] Moreover, in light of the Revolutionary philosophy of freedom for all, Joanne Pope Melish notes, "Revolutionary rhetoric defined 'liberty' as the exercise of natural rights, and 'slavery' as the political condition resulting from the loss of liberty as a consequence of the exercise of power, or perhaps a corruption of will."[236] The idea of forced servitude was now under increasing scrutiny during the transition from the mid to late eighteenth century. What was once accepted as normative and necessary was now a legitimate point of dispute. The understanding of institutionalized slavery as a servile condition forced upon slaves by those in power grew as the Revolution approached. It was a violation of the freedom that Africans naturally held. Consequently, as "Revolutionary philosophy" became an established reality in the colonies, freedom from slavery became an increasing reality with it.[237] Of significance was the antislavery rhetoric and "revolutionary republicanism" that contributed to a growing number of free African slaves.[238]

[234]Davis, *Inhuman Bondage*, 156.

[235]Davis, *Inhuman Bondage*, 156.

[236]Joanne Pope Melish, *Disowning Slavery: Gradual Emancipation and "Race" in New England, 1780–1860* (Ithaca, NY: Cornell University Press, 2015), 80.

[237]Franklin, *From Slavery to Freedom*, 96. As Melish states, though there was an amount of antislavery sentiment prior to the time of the Revolution, it was during the Revolution where antislavery as a movement became established: "Although the earliest antislavery protests preceded the movement for independence by more than half a century, it was only in the context of the Revolution that the antislavery movement gained support outside a fringe group of Quakers and other agitators." Melish, *Disowning Slavery*, 50.

[238]Melish, *Disowning Slavery*, 1.

Like the antislavery movement in Europe towards the mid-eighteenth century, public opinion began to reflect the importance of manumission.[239] A significant cause for the change in public thinking was the circulation of antislavery tracts in Massachusetts during the Revolutionary years in light of the colonies being under English control.[240] Yet as "antislavery sentiment grew and became more respectable" during the late eighteenth-century, Robert H. Romer states, "it is unlikely that a significant number of whites in Massachusetts even thought about abolition or that they would have favored bringing slavery to an end if asked."[241] The struggle between the growing acceptability of emancipation and the expectations of an established slave institution would continue while antislavery ideology gained momentum.

The experience of being under English bondage certainly played a role in the desire by antislavery advocates to see enslaved Africans freed since colonists desired political and religious freedom themselves.[242] Davis says, "As the white American colonists rose in revolt against what they perceived as a British effort to 'enslave' them, many, especially in the North, could not escape from recognizing the 'contradiction' of actually owning slaves."[243] Moreover, slaves desired the same liberation as the colonists. This is what led a number of Africans, both slave and free, to fight in the Revolutionary War on behalf of the colonies. In fact, as Franklin asserts, "Negro patriots saw clearly the implications for their own future in their fight against England. They wanted human freedom as well as political independence."[244] Enslaved Africans, according to Melish, identified with the colonist's predicament, viewing themselves as being in "a present state of physical and material

[239]Bonwick, *The American Revolution*, 167. The colonies mirrored the antislavery movement in England in a number of ways by the middle of the eighteenth century. Like England, antislavery sentiment did not arise in the colonies until midcentury. Moreover, the power of profit in light of slavery made abolition a challenging proposition. Nonetheless, once established, abolitionism in England quickly expanded. E. Gordon Rupp, *Religion in England, 1688–1791* (Oxford: Clarendon Press, 1986), 522.

[240]Zilversmit, *The First Emancipation*, 99. Zilversmit notes how "the deepening Revolutionary crisis brought an increasing number of pamphlets declaiming against the inconsistency of holding slaves while invoking the Rights of Man in the ideological struggle with England." Zilversmit, *The First Emancipation*, 99. It is also important to note how "since the beginning of the Revolution, the publication of antislavery essays had been increasing." Zilversmit, *The First Emancipation*, 169.

[241]Romer, *Slavery in the Connecticut Valley of Massachusetts*, 214.

[242]Melish, *Disowning Slavery*, 80.

[243]Davis, *Inhuman Bondage*, 144.

[244]Franklin, *From Slavery to Freedom*, 95.

disempowerment."[245] Consequently, as James Stewart notes, "many whites could not stifle their feelings of guilt as blacks gave their lives in defense of the society that so thoroughly oppressed them. Support for emancipation became the obvious way to make amends."[246] Nonetheless, even as the cry for liberty from the colonies echoed, enslavement of Africans continued in all thirteen colonies.[247]

As the Revolutionary War commenced, slavery as an institution ceased to be blindly accepted and advocated.[248] Indeed the American Revolution and antislavery movement became inseparable.[249] As Arthur Zilversmit explains: "Men who opposed the continued slavery of the Negroes could argue convincingly that American liberty and the freedom of Negro slaves were not only compatible, but were inseparable goals."[250] Naturally, a number of enslavers, such as those from New England, "became increasingly aware of the ideological inconsistency of keeping slaves while fighting for liberty."[251] For many enslavers, it no longer made sense to continue to enslave Africans in light of the desire to be freed themselves.[252]

While the ideology of liberty during and after the War for Independence should have theoretically pushed slavery and the slave trade towards extinction, both cruelties would continue into the nineteenth century. The differences between the North and South were stark. Where slavery was

[245] Melish, *Disowning Slavery*, 80. Additional proof of the despondent state of slaves was the publishing of material after the war, "purportedly written by slaves," evidencing the sorrow they lived through as people in bondage. Zilversmit, *The First Emancipation*, 171.

[246] Stewart, *Holy Warriors*, 21.

[247] Stewart, *Holy Warriors*, 5.

[248] Zilversmit, *The First Emancipation*, 108.

[249] Zilversmit, *The First Emancipation*, 109.

[250] Zilversmit, *The First Emancipation*, 109. Hopkins is a prime example. See Samuel Hopkins, "A Dialogue Concerning the Slavery of the Africans," in *The Works of Samuel Hopkins, D.D.*, vol. 2 (Boston: Doctrinal Tract and Book Society, 1854). Hopkins's understanding of slavery and the slave trade will be detailed in chapter five.

[251] Zilversmit, *The First Emancipation*, 117–18.

[252] For enslaved Africans, the hope was not only liberation from institutionalized slavery, but equality with the colonists and all of the rights that come with being equals. Melish explains: "To people of color, Revolutionary natural rights and antislavery rhetoric clearly promised an unambiguous state of freedom identical to that of persons who had never been enslaved. Slaves anticipated that once they were emancipated, they would be *free*, not merely 'freed.' To them, Revolutionary rhetoric promised not only autonomy but also prospects for civic participation and even leadership. After all, one of the most profound changes in social beliefs effected by the Revolution was the erosion of unquestioning faith in the hierarchical social order." Melish, *Disowning Slavery*, 82.

declining in the North as the emancipation of slaves became an increasing reality, there was resistance in the South.[253] Southern enslavers feared loss of authority in light of growing abolitionist sentiment, but continued to depend financially and psychologically on the reality of slavery as an institution.[254] Though emancipation and "antislavery societies became more widespread after the war," the idea of abolition, especially in the South, was opposed.[255] Much of the opposition was due to economic concerns.[256] Franklin explains:

> Despite the effort of antislavery leaders to deal a death blow to slavery after the War for Independence, they were unable to do so. Resistance to their abolitionist schemes hardened in the Southern states, where so much capital was invested in slaves and where already a new economic importance was being attached to the institution. In the 1780s, moreover, there was

[253]Stewart explains the changing landscape of slavery in the North during the Revolutionary years: "With antislavery activism and national patriotism now so fully intertwined, slavery slowly began to unravel throughout the North. In 1774, Quakers led by Anthony Benezet bombarded the Continental Congress with antislavery demands and finally obtained its consent to stop all slave importations. The following year, Philadelphia Quakers organized the first association devoted exclusively to abolition, the Society for the Relief of Free Negroes Unlawfully Held in Bondage. Sympathetic to the Quaker zeal for useful improvements in the name of economic progress, powerful politicians, manufacturing magnates, and lawyers—the dynamic commercial and professional sectors of Northern society—likewise took up the abolitionist cause. Only a few of these urban entrepreneurs owned slaves, and very few of the North's significant men of wealth depended on slavery for social position or economic advancement. Slaves also were too few to pose a serious threat to white supremacy once they had been granted their freedom. Social harmony and economic betterment would be enhanced, leading whites maintained, once emancipation removed motives for rebellion. The impressive programs of self-education and moral uplift now being undertaken by Northern free blacks deepened these impressions considerably. Under these circumstances, the forces of abolitionism proved irresistible in the end. By 1784, every Northern state save New York and New Jersey had enacted laws providing for gradual emancipation; by 1804, these two states, too, had passed such bills. Of course, racism and the economic interest of slaveholders generated stubborn obstruction. Northern abolition, moreover, led always to segregation and denials of political rights and terrible moments of violent white racism, not to genuine equality. Yet, for the only time in American history, abolitionists black and white had succeeded in peacefully merging with those who controlled the levers of power." Stewart, *Holy Warriors*, 22–23.

[254]Stewart, *Holy Warriors*, 23. Enslavers understood that "the Revolution had set many people, their own bondspeople included, to an unprecedented questioning of their way of life." Stewart, *Holy Warriors*, 26. Naturally, enslavers felt threatened by the notion of emancipation.

[255]Franklin, *From Slavery to Freedom*, 97–98. This is in contrast to the North, where the meshing of "antislavery activism and national patriotism" caused slavery to gradually cease in the North. Stewart, *Holy Warriors*, 22.

[256]Franklin, *From Slavery to Freedom*, 98.

> the sobering fear that the social program that grew out of the struggle against Britain would get out of hand and uproot the very foundations of social and economic life in America.[257]

Discussing the impact of the economy in the North compared to the South in regards to slavery, Romer notes: "For some reason, perhaps as a result of their different religious traditions as well as the differences in the economies, northerners took the words of the Declaration of Independence more seriously and were more willing to recognize the blatant contradiction involved in fighting for liberty while continuing to enslave blacks."[258] Adding to the economic priority of maintaining slavery by Southern enslavers was the invention of the cotton gin in the late eighteenth century.[259] As a result of the cotton gin, the need for slave labor grew in the South and the influx of slaves increased into the early nineteenth century.[260]

During the years after the Revolutionary War and prior to the Civil War, antislavery leaders in the North "put northern slavery on a path to extinction by appropriating the ideal of equality by creation" while, as Kidd puts it, "the weight of economics and racial prejudice made the antislavery movement anathema to white southerners."[261] The lack of clarity in the Declaration of Independence in regards to slavery certainly did not help the antislavery cause. While the notion of equality based on creation is clearly stated, the lack of clarity in regards to slavery and the fear of slave insurrection was cause for slavery to be ignored by slavery proponents, especially in the South.[262] As a result, while the American Revolution pushed the idea

[257]Franklin, *From Slavery to Freedom*, 98.

[258]Romer, *Slavery in the Connecticut Valley of Massachusetts*, 217.

[259]Franklin, *From Slavery to Freedom*, 105.

[260]Franklin, *From Slavery to Freedom: A History of Negro Americans*, 105.

[261]Kidd, *God of Liberty*, 165.

[262]Franklin elucidates the tension between the personal freedom the Declaration espoused and its vagueness in regards to slavery: "The silence of the Declaration of Independence on the matter of slavery and the slave trade was to make it equally difficult for the abolitionists and proslavery leaders to look to that document for support. Even if Jefferson did say that all men were created equal, it could not be forgotten that the antislavery passages of the Declaration were ruled out altogether. By endowing men with inalienable rights superior to those of positive law, it was, however, a standing invitation to insurrection that few could accept. The implications of the Declaration, however vague, were so powerful that Southern slave owners found it desirable to deny the self-evident truths that it expounded and were willing to do battle with the abolitionists during the period of strain and stress over just what the Declaration meant with regard to society in nineteenth-century America." Franklin, *From Slavery to Freedom*, 89.

of the abolition for both the slave trade and slavery, both continued due to the aforementioned reasons.[263] Thus, "Slavery continued to expand in the southern and southwestern states until brought to an end by the Civil War."[264]

Conclusion

The significance of the social, intellectual, and cultural influences stemming from different historical eras in shaping attitudes and convictions cannot be overstated. For Edwards as a prerevolutionary Puritan, divine revelation trumped both reason and tradition, for godly societal reform would come as a consequence of Spirit indwelt believers living out the truths of Scripture. Unfortunately, the social understanding of hierarchical ordering and consequent social inequality aided the notion of slavery as both normative and acceptable. For Hopkins, while against the natural religion of the Enlightenment, the libertarian and republican principles espoused by Enlightenment sentiment proved to be seminal influences for antislavery ideology during the Revolutionary years. As I argue, Edwards's ethical theology was instrumental for Hopkins's abolitionist stance. First, an understanding of Edwards's ethical theology is needed in order to evidence Hopkins's congruence with Edwards's doctrine of benevolence. Edwards's virtue theory and proslavery position will be discussed next.

[263] Bonwick, *The American Revolution*, 168. The slave trade became illegal in both England and the United States in 1807, yet the law was consistently broken. Franklin, *From Slavery to Freedom*, 109. As mentioned, growth in the cotton industry spurred the need for additional slave labor in the minds of Southern slavery advocates. Consequently, the slave trade continued to supply slaves to the South. Franklin explains: "Despite the state laws prohibiting it, the African slave trade to the United States continued to flourish during the first decade of the national government. The slave interests were in a curious dilemma. On the one hand they feared the wholesale importation of raw and unruly Negroes from Africa or the revolutionary and resourceful Negroes from the Caribbean, while on the other hand they were in desperate need of a larger number of slaves to cultivate the cotton that was now in such great demand. The practicality, if not the venality, of the merchants and planters compelled them to decide in favor of continued importation, hoping that the safeguards erected by the national and state governments would stem any tide of insurrection that might develop in the United States. In defiance of local laws, New England traders carried on a large traffic; while Southern planters were willing to receive slaves from whatever source possible." Franklin, *From Slavery to Freedom*, 108–9.

[264] Bonwick, *The American Revolution*, 168.

Chapter 4: Edwards's Virtue Theory and the Issue of Slavery

In this chapter, I establish Edwards's virtue theory, showing both the philosophical and social/activist aspects of his ethics.[1] For the philosophical aspect, I discuss Edwards's understanding of benevolence to Being in general and self-love. For the social/activist aspects, I consider Edwards's understanding of Christian benevolence. I end the chapter with a discussion on Edwards's proslavery stance. This will result in a holistic view of Edwards's virtue theory, showing Edwards's philosophical argumentation for a creature's union with God and others in a system of existence as well as activism and social concern in his doctrine of benevolence. The rationale for Edwards's agreement with institutionalized slavery in light of his doctrine of benevolence is also established. Doing so prepares for the comparison of Edwards's and Hopkins's ethical theologies in chapter 5, evidencing agreement between the two as well as Hopkins's faithful application of Edwards's doctrine of benevolence for his abolitionist stance. Thus, the argument that Hopkins was more consistent with Edwards's ethical theology regarding the issue of slavery is substantiated.

[1]The need to view both the philosophical and moral components of Edwards's ethics for a proper understanding of Edwards's virtue theory was established in chapter 2.

Benevolence to Being in General

Understanding Edwards's view of God is key to comprehend his philosophically oriented ethics.[2] Edwards develops his view of God philosophically in the *Two Dissertations* as he responds to the growing popularity of moral sense philosophy.[3] Comments on where Edwards is situated within eighteenth century moral sense conversations are important before examining the *Two Dissertations* as Edwards was engaged with key moral sense theorists of the day. Francis Hutcheson is critical as he is the main interlocutor for Edwards's second dissertation, *TV*.[4] Joseph T. Cochran notes from Hutcheson's *An Inquiry into the Original of our Ideas of Beauty and Virtue* the distinction Hutcheson makes between moral sense and internal sense. In the Preface

[2]Fiering observes the lack of scriptural support in *TV*: "Edwards's dissertation on *The Nature of True Virtue* is about God to be sure, but it is an extraordinary fact that Scripture is never cited in the work, nor does Edwards draw on the theological tradition for support." Norman Fiering, *Jonathan Edwards's Moral Thought and Its British Context* (Chapel Hill: University of North Carolina Press, 1981), 9. Thus, the metaphysical language and argumentation employed by Edwards makes sense. Regarding the interpretation of the *Two Dissertations*, Danaher states: "While many commentators on Edwards view the *Two Dissertations* as an attempt to construct a freestanding metaphysics, I argue that these writings are best viewed as an apologetic effort that engages moral sense philosophy, particularly the form it takes in the work of Francis Hutcheson (1694–1746)." William J. Danaher, *The Trinitarian Ethics of Jonathan Edwards* (Louisville, KY: Westminster John Knox, 2004), 201. Given the language Edwards uses, both the philosophical nature of the works and the apologetic approach taken by Edwards are at play. Both were noted in chapter 2.

[3]Discussing similarities and differences between Hutcheson and Shaftsbury, the two moral philosophers Edwards was primarily responding to in *TV*, regarding their understanding of natural moral sense, Schneewind explains Hutcheson, like Shaftsbury, "holds that kind of goodness we praise as 'moral' is possible only for reflective beings who have a disposition to feel approval or disapproval of impulses and motives. Unlike Shaftsbury's moral faculty, the Hutchesonian moral sense approves of only one basic motive: benevolence, which for Hutcheson is a stand-in for Christian *agape*, or disinterested love, directed to others regardless of any merit on their part. We approve of temperance, prudence, courage, and justice only because we think that they are dispositions people need in order to forward the good of others (*Inquiry II* II.I). Virtue is thus benevolence, as approved by the moral sense. The virtuous agent will perform actions that tend to make other people happy. Both agents and actions gain their moral significance from the agent's motive, not from the acts or results due to it. Happiness is naturally good, but its moral goodness is due to its being what the morally approved motive causes." J. B. Schneewind, *The Invention of Autonomy: A History of Modern Moral Philosophy* (Cambridge: Cambridge University Press, 1998), 334. Hence the idea of divine aid for benevolent practice is rejected. Schneewind continues and says that "the degree of virtue depends only on how much benevolence people feel, and how earnestly they express it. The more benevolence they feel and the more they act from it, the more virtuous they are." Schneewind, *The Invention of Autonomy*, 334. According to eighteenth century moral sense philosophy, the end of the moral life is man.

[4]Joseph T. Cochran, "Imitating the Virtue Ethic of Jonathan Edwards and William James," *Bulletin for Ecclesial Theology* 9, no. 2 (2022): 21.

to *Inquiry*, Hutcheson asserts that "any Forms, or Ideas which occur to our Observation, the Author chuses to call Senses; distinguishing them from the Powers which commonly go by that Name, by calling our Power of perceiving the Beauty of Regularity, Order, Harmony, an Internal Sense." He then states, "that Determination to be pleas'd with the Contemplation of those Affections, Actions, or Characters of rational Agents, which we call virtuous, he marks by the name of a Moral Sense." [5] Hutcheson's understanding of internal sense is akin to Edwards's understanding of an "inferior" or "secondary" beauty.[6] While Edwards recognized that everyone could recognize beauty to some degree, "Edwards contended a 'natural man' could not comprehend spiritual beauty. The spiritual beauty of Edwards did not correspond one bit to the moral sense of Hutcheson. Spiritual beauty was a gracious gift extended from One who was absolutely benevolent."[7] Spiritual beauty of course is superior and only apprehended by a believer.[8]

It is clear that Edwards worked from a theocentric foundation rather than that which is rooted in natural or innate moral sense for a truly virtuous life. In fact, according to David C. Brand, Edwards thought natural moral sense philosophy without reference to divine glory was "defective."[9] The Earl of Shaftsbury was another important conversation partner for Edwards. Conforti points out that both Hutcheson and Shaftsbury "rested their sanguine hopes for mankind on belief in an innate 'moral sense' capable of regulating the behavior of individuals without the need for supernatural grace."[10] Specifically for Shaftsbury, because of innate moral sense, one is naturally inclined toward morality and can recognize that which is ethical

[5]Francis Hutcheson, *An Inquiry into the Original of our Ideas of Beauty and Virtue; In Two Treatises*, Rev. ed. (Indianapolis: Liberty Fund, 2008), 8–9.

[6]Cochran, "Imitating the Virtue Ethic of Jonathan Edwards and William James," 21–22.

[7]Cochran, "Imitating the Virtue Ethic of Jonathan Edwards and William James," 22–23.

[8]Cochran, "Imitating the Virtue Ethic of Jonathan Edwards and William James," 22. Discussing how Edwards believed conversion was necessary for one to live a truly virtuous life, Elizabeth Agnew Cochran notes, "Both because true virtue is more proper to God's nature than to human nature and because sin damages our moral capacities, human beings require God's assistance in order to exercise true virtue." Elizabeth Agnew Cochran, "Ethics" in *Oxford Handbook of Jonathan Edwards*, ed. Douglas A Sweeney and Jan Stievermann (Oxford: Oxford University Press, 2021), 287.

[9]David C. Brand, *Profile of the Last Puritan: Jonathan Edwards, Self-Love, and the Dawn of the Beatific*, American Academy of Religion 73 (Atlanta: Scholars Press, 1991), 45.

[10]Joseph A. Conforti, *Samuel Hopkins and the New Divinity Movement: Calvinism, the Congregational Ministry, and Reform in New England Between the Great Awakenings* (Grand Rapids: Christian University Press, 1981), 113.

and unethical.[11] In short, while Edwards agreed that everyone has "partial loves," only a converted individual has a "spiritual sense" that enables him to pursue true virtue.[12]

Hopkins knew well the moral sense issues at hand. In the preface to the original edition of the *Two Dissertations*, Hopkins writes concerning Edwards's perspective, "The notions that some men entertain concerning God's end in creating the world, and concerning true virtue, in our late author's opinion, have a natural tendency to corrupt Christianity, and to destroy the gospel of our Divine Redeemer."[13] Hopkins continues, explaining that it was thus "in the exercise of a pious concern for the honor and glory of God, and a tender respect to the best interests of his fellow men," that Edwards decided to write the *Two Dissertations*.[14] From Hopkins's remarks, Edwards's desire to portray a genuinely Christian understanding of God and virtue is made evident.

Edwards makes clear that God is the ultimate being in the universe. In *CEW*, Edwards discusses God's own self-regard in relation to the end of God's creation. Edwards writes, "That if God himself be in any respect properly capable of being his own end in the creation of the world, then it is reasonable to suppose that he had respect to *himself* as his last and highest end in this work; because he is worthy in himself to be so, being infinitely the greatest and best of beings."[15] Edwards continues, elaborating on God's supreme worth, explaining that "if God esteems, values, and has respect to things according to their nature and proportions, he must necessarily have the greatest respect to himself."[16] Edwards indicates that there is a quality to God's essence that is unmatched. There is no equivalent to God and therefore, God is of most worth. Thus, Edwards can make a clear distinction of God's worth compared to created beings since there is truly no comparison. Pointing once again to the issue of regard, Edwards notes how

[11]Conforti, *Samuel Hopkins and the New Divinity Movement*, 113.

[12]Cochran, "Ethics," 287.; Elizabeth Agnew Cochran, *Receptive Human Virtues: A New Reading of Jonathan Edwards's Ethics* (University Park, PA: Penn State University Press, 2011), 106.

[13]Samuel Hopkins, "Hopkins' Preface," in *Ethical Writings*, ed. Paul Ramsey, vol. 8, *The Works of Jonathan Edwards* (New Haven, CT: Yale University Press, 1989), 402.

[14]Hopkins, "Hopkins' Preface," 402.

[15]Jonathan Edwards, "Concerning the End for Which God Created the World," in *Ethical Writings*, ed. Paul Ramsey, vol. 8, *The Works of Jonathan Edwards* (New Haven, CT: Yale University Press, 1989), 421.

[16]*WJE*, 8:421.

God far exceeds all which is in creation.[17] The essence of God, his character, sets him apart as the one who is owed most regard.

Edwards makes similar statements in *TV*. Discussing how God has "the greatest share of virtuous benevolence," because he has "the greatest share of universal existence," Edwards concludes that God "is infinitely the greatest being."[18] Consequently, everything else in creation and "throughout the whole universe, is as nothing in comparison of the Divine Being."[19] Edwards makes a distinction between the Creator and the created order, placing God in his rightful supreme position. Edwards continues with the Creator versus creation distinction:

> Because God is not only infinitely greater and more excellent than all other being, but he is the head of the universal system of existence; the foundation and fountain of all being and all beauty; from whom all is perfectly derived, and on whom all is absolutely and perfectly dependent; *of whom*, and *through whom*, and *to whom* is all being and all perfection; and whose being and beauty is as it were the sum and comprehension of all existence and excellence: much more than the sun is the fountain and summary comprehension of all the light and brightness of the day.[20]

Edwards points to how God is the source of all creation and therefore, the greatest as the origin of all creation. The biblical language is clear as Edwards describes God's authorship of all things. In *CEW*, divine distinction is once again made evident:

> But if God be indeed so great, and so excellent, that all other beings are as nothing to him, and all other excellency be as nothing and less than nothing, and vanity in comparison of his; and God be omniscient and infallible and perfectly knows that he is infinitely the most valuable Being; then it is fit that his heart should be agreeable to this, which is indeed the true nature

[17] *WJE*, 8:423–24.

[18] Jonathan Edwards, "The Nature of True Virtue," in *Ethical Writings*, vol. 8, *The Works of Jonathan Edwards* (New Haven, CT: Yale University Press, 1989), 550.

[19] *WJE*, 8:550.

[20] *WJE*, 8:551. Edwards's understanding of a "system of existence" will be discussed later in this chapter.

> and proportion of things and agreeable to this infallible and all-comprehending understanding which he has of them, and that perfectly clear light in which he views them: and so 'tis fit and suitable that he should value himself infinitely more than his creatures.[21]

It is not that Edwards denigrates the created order. He believes that God values his creation, which will be made evident when discussing Edwards's understanding of a system of created beings. Rather, in comparison to God and his character inherent in his essence, creation is as nothing. It is an elevation of God rather than a deprecation of creation. So, for Edwards, creatures "are infinitely less worthy of supreme and ultimate regard" when compared to God, recognizing God as "the highest Being, and infinitely greater and more worthy than all others," a being without equal.[22]

Edwards further supports the Creator versus creation distinction by arguing how God existed prior to creation. Regarding divine causation for creaturely existence, Edwards explains how "God can't so properly be said to make the creature his end, as himself. For the creature is not as yet considered as existing. This disposition or desire in God must be prior to the existence of the creature, even in intention and foresight. For it is a disposition that is the original ground of the existence of the creature; and even of the future intended and foreseen existence of the creature."[23] The creature is a result of God's existence as Creator. Thus, it is impossible for God to make the creature his end since that would exalt man over his Creator. Simply put, God is owed the highest regard compared to those who are dependent on him.

A little later Edwards argues that "God is to be considered as first and original in his regard; and the creature is the object of God's regard consequentially and by implication as being as it were comprehended in God," pointing once again to God as the creature's cause of existence.[24] This insight is expanded when Edwards shows scriptural support for such points. Finding support from passages such as Rom 11:36, Col 1:16, Heb 2:10, and Prov 16:4, Edwards asserts: "And when God is so often spoken of as the last end as well as the first, and the end as well as the beginning, what is meant

[21] *WJE*, 8:451.

[22] *WJE*, 8:452.

[23] *WJE*, 8:438.

[24] *WJE*, 8:440–41.

(or at least implied) is, that as he is the first efficient cause and fountain from whence all things originate, so he is the last final cause for which they are made; the final term to which they all tend in their ultimate issue."[25] The cause of creaturely existence is only found in the Creator who existed before creation. The moral sense philosophy Edwards was reacting to in the *Two Dissertations* is made evident in regards to God's end: "The doctrine that makes God's creatures and not himself to be his last end is a doctrine the farthest from having a favorable aspect on God's absolute self-sufficience and independence."[26] Therefore, God is not dependent on anything external from himself but rather self-dependent.[27]

Edwards's understanding of God making himself and his glory his end is apparent in *CEW*. Like God's self-regard and consequent worth as the greatest being, Edwards identifies proper respect of God for himself. Edwards explains, "That if God himself be in any respect properly capable of being his own end in the creation of the world, then it is reasonable to suppose that he had respect to *himself* as his last and highest end in this work; because he is worthy in himself to be so, being infinitely the greatest and best of beings."[28] That God recognizes the inherent worth in himself as the greatest being warrants himself to be his end in creation. And the idea of God's worthiness of being his own end is intimately connected to his glory.

Edwards defines God's glory, or more specifically, God's "internal glory," stating: "When the word is used to signify what is within, inherent or in the possession of the subject, it very commonly signifies excellency, or great valuableness, dignity, or worthiness of regard."[29] It goes back to God's worth as the greatest being. God's glory cannot be separated from God himself. Accordingly, God's glory can be seen as God's end. Referring to Isa 48:11, Edwards writes, "Which is as much as to say, I will obtain my end, I will not forego my glory: another shall not take this prize from me. 'Tis pretty evident here that God's name and his glory, which seems to intend the same thing . . . are spoken of as his last end in the great work mentioned, not as an inferior subordinate end, subservient to the interest of others."[30] Scripture substantiates the intimate connection between "God's name and

[25] *WJE*, 8:467.

[26] *WJE*, 8:450.

[27] *WJE*, 8:450.

[28] *WJE*, 8:421.

[29] *WJE*, 8:513.

[30] *WJE*, 8:475.

his glory," as the two often times "signify the same thing in Scripture."[31] Edwards seems to be stressing the identity of God. Just as God's glory is an inherent reality within the very essence of God, the name of God points to the one who holds this glory.

It makes sense, then, that Edwards points to God's glory as the end of creation.[32] Moreover, God's glory can be seen as a result of creation: "The good attained in the use of a thing, made for use, is the result of the making of that thing, as the signifying the time of day, when actually attained by the use of a watch, is the consequence of the making of the watch. So that 'tis apparent that the glory of God is a thing that is actually the result and consequence of the creation of the world."[33] Having provided scriptural support to substantiate the point, Edwards illustrates divine glory as the result of creation by comparing it to the time a watch provides. In short, Edwards seems to be saying that God's glory is displayed in creation.

This leads us to God's creation of man for his glory. Highlighting Isa 43:6-7, Isa 60:21, and Isa 61:3, Edwards asserts, "In these places we see that the glory of God is spoken of as the end of God's saints, the end for which he makes them, i.e. either gives them being, or gives them a being as saints, or both. It is said that God has 'made' and 'formed' them to be his sons and daughters, *for his own glory:* that they are trees of his planting, the work of his hands, as trees of righteousness, *that he might be glorified*."[34] The purpose for which God made man is evident: to display divine glory. This is seen especially when believers are expressing genuine religion through life. As a result, virtue is made evident.[35] In *TV*, Edwards explains how one that has virtue in mind and heart will recognize God's glory as his end:

> By these things it appears that a truly virtuous mind, being as it were under the sovereign dominion of *love to God*, does above all things seek the *glory of God*, and makes *this* his supreme, governing, and ultimate end: consisting in the expression of God's perfections in their proper effects, and in the manifestation of God's glory to created understandings, and the communications of the infinite fullness of God to the creature; in the creature's

[31] *WJE*, 8:523.

[32] *WJE*, 8:481.

[33] *WJE*, 8:492.

[34] *WJE*, 8:476.

[35] *WJE*, 8:479.

highest esteem of God, love to God, and joy in God, and in the proper exercises and expressions of these.[36]

A creature that genuinely loves God and is in union with him will make God and his glory his end. This is because he recognizes who God is as the greatest being. Hence, God is man's "supreme end" as the creature is to bring God glory.[37]

Having established God as the greatest being and therefore, God and his glory as the end of creation, we now turn to what Edwards meant by benevolence to Being in general. Edwards discusses his understanding of benevolence to Being in general in *TV*.[38] Edwards writes, "True Virtue most essentially consists in benevolence to Being in general. Or perhaps to speak more accurately, it is that consent, propensity and union of heart to Being in general, that is immediately exercised in a general good will."[39] Ramsey points to Edwards's understanding of "consent, propensity and union of heart" to refer to Edwards's "*definition* of 'benevolence.' "[40] This makes sense since Edwards replaces the word "benevolence" with "consent, propensity and union of heart" in the next sentence.[41] Cochran helpfully notes how "Edwards frequently interchanged the concept of action and motion with the ideas: disposition, inclination, exercise, propensity, and

[36] *WJE*, 8:559.

[37] *WJE*, 8:533.

[38] Also see Jonathan Edwards, " 'Controversies' Notebook: The Nature of True Virtue," in *Writings on the Trinity, Grace, and Faith*, ed. Sang Hyun Lee, vol. 21, *The Works of Jonathan Edwards* (New Haven, CT: Yale University Press, 2003), 312–27. While the language and argumentation are philosophically driven in *TV*, Edwards nonetheless provides practical ramifications. For example, Edwards discusses the action of justice by one who has benevolence: " 'Tis true that benevolence to Being in general, when a person hath it, will naturally incline him to justice, or proportion in the exercises of it." *WJE*, 8:571.

[39] *WJE*, 8:540. Importantly, Ramsey notes that using the capital B in Being is a reference to God. Ramsey explains how "in editing the text I retain 'Being in general' and 'Being simply considered' in all instances; and also the capitalization of 'Being' alone where it is obviously a reference to God." Paul Ramsey, "Editor's Introduction," in *Ethical Writings*, vol. 8, *The Works of Jonathan Edwards* (New Haven, CT: Yale University Press, 1989), 117. Ramsey also says, "It is a sufficient defense of my retention of the capitals to argue simply that, where I do so, the word is used in the context as a reference to God, not as a name for God." *WJE*, 8:118. While the capital B is used to reference God, Ramsey uses the lowercase b "when *being* plainly refers to finite beings, and where the word is plainly used more as a metaphysical concept than as a reference to God." *WJE*, 8:117. I take this to mean that "being" refers to creatures or the idea of existence, given Edwards at times describes the system made up of God and creatures as one of existence or being.

[40] *WJE*, 540, n. 6.

[41] *WJE*, 540.

habit."[42] God's disposition is active and like God, human beings are active and relational, seeking union.[43]

Who is the creature united to? Edwards claims that "every intelligent being is some way related to Being in general, and is a part of the universal system of existence; and so stands in connection with the whole; what can its general and true beauty be, but its union and consent with the great whole?"[44] Edwards specifies what he means by "intelligent being" in union to Being in general as denoting "*intelligent* Being in general. Not inanimate things, or beings that have no perception or will, which are not properly capable objects of benevolence."[45] While the reference is God, Edwards seems to be implying an interconnectedness between creatures, a special bond, or more specifically, that which unites them as a "universal system of existence."[46] Edwards highlights God's place in the system of existence in *TV*, chapter one, stating that "if Being, simply considered, be the first object of a truly virtuous benevolence, then that Being who has *most* of being, or has the greatest share of existence, other things being equal, so far as such a being is exhibited to our faculties or set in our view, will have the *greatest* share of the propensity and benevolent affection of the heart."[47]

Similarly in chapter two of *TV*, Edwards explains the Being and creature dynamic in light of the system of existence. God, as the greatest being, has most ownership of all existence.[48] Edwards seems to be implying that God as the supreme being is intimately connected to the great system of being or existence. Because God is the greatest of all beings, he possesses the greatest portion of existence. This in no way takes away from the legitimacy of a system of created existence for Edwards, for creatures are united to God.

[42]Cochran, "Imitating the Virtue Ethic of Jonathan Edwards and William James," 24.

[43]McClymond and McDermott, *The Theology of Jonathan Edwards*, 530.

[44]*WJE*, 8:541.

[45]*WJE*, 8:542.

[46]*WJE*, 8:541. Fiering importantly notes, "God is also properly designated 'being in general,' because God's being is itself the cause of all created essences. All existence, all being, derives from God, who is the one self-sufficient being. It seems clear that Edwards meant by 'being in general' the transcendent God *plus* His ordered creation." Fiering, *Jonathan Edwards's Moral Thought and Its British Context*, 326. Discussing *TV* and the system discussed, McDermott puts it this way: "Edwards described the structure of being as a vast network of interrelations wherein every entity is related to every other." Gerald R. McDermott, *One Holy and Happy Society: The Public Theology of Jonathan Edwards* (University Park, PA: Penn State University Press, 1992), 101.

[47]*WJE*, 8:545–46.

[48]*WJE*, 8:550.

The self-communication of God to creatures, which will be discussed later, contributes to this idea as creatures embody the presence of God. Edwards illustrates the idea of union further:

> When I say, true virtue consists in love to Being in general, I shall not be likely to be understood, that no one act of the mind or exercise of love is of the nature of true virtue but what has Being in general, or the great system of universal existence, for its *direct* and *immediate* object; so that no exercise of love or kind affection to any one particular being, that is but a small part of this whole, has anything of the nature of true virtue. But, that the nature of true virtue consists in a disposition to benevolence towards Being in general: though, from such a disposition may arise exercises of love to particular beings, as objects are presented and occasions arise.[49]

Again, Edwards equates "Being in general" to "the great system of universal existence."[50] Likewise in *CEW*, Edwards argues that God or Being "comprehends all entity, and all excellence in his own essence. The first Being, the eternal and infinite Being, is in effect, *Being in general;* and comprehends universal existence, as was observed before."[51] The ontological nature of Edwards's description is made clear by creatures embracing harmony in relationship as a system of intelligent beings with God as their head. God is Being in general because creatures are in union with God. To be united to God, because he is connected with creatures, is to also be united to others in a system of existence. Edwards illustrates the point: "If the Deity is to be looked upon as within that system of beings which properly terminates our benevolence, or belonging to that whole, certainly he is to be regarded as the *head* of the system, and the *chief* part of it; if it be proper to call him a *part* who is infinitely more than all the rest, and in comparison of whom and without whom all the rest are nothing, either as to beauty or existence."[52] Edwards makes a similar argument for the inseparableness of God and creatures in Miscellany 117. Discussing God's endless love and the extension of love to "being in general," Edwards explains,

[49] *WJE*, 8:541–42.

[50] *WJE*, 8:541.

[51] *WJE*, 8:461.

[52] *WJE*, 8:553–54.

> Then there must have been an object from all eternity which God infinitely loves. But we have showed that all love arises from the perception, either of consent to being in general, or consent to that being that perceives. Infinite loveliness, to God, therefore, must consist either in infinite consent to entity in general, or infinite consent to God. But we have shown that consent to entity and consent to God are the same, because God is the general and only proper entity of all things. So that 'tis necessary that that object which God infinitely loves must be infinitely and perfectly consenting and agreeable to him; but that which infinitely and perfectly agrees is the very same essence, for if it be different it don't infinitely consent.[53]

Divine and creaturely consent or union creates an inseparable bond between God and the system of existence. God's primary position and the creature's dependent position in the system are noted. Therefore, Edwards likens God and creatures as being one without sacrificing God's place as the foundation for existence.

Specifically for Edwards, there are two objects of benevolence. God is first, for "the primary object of virtuous love is Being, simply considered; or that true virtue primarily consists, not in love to any particular beings, because of their virtue or beauty, nor in gratitude, because they love us; but in a propensity and union of heart to Being simply considered; exciting 'absolute Benevolence' (if I may so call it) to Being in general."[54] Edwards refers to his prior discussion on "love of *complacence*," which "primarily consists in any love to its object for its beauty" and "*gratitude*," which consists in "one being's benevolence to another for his benevolence to him."[55] He then explains that love or union to God, "Being simply considered," is the cause for love to "Being in general."[56] So, if the "*first* object of a virtuous benevolence is *Being*, simply considered: and if Being, *simply* considered, be its object, then Being *in general* is its object; and the thing it has an ultimate propensity to, is the *highest good* of Being in general."[57] Edwards again

[53]Jonathan Edwards, *Misc 117,* in *The "Miscellanies," a-500*, ed. Thomas A. Schafer, vol. 13, *The Works of Jonathan Edwards* (New Haven, CT: Yale University Press, 1994), 283.

[54]*WJE*, 8:544.

[55]*WJE*, 8:543–44.

[56]*WJE*, 8:544.

[57]*WJE*, 8:545.

shows the close connection between God and the system of existence. If one loves and is united to God, the head of the system, one is in turn united to others.

Edwards transitions to his discussion on the second object of benevolence, explaining, "Pure benevolence in its *first* exercise is nothing else but being's uniting, consent, or propensity to Being; appearing true and pure by its extending to Being in general, and inclining to the general highest good, and to each being, whose welfare is consistent with the highest general good, in proportion to the degree of *existence*—understand, other things being equal."[58] Edwards again defines benevolence as indicating union and its inclination to seek the good of the whole. The whole is what Edwards means by *benevolent* being. He means the creatures that make up the system of being or existence, the second object of benevolence. This is made clear by the ensuing discussion on creatures or being in regards to benevolence. Edwards writes,

> When anyone under the influence of general benevolence sees another being possessed of the like general benevolence, this attaches his heart to him, and draws forth greater love to him, than merely his having existence: because so far as the being beloved has love to Being in general, so far his own being is, as it were, enlarged; extends to, and in some sort comprehends, Being in general: and therefore he that is governed by love to Being in general, must of necessity have complacence in him, and the greater degree of benevolence to him, as it were out of gratitude to him for his love to general existence, that his own heart is extended and united to, and so looks on its interest as its own.[59]

Once again, Edwards stresses union, specifically union to the whole. Divine and creaturely union is a result of God's self-extension. Also in *TV*, Edwards explains:

> Virtue, as I have observed, consists in the cordial consent or union of being to Being in general. And, as has also been observed, that frame of mind, whereby it is disposed to relish and be pleased with the view of this, is benevolence or union of

[58] *WJE*, 8:546.

[59] *WJE*, 8:546–47.

> heart itself to Being in general, or a universally benevolent frame of mind: because he whose temper is to love Being in general, therein must have a disposition to approve and be pleased with love to Being in general.[60]

For Edwards, true virtue involves love for God and others. This includes a creature's temperament of mind. As the believer loves God and is united to him, he is truly made one with God and others.[61]

Edwards elaborates on the creature's union with God and others in a system of existence in *CEW*. Again, Edwards makes clear, "The first Being, the eternal and infinite Being, is in effect, *Being in general;* and comprehends universal existence," as God comprises creatures.[62] The system of God and creatures is made obvious by Edwards immediately discussing divine communication to creatures. In terms of the system's character, Edwards indicates that the whole is greater than the parts. Upon discussing how God has the greatest "regard to himself," Edwards explains the importance of viewing the system holistically, saying that the "greater, or more existence should have a greater share than less, that a greater part of the whole should be more looked at and respected than the lesser in proportion (other things being equal) to the measure of existence," giving value to the mass rather than to a "lesser" portion.[63] Edwards continues, discussing God's decision to give more value to the whole than the parts of the system:

> Such an arbiter, in considering the system of created intelligent beings by itself, would determine that the system of created intelligent beings by itself, would determine that the system in general, consisting of many millions, was of greater importance, and worthy of a greater share of regard, than only one individual. For however considerable some of the individuals might be, so that they might be much greater and better, and have a greater share of the sum total of existence and excellence than another individual, yet no one exceeds others so much as to countervail all the rest of the system.[64]

[60] *WJE*, 8:620.

[61] *WJE*, 8:19.

[62] *WJE*, 8:461.

[63] *WJE*, 8:422–23.

[64] *WJE*, 8:423.

According to Edwards, in God's economy, while the individual is valued in the system, the system itself takes precedence. Edwards specifies the system further by contrasting it with what he names as "private system."[65] Edwards explains,

> if any being or beings have by natural instinct, or any other means, a determination of mind to benevolence extending only to some particular persons or private system, however large that system may be, or however great a number of individuals it may contain, so long as it contains but an infinitely small part of universal existence, and so bears no proportion to this great and universal system: such limited private benevolence, not arising from nor being subordinate to benevolence to Being in general, cannot have the nature of true virtue.[66]

In other words, the priority is the system of existence that is universal. For Edwards, if love is extended only to a portion of the whole or a system within a system is created, it is a result of love that is private in nature and thus, void of genuine virtue. However, "If that private system contained the sum of universal existence, then their benevolence would have true beauty; or, in other words, would be beautiful all things considered: but now it is not so."[67] Strictly speaking, for Edwards, benevolence is only genuine if directed to the system as a whole, thus valuing the universality of existence over "an infinitely small part of it."[68]

In *CEW*, moving from a system comprising of creatures only to a universal system that includes God, Edwards writes, "And if this judge consider not only the system of created beings, but the system of being in general, comprehending the sum total of universal existence, both Creator and creature; still every part must be considered according to its weight and importance, or the measure it has of existence and excellence."[69] God is to be viewed with highest esteem.[70] This by in large is why Edwards views regard to God as needing to be measured appropriately when the universal

[65] *WJE*, 8:601.

[66] *WJE*, 8:601–2.

[67] *WJE*, 8:610.

[68] *WJE*, 8:610.

[69] *WJE*, 8:423.

[70] *WJE*, 8:423–24.

system is considered.[71] Edwards then discusses the sovereign role of God governing the universe.[72] It is a reminder of God as the head and authority of the system of existence.

Elaborating on God's highest regard for himself, Edwards writes, "And if it be thus fit that God should have a supreme regard to himself, then it is fit that this supreme regard should appear, in those things by which he makes himself known, or by his *word* and *works;* i.e. in what he says, and in what he does."[73] Edwards continues and specifies how God displays himself in light of divine self-regard:

> And if it was God's intention, as there is great reason to think it was, that his works should exhibit an image of himself their author, that it might brightly appear by his works what manner of being he is, and afford a proper representation of his divine excellencies, and especially his *moral* excellence, consisting in the *disposition of his heart;* then 'tis reasonable to suppose that his works are so wrought as to show this supreme respect to himself wherein his moral excellency does primarily consist.[74]

God desires to show himself by way of his attributes and moral character. Specifically, the works of God reflect the type of God he is. These works, then, exhibit God's proper self-regard.

This head of the system, in union with the system, communicates himself to creatures that make up the system.[75] In *CEW*, the relationship between divine and creaturely union through divine communication is explained. Discussing God's aim for "the creature's excellency and happiness" when "creating the world," Edwards explains, "As the creature's good was viewed in this manner when God made the world for it, viz. with respect to the whole of the eternal duration of it, and the eternally progressive union and communion with him; so the creature must be viewed as in infinite and strict union with himself."[76] Edwards continues, stating, "In this view it

[71] *WJE*, 8:424.

[72] *WJE*, 8:424–25.

[73] *WJE*, 8:422.

[74] *WJE*, 8:422.

[75] For a detailed analysis on Edwards's understanding of divine communication and self-enlargement, see Sang Hyun Lee, *The Philosophical Theology of Jonathan Edwards* (Princeton, NJ: Princeton University Press, 1988), 170–210.

[76] *WJE*, 8:459.

appears that God's respect to the creature, in the whole, unites with his respect to himself."[77] The union is explained ontologically. The existence of the creature is always viewed in light of the existence of God. And if God and his glory are indeed the end of creation, then divine communication to creatures united to him results in the same end. This is why Edwards can write about the communication and display of God's glory in the creature as displaying his own glory as their Creator:

> That God in seeking his glory, therein seeks the good of his creatures: because the emanation of his glory (which he seeks and delights in, as he delights in himself and his own eternal glory) implies the communicated excellency and happiness of his creature. And that in communicating his fullness for them, he does it for himself: because their good, which he seeks, is so much in union and communion with himself. God is their good. Their excellency and happiness is nothing but the emanation and expression of God's glory: God in seeking their glory and happiness, seeks himself: and in seeking himself, i.e. himself diffused and expressed (which he delights in, as he delights in his own beauty and fullness), he seeks their glory and happiness.[78]

According to Edwards, the display of divine glory and happiness is correspondent to the creaturely display of happiness and glory. So the creature is very much a bearer of the divine image. Hence the closeness of union is stressed.

The communication of God's attributes further establishes the idea of divine and creaturely union. Because God values his attributes, "he delights in their proper exercise and expression."[79] Hence, "the glorious perfections of God should be known, and the operations and expressions of them seen by other beings besides himself."[80] Edwards makes clear, by God

[77] *WJE*, 8:459.

[78] *WJE*, 8:459. Fiering explains the role of God's glory as the end of creation and the creature's involvement to support that end: "God's end is His own glory, and human beings are given an opportunity to participate in this glory through consent of heart to being in general. The creation is not subordinate to man's finite ends; man must subordinate himself to the infinite purposes of the Creator." Fiering, *Jonathan Edwards's Moral Thought and Its British Context*, 332–33.

[79] *WJE*, 8:430.

[80] *WJE*, 8:430–31. I take it that Edwards meant "attributes" and "perfections" to indicate the same thing as both words point to the character of God.

communicating his perfections to creatures, God is in fact communicating himself. As God delights "in the expressions of his perfections, he manifests a delight in his own perfections themselves: or in other words, he manifests a delight in himself; and in making these expressions of his own perfections his end, *he makes himself his end*."[81] God equals his perfections as he desires to communicate those perfections or himself to creatures. Thus, God's self-love is made evident as he makes himself the end of creation.[82] Edwards continues, saying it is "fit that he should take delight in his own excellencies' being seen, acknowledged, esteemed, and delighted in. This is implied in a love to himself and his own perfections. And in seeking this, and making this his end, he seeks himself, and makes himself his end."[83] By communicating the good of himself, God demonstrates upmost self-regard.[84] Via divine communication, God makes himself his end and the end of creation.

Specifically, divine communication, according to Edwards, was God's goal from the beginning: "And 'tis farther to be considered that the thing which God aimed at in the creation of the world, as the end which he had ultimately in view, was the communication of himself, which he intended throughout all eternity."[85] Edwards continues, "And if we attend to the nature and circumstances of this eternal emanation of divine good, it will more clearly show how in making this his end, God testifies a supreme respect to himself, and makes himself his end."[86] Edwards refers again to God's proper self-regard as a result of God's self-communication. Hence, God is the goal and therefore, the end of creation.

Additionally, God's communication of himself to creatures is the greatest work for divine display. Edwards's understanding of God's self-enlargement is key to rightly delimit God's communication of himself to creatures. Consistently referring to God as Being in general, Edwards explains God's union with creatures further by God's enlargement of himself to include creatures: "God in his benevolence to his creatures, can't have his heart enlarged in such a manner as to take in beings that he finds, who are originally out of himself, distinct and independent. This can't be in an infinite being, who exists alone from eternity. But he, from his goodness, as it were enlarges

[81] *WJE*, 8:437.

[82] *WJE*, 8:438.

[83] *WJE*, 8:437–38.

[84] *WJE*, 8:438.

[85] *WJE*, 8:443.

[86] *WJE*, 8:443.

himself in a more excellent and divine manner."[87] Edwards specifies the manner in which God enlarges himself for the sake of creatures: "This is by communicating and diffusing himself; and so instead of finding, making objects of his benevolence: not by taking into himself what he finds distinct from himself, and so partaking of their good, and being happy in them; but by flowing forth, and expressing himself in them, and making them to partake of him, and rejoicing in himself expressed in them, and communicated to them."[88] The metaphysical nature of Edwards's language is clear. Edwards is obviously not referring to a spatial enlargement of God's being, but rather God's connection to creatures by way of divine emanation or communication as an act of benevolence towards them.[89] As a result, God is found in creatures as he reaches out to them. Again, the divine disposition is one that actively seeks union and relationship.

Thus, what is communicated is the very essence of God, his character, and his attributes. The creature experiences "the emanation of divine fullness" as God communicates his "virtue and holiness to the creature."[90] Specifically, it is "a communication of God's holiness; so that hereby the creature partakes of God's own moral excellency, which is properly the beauty of the divine nature."[91] This results in a creature's "participation of what is in God" as "God and his glory are the objective ground of it."[92] Creaturely participation would not be possible without God first communicating himself to creatures. As a result, God is made manifest in and through the creature. There is now unition of the Creator and the created.[93] Also, God's communication

[87]*WJE*, 8:461.

[88]*WJE*, 8:461–62.

[89]McDermott makes a similar argument when explaining God's personal extension to creatures: "Although he does not add to his actuality, God is continually involved in a process of self-extension by creating, and then relating to, other beings." McDermott, *One Holy and Happy Society*, 97.

[90]*WJE*, 8:442.

[91]*WJE*, 8:442.

[92]*WJE*, 8:442.

[93]*WJE*, 8:442–43. Edwards makes an important point in regards to divine communication by noting how the creature reflects the glory of God back to God himself: "The emanation or communication of the divine fullness, consisting in the knowledge of God, love to God, and joy in God, has relation indeed both to God and the creature: but it has relation to God as its fountain, as it is an emanation from God; and as the communication itself, or thing communicated, is something divine, something of God, something of his internal fullness; as the water in the stream is something of the fountain; and as the beams are of the sun. And again, they have relation to God as they have respect to him as their object: for the

of himself is always for the good of the creature as God demonstrates the highest regard for himself.[94] Again, God's end is the creature's end.

The idea of union is further considered when Edwards discusses divine love. Edwards writes, "That in God the love of himself, and the love of the public are not to be distinguished, as in man, because God's being as it were comprehends all. His existence, being infinite, must be equivalent to universal existence. And for the same reason that public affection in the creature is fit and beautiful, God's regard to himself must be so likewise."[95] Edwards seems to indicate divine omnipresence by way of creation. One cannot spatially locate God because God encompasses the created order. Therefore, as it pertains to creatures, the union points to the amalgamation of God's self-love and love for the community. Edwards continues with the theme of union, discussing the matter of holiness:

> In God, the love of what is fit and decent, or the love of virtue, can't be a distinct thing from the love of himself—because the love of God is that wherein all virtue and holiness does primarily and chiefly consist, and God's own holiness must primarily consist in the love of himself, as was before observed. And if God's holiness consists in love to himself, then it will imply an approbation of and pleasedness with the esteem and love of him in others. For a being that loves himself, necessarily loves Love to himself. If holiness in God consist chiefly in love to himself,

knowledge communicated is the knowledge of God; and so God is the object of the knowledge: and the love communicated, is the love of God; so God is the object of that love: and the happiness communicated, is joy in God; and so he is the object of the joy communicated. In the creature's knowing, esteeming, loving, rejoicing in, and praising God, the glory of God is both exhibited and acknowledged; his fullness is received and returned. Here is both an *emanation* and *remanation*. The refulgence shines upon and into the creature, and is reflected back to the luminary. The beams of glory to their original. So that the whole is *of* God, and *in* God, and *to* God; and God is the beginning, middle and end in this affair." *WJE*, 8:531. It seems that Edwards is also highlighting creaturely participation as the creature reciprocates God's extension of himself. Delattre rightly reminds us of the source: "The fullness of God, in Edwards' view, consists summarily in God's knowledge, holiness, and happiness; and the fulfillment of human life consists in our participation in that very same knowledge, holiness, and happiness. To understand or even rightly describe the Christian life, one must begin with the divine life." Roland A. Delattre, "The Theological Ethics of Jonathan Edwards: An Homage to Paul Ramsey," *Journal of Religious Ethics* 19, no. 2 (1991): 76.

[94] *WJE*, 8:531.

[95] *WJE*, 8:455.

> holiness in the creature must chiefly consist in love to him. And if God loves holiness in himself, he must love it in the creature.[96]

Edwards explains that God's love for holiness and love for himself are the same because holiness resides in God's love. In light of creaturely and divine union, creaturely holiness, then, is inherent in his love to God. Moreover, God's love for "holiness in himself" is the same as love for holiness "in the creature."[97] Thus, God views the creature as one with himself.

Self-Love

Edwards's understanding of self-love is another important area to probe to comprehend Edwards's philosophical ethics. As stated at the beginning of this chapter, the eighteenth century British moral sense philosophy he was responding to, known as benevolism, affirmed an innate moral sense in humanity to naturally pursue benevolence and virtue.[98] Edwards likened natural moral sense to human conscience and "a kind of self-love, which of themselves could not produce benevolence."[99] While recognizing the importance of natural self-love, Edwards recognizes a self-love that is sourced in God. Specifically for Edwards, there are two types of self-love. The importance lies in his signification of self-love in order to develop a definition of "divine love."[100] Edwards explains the nature of self-love by describing one that embraces personal happiness versus one that is private in nature.

The love of one's own happiness is a happiness consisting in the happiness of others. First, Edwards defines this self-love as "his loving whatsoever is grateful or pleasing to him. Which comes only to this, that self-love is a man's liking, and being suited and pleased in that which he likes, and which pleases him; or that 'tis a man's loving what he loves."[101] Edwards continues and importantly notes, "For whatever a man loves, that thing is grateful and pleasing to him, whether that be his own peculiar happiness,

[96] *WJE*, 8:455–56.

[97] *WJE*, 8:456.

[98] McClymond and McDermott, *The Theology of Jonathan Edwards*, 533; Cochran, "Imitating the Virtue Ethic of Jonathan Edwards and William James," 21.

[99] McClymond and McDermott, *The Theology of Jonathan Edwards*, 534.

[100] John E. Smith, *Jonathan Edwards: Puritan, Preacher, Philosopher* (Notre Dame: University of Notre Dame Press, 1992), 101.

[101] *WJE*, 8:575.

or the happiness of others."[102] Loving the happiness in others is key. It is a self-love that is selfless in nature, recognizing "our love to the person is the cause of our delighting, or being happy in his happiness."[103] Edwards in *CEW* writes, "In some sense, the most benevolent generous person in the world seeks his own happiness in doing good to others, because he places his happiness in their good."[104] Edwards explains that this is possible "by our hearts being first united to them in affection, so that as it were, we look on them as ourselves," once again stressing the idea of union.[105] As a result, seeing the happiness in others brings happiness to the one extending love.[106]

Private self-love, on the other hand, regards oneself only. Edwards describes this type of self-love as "a man's regard to his confined *private self*, or love to himself with respect to his *private interest*."[107] Edwards continues, "By 'private' interest I mean that which most immediately consists in those pleasures, or pains, that are *personal*."[108] Attention is restricted to the individual self. Thus, private self-love considers no other. This is why, in *CEW*, Edwards likens "confined self-love" as selfish in nature.[109] It is therefore "opposite to a general benevolence" because one's regard does not extend beyond oneself.[110] So strong are the inclinations for self that this self-love can result in a man loving others because they love him.[111] It is still about the interests of oneself and not others.

In *TV*, Edwards associates selfish self-love with sin: "So with respect to natural *gratitude*, though there may be no virtue merely in loving them that love us, yet the contrary may be an evidence of a great degree of depravity,

[102] *WJE*, 8:575.

[103] *WJE*, 8:577.

[104] *WJE*, 8:461.

[105] *WJE*, 8:577. Edwards also discusses love to others with the idea of self-enlargement: "A man's self is as it were extended and enlarged by love. Others so far as beloved do, as it were, become parts of himself; so that wherein their interest is promoted he looks on his own as promoted, and wherein their interest is touched his is touched." Jonathan Edwards, "Charity and Its Fruits," in *Ethical Writings*, ed. Paul Ramsey, vol. 8, *The Works of Jonathan Edwards* (New Haven, CT: Yale University Press, 1989), 263. It is another example of the importance Edwards gives to union with one's neighbor.

[106] *WJE*, 8:577.

[107] *WJE*, 8:577.

[108] *WJE*, 8:577.

[109] *WJE*, 8:461.

[110] *WJE*, 8:461.

[111] *WJE*, 8:578–79.

as it may argue a higher degree of selfishness, so that a man is come to look upon himself as *all*, and others as nothing, and so their respect and kindness as nothing."[112] It is prideful to take on such a posture, viewing oneself as the only one worthy of consideration.[113] As Edwards explains, such selfishness is an indication of sin. In fact, "All sin has its source from selfishness, or from self-love, not subordinate to regard to Being in general."[114] In sermon seven of *Charity and Its Fruits*, Edwards discusses the relationship between selfish self-love and sin. According to Edwards, "The ruin which the Fall brought upon the soul of man consists very much in that he lost his nobler and more extensive principles, and fell wholly under the government of self-love."[115] Edwards goes on and explains what he means by the "nobler" or "more extensive principles," stating, "As in other respects, so in this, that whereas before his soul was under the government of that noble principle of divine love whereby it was, as it were, enlarged to a kind of comprehension of all his fellow creatures; and not only so, but was not confined within such strait limits as the bounds of the creation but was extended to the Creator," thus dependent on God.[116] In other words, before the Fall, greater principles opposite of selfishness were in control. Edwards then discusses the consequences of the Fall in regards to the greater principles:

> But as soon as he had transgressed, those nobler principles were immediately lost and all this excellent enlargedness of his soul was gone and he thenceforth shrunk into a little point, circumscribed and closely shut up within itself to the exclusion of others. God was forsaken and fellow creatures forsaken, and man retired within himself and became wholly governed by narrow, selfish principles. Self-love became absolute master of

[112] *WJE*, 8:615.

[113] *WJE*, 8:615.

[114] *WJE*, 8:614. Earlier, Edwards made the point, discussing the opposition of selfishness to benevolence to Being in general. Having discussed the need to love God in order for virtue to be genuine, Edwards explains, "And therefore let it be supposed that some beings, by natural instinct or by some other means, have a determination of mind to union and benevolence to a *particular person* or *private system*, which is but a small part of the universal system of being: and that this disposition or determination of mind is independent on, or not subordinate to, benevolence to *Being in general*. Such a determination, disposition, or affection of mind is not of the nature of true virtue." *WJE*, 8:554.

[115] *WJE*, 8:252.

[116] *WJE*, 8:253.

> his soul, the more noble and spiritual principles having taken warning and fled.[117]

When sin entered the world, the greater, noble, or spiritual principles went away, leaving self-love in control. Without the greater principles governing the principles of self-love, the creature was now controlled by selfishness. Edwards makes similar arguments in *Original Sin*, discussing principles which are natural versus principles which are supernatural. Referring to Adam, Edwards writes,

> The case with man was plainly this: when God made man at first, he implanted in him two kinds of principles. There was an *inferior* kind, which may be called *natural*, being the principles of mere human nature; such as self-love, with those natural appetites and passions, which belong to the nature of man, in which his love to his own liberty, honor and pleasure, were exercised: these when alone, and left to themselves, are what the Scriptures sometimes call *flesh*. Besides these, there were *superior* principles, that were spiritual, holy and divine, summarily comprehended in divine love; wherein consisted the spiritual image of God, and man's righteousness and true holiness; which are called in Scripture the *divine nature*.[118]

Edwards continues and clarifies the distinction between the two principles: "These superior principles were given to possess the throne, and

[117] *WJE*, 8:253. Edwards also likens selfish self-love as inordinate due to the absence of the greater principles. Edwards explains, "Man before the Fall loved himself or his own happiness, I suppose, as much as after his fall. But then a superior principle of divine love had the throne, it being in such strength that it wholly regulated and directed self-love. But since the Fall this principle of divine love has lost its strength, or rather is dead. So that self-love continuing in its former strength, and having no superior principle to regulate it, becomes inordinate in its influence, and governs where it should be only a servant." *WJE*, 8:256. It is important to remember here Edwards's understanding of a self-love that is selfless versus one that is selfish in nature, which is inordinate. In a similar way, Edwards likens the natural principles reigning due to the absence of spiritual principles as a fire, which was once contained, now consuming a house. Edwards notes how after the Fall, "Man did immediately set up himself, and the objects of his private affections and appetites, as supreme; and so they took the place of God. These inferior principles are like a fire in an house; which, we say, is a good servant, but a bad master; very useful while kept in its place, but if left to take possession of the whole house, soon brings all to destruction." Jonathan Edwards, *Original Sin*, ed. Clyde A. Holbrook, vol. 3, *The Works of Jonathan Edwards* (New Haven, CT: Yale University Press, 1970), 382–83. As a consequence of selfishness, man and self-regard are the priority at the expense of benevolence to Being in general.

[118] *WJE*, 3:381.

maintain an absolute dominion in the heart: the other, to be wholly subordinate and subservient."[119] According to Edwards, Adam was born with both natural and spiritual principles, with the spiritual reigning over the natural. As a result of the Fall, the natural principles were left to themselves. Edwards writes, "These divine principles thus reigning, were the dignity, life, happiness, and glory of man's nature. When man sinned, and broke God's Covenant, and fell under his curse, these superior principles left his heart: for indeed God then left him; that communion with God, on which these principles depended, entirely ceased; the Holy Spirit, that divine inhabitant, forsook the house."[120] The spiritual principles left and man was now severed from God, experiencing broken communion as the natural principles began to reign. Edward explains, "The inferior principles of self-love and natural appetite, which were given only to serve, being alone, and left to themselves, of course became reigning principles; having no superior principles to regulate or control them, they became absolute masters of the heart."[121] It makes sense, then, that selfish self-love would reign in man, being void of the greater principles to govern the natural.

As a result, for Edwards, a creature places himself not only in opposition to Being in general, but specifically elevates himself above the whole. As Edwards notes, discussing affections that are private, "For he that is influenced by private affection, not subordinate to regard to Being in general, sets up its particular or limited object *above* Being in general; and this most naturally tends to enmity against the latter, which is by right the great supreme, ruling, and absolutely sovereign object of our regard."[122] The opposition is to both God and the universal system of intelligent creatures or existence. By elevating himself above Being in general, the creature idolizes self rather than God.[123] Edwards further explains,

> From these things, I think, it is manifest that no affection limited to any private system, not dependent on, nor subordinate to Being in general can be of the nature of true virtue; and this, whatever the private system be, let it be more or less extensive,

[119]*WJE*, 3:382. For further discussion on Edwards's understanding of the natural/inferior versus spiritual/greater principles, see "Miscellanies," no. 301, in *WJE*, 13:387–89.

[120]*WJE*, 3:382.

[121]*WJE*, 3:382.

[122]*WJE*, 8:555.

[123]*WJE*, 8:181.

> consisting of a greater or smaller number of individuals, so long as it contains an infinitely little part of universal existence, and so bears no proportion to the great all-comprehending system. And consequently, that no affection whatsoever to any creature, or any system of created beings, which is not dependent on, nor subordinate to a propensity or union of the heart to God, the Supreme and Infinite Being, can be of the nature of true virtue.[124]

An affection that is subordinate to one's love to God, the head of the system, is then subordinate to the universal system. Therein lies genuine virtue. On the contrary, "As it is with *selfishness*, or when a man is governed by a regard to his own private interest, independent of regard to the public good, such a temper exposes a man to act the part of an enemy to the public."[125] Such an attitude does not seek "the good of the public."[126] According to Edwards, what is needed is "favoring Being in general," knowing that it is "the chief and most essential good that is in virtue," which is opposed to selfishness.[127] One needs to look beyond himself and in Christian benevolence, extend his concern and attention to others. In light of benevolence to Being in general, he is to love God and all intelligent beings that make up the universal system of being or existence. In sum, by distinguishing self-love that is selfless versus one that is private or selfish, "divine love" is clearly understood, for the self-love that is selfless comes "from a heart *well disposed* and *inclined*" towards virtue.[128] Having discussed Edwards's philosophically oriented ethics, it is important to begin considering the activism and social nature in Edwards's theological ethics to provide a holistic account of his virtue theory.

[124] *WJE*, 8:556–57.

[125] *WJE*, 8:555.

[126] *WJE*, 8:555.

[127] *WJE*, 8:555.

[128] Jonathan Edwards, *Freedom of the Will*, ed. Paul Ramsey, vol. 1, *The Works of Jonathan Edwards* (New Haven, CT: Yale University Press, 2009), 321.

Benevolence, Charity, and Love

Edwards uses the words charity, love, and benevolence as synonymous terms. In *TV*, Edwards asserts, "The general nature of true virtue is love."[129] For Edwards, the foundation for charity is always God, who is the source of genuine virtue. Thus, Fiering rightly notes that "true virtue (or holy love, or Christian charity—the terms all have the same meaning) has an altogether distinct foundation, that there is a *qualitative* difference between it and all merely natural social benevolence."[130] Edwards expounds on his understanding of Christian love in the sermon series *CF*. Specifically, it is Edwards's exposition of love as found in 1 Cor 13.

In sermons one through three, Edwards defines charity, benevolence, or love and discusses the source of that love.[131] Beginning with sermon one, having discussed the importance of charity as represented in the New Testament, Edwards gives a definition: "The word properly signifies love, or that disposition or affection by which one is dear to another. The word *agape* in the original, which is translated 'charity,' might as well have been rendered 'love,' for this is the proper English of it. So that charity in the New Testament is the very same as Christian love."[132] This charity is extended to both God and creatures.[133] Accordingly, Edwards establishes the nature of charity as others focused. It is a love that is distinct because it has God

[129]*WJE*, 8:609.

[130]Fiering, *Jonathan Edwards's Moral Thought and Its British Context*, 172.

[131]*WJE*, 8:59. Edwards preached the *CF* sermons in 1738. For the date of *CF*, see *WJE*, 8:1–2.

[132]*WJE*, 8:129.

[133]*WJE*, 8:129–30. Edwards establishes a creature's love to God as the basis to love others. Edwards states, "Love to God is the foundation of a gracious love to men." *WJE*, 8:133. A little later Edwards asserts, "From love to God springs love to man," referencing 1 John 5:1. *WJE*, 8:142. It is important to note that this love, according to Edwards, comes from a single principle in the believer's heart: "A Christian love to God, and Christian love to men, are not properly two distinct principles in the heart. These varieties are radically the same: the same principle flowing forth towards different objects, according to the order of their existence. God is the first cause of all things, and the fountain and source of all good; and men are derived from him, having something of his image, and are the objects of his mercy. So the first and supreme object of divine love is God: and men are loved either as the children of God or his creatures, and those that are in his image, and the objects of his mercy; or in some respects related to God, or partakers of his loveliness, or at least capable of his happiness." Jonathan Edwards, "Treatise on Grace," in *Writings on the Trinity, Grace, and Faith*, ed. Sang Hyun Lee, vol. 21, *The Works of Jonathan Edwards* (New Haven, CT: Yale University Press, 2003), 172. Ramsey rightly notes in regard to the *CF* sermons, "The love of which Edwards speaks is *one* in principle (*principium*, spring or source) flowing out toward diverse objects. One and the same Spirit infuses love, influences the heart to love God and fellow man." *WJE*, 8:59.

as its source.[134] More specifically, it is God's "Spirit influencing the heart," causing a creature to love Christianly, which is a love that is singular in principle.[135] In other words, Christian love is singular in principle because it has God as its source, namely the Spirit. The nature of the Spirit is "a spirit of love. And therefore when the Spirit of God enters into the soul, love enters. God is love, and he who has God dwelling in him by his Spirit will have love dwelling in him."[136] So the love within a believer is singular because it is Spirit produced, expressing itself to both God and creatures.[137] This will lead a creature to engage in "all duties towards their neighbors," such as "acts of justice," thinking of others as greater, and showing concern for the poor and broken-hearted.[138] Thus, Edwards begins to establish the expression of activism as a product of Christian benevolence.

In regard to showing concern for the poor, Edwards elaborated on this theme in an earlier sermon titled *Duty of Charity to the Poor*, which he preached in 1733. Giving to those in need is an effect of loving one's neighbor. Edwards explains,

> Loving our neighbor as ourselves is the sum of the moral law respecting our fellow creatures, and helping of them and contributing to their relief is the most natural expression of this love. It is vain to pretend to a spirit of love to our neighbor when it grieves us to part with anything for their help when under calamity. They that love only in word and in tongue, and not in deeds, have no love in truth; any profession without it is a vain pretense.[139]

Contrarily, genuine Christian benevolence will result in sacrificial giving. Moreover, the believer is to give generously, recognizing that no individual

[134] *WJE*, 8:131–34.

[135] *WJE*, 8:132. Edwards explains the singular nature of principle in Christian love: "All Christian love is one as to its principle. About whatever object it is exercised, it is the same spring and fountain in the heart though it may flow out towards diverse objects." *WJE*, 8:132.

[136] *WJE*, 8:132.

[137] *WJE*, 8:133.

[138] *WJE*, 8:135–36.

[139] Jonathan Edwards, "The Duty of Charity to the Poor," in *Sermons and Discourses, 1730–1733*, ed. Mark Valeri, vol. 17, *The Works of Jonathan Edwards* (New Haven, CT: Yale University Press, 1999), 376. For the date of this sermon, see Mark Valeri, Introduction to "The Duty of Charity to the Poor," in *Sermons and Discourses, 1730–1733*, ed. Mark Valeri, vol. 17, *The Works of Jonathan Edwards* (New Haven, CT: Yale University Press, 1999), 369.

should be in need given the presence of Christians.[140] Edwards believes Scripture as a whole implores the Christian to "this duty of charity to the poor."[141]

In sermon two of *CF*, Edwards differentiates charity and spiritual gifts according to 1 Cor 14:1 and establishes charity as superior compared to the "extraordinary gifts" given by the Spirit.[142] The Spirit produces "saving grace" in the believer's heart so both the presence of the Spirit and holiness are intrinsic realities within the believer.[143] The God-centeredness of Edwards's moral thought is evident. A pattern has already been established: the source of the moral life is God. This is further explicated by Edwards's comments on the relation of a creature's happiness to holiness and union with God. Edwards states, "Man's highest happiness consists in holiness. It is by this the reasonable creature is united to God, the fountain of all good. Happiness does so essentially consist in knowing and loving and serving God, and having a holy and divine temper of soul, and the lively exercises of it," causing the creature to be happy.[144] Edwards indicates that God is the reason for the believer's joy. The Christian, in union with God, relates to and lives for God as he is Spirit enabled, causing him to be happy. This makes sense because, for Edwards, God is the creature's end. And the saving grace within the believer will always lead to living a life unto God and in turn, doing good to others.[145] For Edwards, devotion to God will prompt an outward focus, leading to practical ministry.

Edwards continues with the theme of grace in sermon three. More specifically, Edwards differentiates actions arising from "natural principles"

[140] *WJE*, 17:373–74.

[141] *WJE*, 17:375.

[142] *WJE*, 8:151–57.

[143] *WJE*, 8:157–58. Edwards elaborates: "This blessing of the saving grace of God is a quality inherent in the nature of him who is the subject of it. This gift of the Spirit of God, working a saving Christian temper and exciting gracious exercises, confers a blessing which has its seat in the heart; a blessing which makes a man's heart and nature excellent." *WJE*, 8:157. Edwards equates this saving grace in the believer's heart with holiness, explaining that "holiness consists in having grace in the heart: grace and holiness are the same thing." *WJE*, 8:158. Thus, considering the source is the Spirit, holiness becomes a part of the believer's nature.

[144] *WJE*, 8:161.

[145] Living for God and doing good to one's neighbor is how Edwards ends sermon two: "How should such as you, who are so highly privileged, at all times carry towards God, in all filial love, thankfulness, strict obedience, quiet submission! And how should you live towards your neighbors, walking humbly, inoffensively, meekly, charitably, doing good to all, to their souls and bodies as you have opportunity, always fervent in spirit, serving the Lord, with the greatest and most earnest diligence." *WJE*, 8:173. By serving the Lord, the believer will serve others.

versus those that arise from "sincerity in the heart" as he focuses on 1 Cor 13:3.[146] What Edwards means by sincerity is that which is a result of Christian love: "Charity or love is something which has its seat in the heart, and is that in which sincerity does consist; and all that is saving and distinguishing summarily consists in it."[147] Without charity, actions or sufferings arising from mere "moral nature" are not Christian and therefore, void of God's approval.[148] Moreover, the actions or sufferings lack virtue because the act or suffering is not directed to God but focused on self.[149] Edwards concludes the sermon by focusing on four results of sincerity in the heart: (1.) a creature's words/actions, (2.) a joyful willingness to choose appropriate obedience (i.e. children to parents), God, and holiness, (3.) integrity, and (4.) purity.[150] Edwards sums up the need for charity in the heart: "He only can bestow it. It is something far above the unassisted power of nature; for though there may be great performances, and great sufferings too, yet without sincere love they are all in vain."[151] For Edwards, actions and sufferings to be truly virtuous must be Spirit induced. It is only the believer that has sincere charity in the heart.[152]

From sermons one through three, we see both the God-centered foundation and practical dimensions of Edwards's ethical theology. Moving on, sermons four through ten "primarily concern the fruits of charity in disposition and action toward men."[153] Sermons four and seven will be discussed at the end, which details Edwards's understanding of benevolence as self-sacrificing in nature.

In sermon five, covering 1 Cor 13:4, Edwards explains how Christian benevolence is void of envy. Edwards focuses on the affluence and material goods of others and shows how the nature of Christian love is not envious

[146] *WJE*, 8:176–78.

[147] *WJE*, 8:180.

[148] *WJE*, 8:178. While the context is the need for sincerity in the heart for actions to be God-honoring, Edwards does highlight, as he did in sermon one, Christian concern for the poor. Edwards writes, "Here is one of the highest kinds of external performances mentioned, viz. a man's giving all his goods to feed the poor. Giving to the poor is a duty very much insisted on in the Word of God, and particularly under the Christian dispensation." *WJE*, 8:174.

[149] *WJE*, 8:179–81.

[150] *WJE*, 8:182–83.

[151] *WJE*, 8:184.

[152] *WJE*, 8:184.

[153] *WJE*, 8:60.

towards such ends.[154] If a creature is against the happiness of another because he is then brought to a lower position in comparison, the creature is an envious creature.[155] This is because there is "a disposition in men to be singular in happiness; they love to be distinguished in their advancement."[156] Edwards was aware of the dangers of selfish self-love as highlighted in sermon seven. Yet, Edwards states, "a Christian spirit is contrary to such a spirit," referring to an envious spirit.[157] Edwards is clear that believers are to instead be joyful in the success and affluence of other creatures.[158] They are to be marked by gentleness, humility, generosity, and kindness towards others.[159] Christ embodied this reality as He lived a life contrary to an envious attitude.[160] Hence, "The spirit of envy is the very contrary of the spirit of heaven, where all rejoice in the happiness of others," recognizing that charity imbedded within the heart of the believer should lead to a focus on others.[161] Edwards concludes the sermon by stating how we are to "seek the spirit of Christian love, that excellent spirit of divine charity which will lead us always to rejoice in the welfare of others and which will fill our own hearts with happiness."[162] Instead of envy, the believer should desire to see the other flourish.

In a similar vein from his discussion on the contrariness of charity to envy, Edwards turns to the topic of humility as found in 1 Cor 13:4-5 in sermon six. In light of the passage, Edwards importantly notes that Paul "shows how Christian love tends to men's behaving suitably and amiably in every condition. If men are below others, it disposes them not to envy those that are above them; and if they are above others, it disposes them not to be proud of their superiority."[163] In other words, charity is opposite to human

[154] *WJE*, 8:218–19.

[155] *WJE*, 8:219.

[156] *WJE*, 8:219.

[157] *WJE*, 8:221.

[158] *WJE*, 8:222.

[159] *WJE*, 8:223.

[160] *WJE*, 8:224–26.

[161] *WJE*, 8:230.

[162] *WJE*, 8:231. The idea of a creature finding personal happiness in the happiness of others, namely in *TV*, was discussed when covering Edwards's philosophical ethics. It will be discussed further when covering sermon seven.

[163] *WJE*, 8:233.

pride.[164] Humility should encourage the idea of a creature's smallness compared to God as the greatest being and others in higher positions, thus reinforcing the notion of humility.[165] But it is ultimately recognizing the "loveliness of God" that will lead to creaturely humility.[166] Edwards notes, "If the knowledge of God as lovely causes humility, then a respect to God as lovely implies humility. And from this love to God arises a Christian love to men. And it therefore follows that a true love both to God and men implies humility."[167] Love to God produces humility because creatures recognize their place underneath God's greatness, leading them to act humbly towards others.[168]

Because sermon seven will be covered later, we now discuss sermon eight. Edwards discusses how Christian charity is opposite to "an angry spirit" based on 1 Cor 13:5.[169] Edwards explains that while not all anger is unchristian, there are types of anger that are.[170] Unchristian anger is Edwards's focus for the majority of the sermon, capped by reasons for its contrariness to Christian charity. Edwards makes clear that benevolence is opposed to human pride and selfishness.[171] Instead it is about God, his glory, and the well-being of others.[172] As Edwards explains, believers are to "in a great measure forget themselves for God's sake, and Christ's sake; and the end, at which they would aim in their anger, would not be making themselves feared, or getting their own will, but God's glory, and others' good."[173] Hence, Edwards continues with a theme of Christian charity being selfless and outward focused in nature.

[164] *WJE*, 8:233.

[165] *WJE*, 8:234–43.

[166] *WJE*, 8:243–45.

[167] *WJE*, 8:245.

[168] *WJE*, 8:245–46. In contrast to the devil's void of love for God, Edwards writes, "But when love enters the heart, the heart and inclination comply with all that humble respect which becomes the distance between God and us. And so love to men arising from love to God disposes to a humble behavior towards them, giving them all the honor and respect which becomes us." *WJE*, 8:246.

[169] *WJE*, 8:272.

[170] *WJE*, 8:272–78.

[171] *WJE*, 8:279.

[172] *WJE*, 8:279.

[173] *WJE*, 8:279.

Edwards continues to work from 1 Cor 13:5 and addresses how charity is opposite to "a censorious spirit."[174] Specifically, what Edwards means is what is "contrary to a disposition uncharitably to judge others."[175] This type of spirit is expressed by judging others wrongly, such as wrongly claiming hypocrisy in others, believing there is a lack or little evidence of positive qualities in others, and accusing others of wrong actions due to personal jealousy.[176] Edwards transitions and explains how censoriousness, or being over-critical of others, is against a genuine "Christian spirit."[177] It is against "love to our neighbor" and reflects human pride, resulting in a "proud disposition, as though they were free from such faults and blemishes themselves with which they are busy and bitter in charging others, and for which they are censuring and condemning them."[178] Though wrongly claiming hypocrisy in others, the creature with an overly critical spirit is ironically the one with hypocrisy. Edwards concludes the sermon by exhorting his listeners to not speak negatively about his neighbor, to recognize that things are often times more positive regarding others when the truth becomes more apparent, to mind their own business when matters do not concern them, and to remember that God's judgment will come if they wrongly judge others.[179] Broadly speaking, Christian charity will not seek to harm one's neighbor.

In sermon ten, focusing on 1 Cor 13:6, Edwards defines Paul's use of the word "iniquity" as "wickedness in men's deeds or practice" and interprets "the truth" to mean "walking in holy practice."[180] Practice as a result of divine grace is the central point of the sermon. In light of passages such as John 17:19 and Col 1:21-22, "Christ thus redeemed the elect and purchased grace for them to that end, that they might walk in holy practice. He reconciled them to God by his death to redeem them from wicked works, that they might be holy and unblameable in their lives."[181] Moreover, "spiritual knowledge and understanding, which are the immediate foundation of all true grace in

[174]*WJE*, 8:283.

[175]*WJE*, 8:283.

[176]*WJE*, 8:284–86.

[177]*WJE*, 8:288.

[178]*WJE*, 8:288–90.

[179]*WJE*, 8:290–92.

[180]*WJE*, 8:294.

[181]*WJE*, 8:295.

the heart, tends to practice. A true knowledge of God and divine things is a practical knowledge."[182] Accordingly, the believer gifted divine grace in the heart will, from their understanding of God, live a life pleasing to him; a life marked by holiness.[183] While a creature's knowledge is the foundation of grace, the "seat" of grace is the will.[184] Practice, then, will necessarily follow for a creature determines what he acts according to his will.[185] Divine grace is gifted and placed in a creature's heart, working powerfully to bring about "particular Christian graces," which lead to practice.[186] For example, saving faith in Christ inclines a believer to live out his faith and to renounce sin and model holiness by obeying Christ's commands.[187] Edwards continues, explaining how trust in and love to God affects Christian practice, reason informs a creature of practice as proof of benevolence, repentance and humility leads one to Christian practice, etc.[188] Edwards concludes the section by asserting that "every true Christian grace tends to a Christian life and walk; and it appears by these things that all grace has a direct relation to a holy practice," reinforcing the idea of practice as a result of divine grace.[189] In so doing, further evidence helps debunk past claims which portray either the theocentric or philosophical nature of Edwards's ethics as cause for inhibiting activism.

Edwards, in *RA*, details the importance of an active Christian life when discussing the twelfth sign of "holy affections."[190] Specifically, practice is the primary indicator of genuine holiness. Edwards explains, "Christian practice or a holy life is a great and distinguishing sign of true and saving grace. But I may go further, and assert, that it is the chief of all the signs of grace, both as an evidence of the sincerity of professors unto others, and also to their

[182] *WJE*, 8:296.

[183] *WJE*, 8:296.

[184] *WJE*, 8:297.

[185] *WJE*, 8:297–98.

[186] *WJE*, 8:299.

[187] *WJE*, 8:299–301.

[188] *WJE*, 8:301–5. Other types of grace that lead to practice, which Edwards discusses are: "A true fear of God," "a spirit of thankfulness and praise to God," "Christian-mindedness and heavenly-mindedness," "a spirit of Christian love to men," and finally, "a true and gracious hope." *WJE*, 8:305–8.

[189] *WJE*, 8:308.

[190] Jonathan Edwards, *Religious Affections*, ed. John E. Smith, vol. 2, *The Works of Jonathan Edwards* (New Haven, CT: Yale University Press, 2009), 383.

own consciences."[191] The source for the affections, which lead to practice, is the Spirit dwelling within a believer, resulting in divine communication.[192] Thus, practice substantiates one as a Christian. As Edwards states, "Christian practice is the sign of signs, in this sense that it is the great evidence, which confirms and crowns all other signs of godliness."[193] Assuredly, the believer will live out what he believes.

In sermons eleven through fourteen, "Edwards stresses love to God," as he transitions from a focus on love to one's neighbor.[194] To begin, Edwards works from 1 Cor 13:7 and concentrates on the phrase "beareth all things," taking it to mean "suffering for the cause of Christ and religion," which is the central point of the sermon.[195] A believer suffering for Christ or for Christianity gives evidence that such suffering is a "great fruit of charity" or love.[196] A believer selflessly suffers for Christ, willingly enduring regardless of the type or extent of suffering.[197] Edwards provides evidence for his claim by detailing a life marked by subordination to God as the greatest being and the believer's greatest treasure, recognizing earthly suffering as worth the cost for Christ.[198] The tone of the sermon shows the foundational nature of a believer's love for God, indicated by the willingness to suffer as a result of such devotion.

Edwards continues his exposition of 1 Cor 13:7 in sermons twelve and thirteen. For sermon twelve, it is about "faith and hope."[199] Specifically, Edwards shows the interconnectedness of Christian graces, stating that "the graces of Christianity are all linked together or united one to another and within one another," displaying harmony.[200] As a result, there is solidarity and dependence between the graces.[201] Hence, charity, which "is a grace which cherishes and promotes the exercise of other graces," is connected to

[191] *WJE*, 2:406.

[192] *WJE*, 2:392.

[193] *WJE*, 2:444.

[194] *WJE*, 8:60.

[195] *WJE*, 8:313.

[196] *WJE*, 8:314.

[197] *WJE*, 8:315–16.

[198] *WJE*, 8:316–21.

[199] *WJE*, 8:326.

[200] *WJE*, 8:327–28.

[201] *WJE*, 8:329.

all graces.[202] Edwards makes clear that the source is the Holy Spirit through a single work, further highlighting the union of the graces.[203] They are all rooted in "the knowledge of God's excellency," have "the law of God" as their rule, and have God and his glory as their end.[204] So, Edwards shows the contributing nature of love for the other graces with God as the end in view.

In sermon thirteen, Edwards explains what Paul means by "endureth all things" as expressing "the lasting and abiding nature of a principle of true grace or charity; how that, whatever opposition it meets with it does not fail, but remains or endures."[205] Divine grace within a believer withstands evil.[206] This is because genuine grace will persevere, depending on God as God sustains this grace in a Christian's heart.[207] Hence, the focus continues to be God and the believer's dependence on God.

Edwards transitions to 1 Cor 13:8 for sermon fourteen and establishes charity as "unfailing and everlasting."[208] Further, Edwards says that the "miraculous gifts of the Spirit" were present in the church in "those days" and how they "were then common," espousing a cessationist perspective.[209] Contrarily, Christian love lasts into eternity.[210] A prevalent theme in the series, Edwards discusses divine communication and explains how the Spirit communicates himself and the extraordinary gifts, providing a biblical survey of such instances.[211] The church, represented both corporately and individually, possesses love as a "fruit of the Spirit," which goes on into eter-

[202] *WJE*, 8:326, 330–31. Edwards notes that the graces "are related to one grace as the sum of them all; and that is charity, or divine love. This, we have before shown, is the sum of all true Christian grace, however many names we may give the different ways and manners of the exercise of grace; yet if we strictly examine them, they are all related to one. Love is the fulfilling of them all. They are but so many diversifications, and different habitudes and relations and manners of exercise of the same thing. One grace does in effect contain them all. Whence it is no wonder that they are nearly allied, and are always together, and dependent on one another, and implied one in another." *WJE*, 8:333–34.

[203] *WJE*, 8:332.

[204] *WJE*, 8:333.

[205] *WJE*, 8:339–40.

[206] *WJE*, 8:341–43.

[207] *WJE*, 8:344–45, 341.

[208] *WJE*, 8:352.

[209] *WJE*, 8:352–53.

[210] *WJE*, 8:353.

[211] *WJE*, 8:354–58.

nity.[212] For Edwards, love is "the sum of all grace."[213] Hence, recognizing this love gifted by God, believers ought to love God and others in the manner in which Christ loved.[214] It is another example of how Edwards believes Christian ethics should lead to action.

Edwards concludes the sermon series with sermon fifteen by discussing how eternity will be marked by the presence and character of love. It is, as Ramsey notes, "Edwards's remarkable glorification of divine love in every respect: perfect love for one another in indefectible love to God."[215] As Edwards has considered throughout the series, God is "both the cause and source of all holy love" and it is perfect in Heaven.[216] It is a love free from all impurity and therefore "spiritual" in nature.[217] Like benevolence on earth, it reaches out to God and neighbor in Heaven: "Love naturally desires to express itself; and in heaven the love of the saints shall be at liberty to express itself as it desires, either towards God or one another."[218] So love is not only perfect, but continues to be active in eternity. As believers "love one another, they have not only their own but each other's prosperity to rejoice in, and are by love made partakers of each other's glory."[219] Christians continue to show deference to one another in eternity. As Edwards asserts upon discussing the effect of love,

> And we have reason to think that they are employed so as in some way to be subservient to each other's happiness under God; because they are represented in Scripture as united together as one society, which can be for no other purpose but mutual subserviency. And they are thus mutually subservient by a most

[212] *WJE*, 8:358.

[213] *WJE*, 8:360.

[214] *WJE*, 8:365.

[215] *WJE*, 8:60–61.

[216] *WJE*, 8:369, 367. Edwards expands on God as the source of love, explaining, "The heart of God is the original seat or subject of it. Divine love is in him not as a subject which receives from another, but as its original seat, where it is of itself. Love is in God as light is in the sun, which does not shine by a reflected light as the moon and planets do; but by his own light, and as the fountain of light. And love flows out from him towards all the inhabitants of heaven." *WJE*, 8:373.

[217] *WJE*, 8:374.

[218] *WJE*, 8:379.

[219] *WJE*, 8:381–82.

> excellent and perfectly amiable behavior, one towards another, as a fruit of their perfect love one to another.[220]

The union is perfected as believers continue to reach out towards their neighbors. This benevolence, while imperfect on earth, is training for the perfection of love awaiting every believer: "By living a life of love, you will be in the way of heaven. As heaven is a world of love, so the way to heaven is the way of love. This will best prepare for heaven, and make you meet for an inheritance with the saints in that land of light and love. And if ever you arrive in heaven, faith and love must be the wings which must carry you there."[221]

Edwards discusses charity in like-manner in other sermons. In 1741, Edwards preached a sermon titled *Much in Deeds of Charity*. In this sermon, Edwards expounds on seeking "spiritual discoveries in a right way" by not only praying, but also engaging in "deeds of charity or works of love."[222] What Edwards has in mind is giving materially and doing "according to our abilities and opportunities."[223] It consists in "living in deeds and fruit of love and charity."[224] The Christian is to engage both spiritually and with action: "It is not only to read and to pray and to go to meeting and to meditate, but is to attend all the duties which God has required of us, both towards God and towards our neighbor."[225] Edwards once again brings up giving to the poor, which is a way to spiritual discoveries.[226] Towards the end of the sermon, Edwards states, "There is nothing seems to be more inviting, as it were, to the God of love to dwell among a people, than the prevailing of such a spirit and practice: their abounding in deeds of love."[227] The sermon is yet another example of charity being expressed in practical action towards helping one's neighbor.

[220] *WJE*, 8:384.

[221] *WJE*, 8:396–97.

[222] Jonathan Edwards, "Much in Deeds of Charity," in *The Sermons of Jonathan Edwards: A Reader*, ed. Wilson H. Kimnach, Kenneth P. Minkema, and Douglas A. Sweeney (New Haven, CT: Yale University Press, 1999), 198. For the date of this sermon, see Edwards, "Much in Deeds of Charity," 197.

[223] Edwards, "Much in Deeds of Charity," 198.

[224] Edwards, "Much in Deeds of Charity," 200.

[225] Edwards, "Much in Deeds of Charity," 203.

[226] Edwards, "Much in Deeds of Charity," 205.

[227] Edwards, "Much in Deeds of Charity," 211.

In another sermon, *The Spirit of the True Saints Is a Spirit of Divine Love*, preached sometime in the 1730s, Edwards examines what divine love is, how it resides in believers, and how it is practiced.[228] This love, gifted by God to the believer, is expressed by loving God supremely and loving others, both saved and unsaved.[229] Christian love "is not a loving in word and in tongue but a loving in deed and in truth."[230] Edwards continues, "He who has a true love to an earthly friend and is a sincere, hearty friend, he will be willing to do for him, willing to give to him, yea he will be willing to suffer for him. So those who have a true love they show love to him, will serve him and seek his glory, willing to give freely and liberally to him."[231] Edwards again provides evidence of serving and giving, of doing and providing for the sake of another as a fruit of charity. Edwards encourages his listeners "to be much in the exercise of this divine love. God has been pleased to implant this divine seed to infuse this holy principle into your heart and thereby has received you and sanctified you, has mortified lust, and assimilated you in a degree to angels. Labor therefore to be much in the exercise of it," living out God's love towards others.[232] This includes those that are wicked: "Love wicked men with a love of pity, weep and pray for them and seek the good of their souls and also the good of their bodies."[233] The believer is to help for both spiritual and temporal needs.[234] Likewise, love for one's enemy is necessary for the Christian.[235] In other words, "Labor to live a life of love."[236] As highlighted in this sermon, it is not just divine love dwelling in the heart by way of God's Spirit, but also love expressed in action.

Elsewhere, Edwards discusses the need to imitate the love found in Christ:

[228]Jonathan Edwards, "The Spirit of the True Saints Is a Spirit of Divine Love," in *The Glory and Honor of God: Volume 2 of the Previously Unpublished Sermons of Jonathan Edwards*, ed. Michael D. McMullen (Nashville, TN: Broadman & Holman, 2004), 298. For the date of this sermon, see Michael D. McMullen, Introduction to "The Spirit of the True Saints Is a Spirit of Divine Love," in *The Glory and Honor of God: Volume 2 of the Previously Unpublished Sermons of Jonathan Edwards*, ed. Michael D. McMullen (Nashville, TN: Broadman & Holman, 2004), 297.

[229]Edwards, "The Spirit of the True Saints Is a Spirit of Divine Love," 298–307.

[230]Edwards, "The Spirit of the True Saints Is a Spirit of Divine Love," 326.

[231]Edwards, "The Spirit of the True Saints Is a Spirit of Divine Love," 326.

[232]Edwards, "The Spirit of the True Saints Is a Spirit of Divine Love," 331–32.

[233]Edwards, "The Spirit of the True Saints Is a Spirit of Divine Love," 342.

[234]Edwards, "The Spirit of the True Saints Is a Spirit of Divine Love," 342.

[235]Edwards, "The Spirit of the True Saints Is a Spirit of Divine Love," 342.

[236]Edwards, "The Spirit of the True Saints Is a Spirit of Divine Love," 333.

> But he that with all his heart embraces that divine grace and love which is manifested in Christ's salvation, must of necessity therein embrace all holiness: for he must entirely delight in such a thing, viz. love, and must desire to imitate that divine love manifested in Christ, to have it in his heart and to imitate it in his practice, to make returns of love for love, and so to love God and Christ and imitate his love to men. But such a love to God and man is the sum of all holiness in man.[237]

Such love does not lay dormant but is applied towards others. This results in works, which provide proof of godliness: "Good works of charity are often especially insisted on as evidential."[238] Christians will act and produce works, for, "The fruits of grace in the life must needs be the proper evidences of it."[239] Moreover, "Love and charity is the primary fruit of the Spirit."[240] As a result, love for others "is particularly given as a sign of grace."[241] Similarly in *RA*, Edwards explains how in much of Scripture, "love to the brethren is spoken of as a sign of godliness . . . there is no one virtuous affection or disposition so often expressly spoken of as a sign of true grace, as our having love one to another," thus evidencing a genuine work of God in the heart.[242] Caring and providing for the poor is a direct result of such charity.[243]

Edwards also explains the need to give to others from the perspective of lacking charity:

[237]Jonathan Edwards, " 'Controversies' Notebook: Justification," in *Writings on the Trinity, Grace, and Faith*, ed. Sang Hyun Lee, vol. 21, *The Works of Jonathan Edwards* (New Haven, CT: Yale University Press, 2003), 359–60.

[238]Jonathan Edwards, "Signs of Godliness," in *Writings on the Trinity, Grace, and Faith*, vol. 21, *The Works of Jonathan Edwards* (New Haven, CT: Yale University Press, 2003), 473. In *RA*, Edwards writes, "In order to men's being true Christians, it is necessary that they prosecute the business of religion, and the service of God with great earnestness and diligence, as the work which they devote themselves to, and make the main business of their lives. All Christ's peculiar people, not only do good works, but are zealous of good works (Titus 2:14)." *WJE*, 2:387.

[239]*WJE*, 21:474, 476.

[240]*WJE*, 21:490.

[241]*WJE*, 21:490.

[242]*WJE*, 2:437. Also in *RA*, Edwards connects godliness or holiness to genuine virtue and ensuing results: "Holiness comprehends all the true virtue of a good man, his love to God, his gracious love to men, his justice, his charity, and bowels of mercies, his gracious meekness and gentleness, and all other true Christian virtues that he has, belong to his holiness." *WJE*, 2:255. That is, holiness expresses itself in active love towards others.

[243]*WJE*, 21:491.

> If you are uncharitable; if you neglect the welfare of your fellow creatures; if you are not ready, freely and without grudging, to distribute to the needs and necessities of others; if you withhold your hand from doing good to your fellow-Christians upon all occasions for a needless fear of hurting yourself: you act as if you were your own. You are to remember that you have given yourself to God with all that you have; for if you are God's, what you possess is his too, and not your own, neither have you the liberty of disposing of it according to your own inclinations, for your outward ease and prosperity, without respect to God's glory and the good of others.[244]

Because the believer no longer lives for himself but for God and others, he is to freely provide for those in need, acting not uncharitably but charitably. Thus, the Christian is to be marked by generosity.[245] He is to be unselfish, "communicative and open-handed, to be ready to lay out ourselves for the benefit and comfort of others."[246] Edwards continues to explain the believer's selfless disposition: "And this is a disposition abundantly insisted upon in the gospel, to be ready to distribute, willing to communicate, not to look every man on his own things but everyone on the things of others; to love our neighbors as ourselves, to scatter abroad and cast our bread upon the waters."[247] This sacrificial posture towards others is distinctly Christian as "it fills the heart with a noble diffusive love and benevolence to mankind, and makes to love not only in word and in tongue but in deed and in truth."[248] So the believer is to abound "in deeds of love and charity," looking to help

[244]Jonathan Edwards, "Dedication to God," in *Sermons and Discourses, 1720–1723*, ed. Wilson H. Kimnach, vol. 10, *The Works of Jonathan Edwards* (New Haven, CT: Yale University Press, 1992), 561–62. Edwards likely preached this sermon in early 1723. For the date of this sermon, see Wilson H. Kimnach, Introduction to "Dedication to God," in *Sermons and Discourses, 1720–1723*, ed. Wilson H. Kimnach, vol. 10, *The Works of Jonathan Edwards* (New Haven, CT: Yale University Press, 1992), 547–49.

[245]Jonathan Edwards, "True Nobleness of Mind," in *Sermons and Discourses, 1723–1729*, ed. Kenneth P. Minkema, vol. 14, *The Works of Jonathan Edwards* (New Haven, CT: Yale University Press, 1997), 238. Edwards preached this sermon in 1728. For the date of this sermon, see Kenneth P. Minkema, Introduction to "True Nobleness of Mind," in *Sermons and Discourses, 1723–1729*, ed. Kenneth P. Minkema, vol. 14, *The Works of Jonathan Edwards* (New Haven, CT: Yale University Press, 1997), 228.

[246]*WJE*, 14:238.

[247]*WJE*, 14:238.

[248]*WJE*, 14:238.

"one another under our difficulties and straits," being others minded.[249] In the sermon *Mercy and Not Sacrifice*, given in 1740, Edwards says Christians are to live "in love, studying to promote one another's good, abounding in deeds of righteousness and mercy," effectively living out one's faith.[250] Edwards reiterates that love is expressed by acting charitably towards one's neighbor: "Therefore seek to express your love much in this way, by being very much in such deeds of righteousness, faithfulness, mercy and love towards your neighbor."[251]

Having established charity as from God and outward focused, Edwards also discusses love as explicitly self-sacrificing in nature. In sermon four of *CF*, Edwards considers the ideas of suffering willingly and doing good.[252] Believers are to "bear ill received from others" in a meek way.[253] In light of Christian benevolence, this means that the individual wronged should not seek revenge, will exude a gentle spirit, will continue to love, will maintain calm, and will suffer so peace can be established.[254] A believer's love for God will aide him in willingly suffering.[255] In terms of an active response, the Christian is to seek ways in which he can bless others, both spiritually and in practical ways.[256] Edwards sums up the possible ways which a believer can extend good to others:

> Persons may thus contribute to others' good in three ways, viz. first, by giving to them, by bestowing on them those things which

[249] Jonathan Edwards, "Bringing the Ark of Zion a Second Time," in *Sermons and Discourses, 1739–1742*, ed. Harry S. Stout, Nathan O. Hatch, and Kyle P. Farley, vol. 22, *The Works of Jonathan Edwards* (New Haven, CT: Yale University Press, 2003), 260. Edwards preached this sermon in 1740. For the date of this sermon, see Harry S. Stout, Nathan O. Hatch, and Kyle P. Farley, Introduction to "Bringing the Ark of Zion a Second Time," in *Sermons and Discourses, 1739–1742*, ed. Harry S. Stout, Nathan O. Hatch, and Kyle P. Farley, vol. 22, *The Works of Jonathan Edwards* (New Haven, CT: Yale University Press, 2003), 245.

[250] Jonathan Edwards, "Mercy and Not Sacrifice," in *Sermons and Discourses, 1739–1742*, ed. Harry S. Stout, Nathan O. Hatch, and Kyle P. Farley, vol. 22, *The Works of Jonathan Edwards* (New Haven, CT: Yale University Press, 2003), 133. For the date of this sermon, see Harry S. Stout, Nathan O. Hatch, and Kyle P. Farley, Introduction to "Mercy and Not Sacrifice," in *Sermons and Discourses, 1739–1742*, ed. Harry S. Stout, Nathan O. Hatch, and Kyle P. Farley, vol. 22, *The Works of Jonathan Edwards* (New Haven, CT: Yale University Press, 2003), 111.

[251] *WJE*, 22:135.

[252] *WJE*, 8:185.

[253] *WJE*, 8:185–86.

[254] *WJE*, 8:189–92.

[255] *WJE*, 8:192–96.

[256] *WJE*, 8:207–9.

> we have and which they need, or which may be to their benefit; second, by doing for them, by taking pains for them to help them or promote their welfare. Or third, by suffering for them, by bearing their burdens for them, or at least in part that we may make their burdens the lighter.[257]

And the good given should be impartial, extending to all.[258] Additionally, like suffering, the doing of good to one's neighbor should be done willingly.[259] Genuine Christian love will always be "effectual."[260] As Edwards states, "The proper evidence of wishing good to another is doing good to another. What can be plainer than that the proper evidence of the will is the act? The act of the man follows the will wherein the man has power to act. The proper evidence of a man's sincerely desiring the good of another is seeking it in his practice."[261] In sum, humanitarianism is highlighted in Edwards's view of Christian charity as believers are to seek the wellbeing of others spiritually, personally, and materially.

Earlier in his life (1723), from the sermon *Living Peaceably One With Another*, Edwards discusses the proper Christian response to those who cause harm: "We ought to have a love that is true, inward and sincere to our injurers, whether they injure us in our estates, or names, or bodies; whether they injure us by one vice or another, whether by covetousness and a craving after much of the world, or by their malice or backbiting."[262] The Christian is to receive the injury instead of wishing harm on the one injuring.[263] The choice is to suffer because the believer is to sincerely love the one causing harm.

In sermon seven of *CF*, Edwards shows how charity is opposite to selfish self-love. After Edwards talks about how self-love and personal happiness

[257] *WJE*, 8:208.

[258] *WJE*, 8:209–11.

[259] *WJE*, 8:211–12.

[260] *WJE*, 8:213.

[261] *WJE*, 8:213.

[262] Jonathan Edwards, "Living Peaceably One With Another," in *Sermons and Discourses: 1723–1729*, ed. Kenneth P. Minkema, vol. 14, *The Works of Jonathan Edwards* (New Haven, CT: Yale University Press, 1997), 123–24. For the date of this sermon, see Kenneth P. Minkema, Introduction to "Living Peaceably One With Another," in *Sermons and Discourses: 1723–1729*, ed. Kenneth P. Minkema, vol. 14, *The Works of Jonathan Edwards* (New Haven, CT: Yale University Press, 1997), 116.

[263] *WJE*, 14:123.

are perfectly acceptable, he goes on to discuss the nature of self-love that is selfish.[264] Edwards begins by explaining how a "Christian spirit is contrary to a selfish spirit, which consists in self-love which goes out after such objects as are confined and limited, such as a man's own worldly wealth or the honor that is of men, being set up higher than his neighbor in the world—his own worldly ease and convenience, or his pleasing and gratifying his own bodily sense."[265] Personal interest is placed ahead of neighborly interest. Contrarily, Edwards elaborates on selflessness expressed through a concern for others and personal sacrifice for their good.[266] Edwards also discusses the importance of concern for society: "A Christian spirit is contrary to a selfish spirit as it disposes persons to be public spirited. A man of a right spirit is not of a narrow, private spirit; but he is greatly concerned for the good of the public community to which he belongs, and particularly of the town where he dwells."[267] So the concern for an individual neighbor broadens to a concern for the general public. Edwards continues and includes concern for one's country, stating, "A Christian spirited man will be also concerned for the good of his country, and it disposes him to lay out himself for it."[268] That is, the believer is also to exude a national concern, willing to sacrifice for the nation's good. This stems not from selfishness, but genuine benevolence, which is selfless. Edwards says "there is no other-love so much above a selfish principle as Christian love is, there is no love that is so free and disinterested."[269] It is a love that leads to self-sacrifice for the public good.

[264] *WJE*, 8:254–59.

[265] *WJE*, 8:258–59.

[266] *WJE*, 8:259–60.

[267] *WJE*, 8:260. This is especially true for those who hold a position in public office. Edwards explains, "Especially will a Christian spirit dispose those who stand in a public capacity, such as ministers and magistrates and all public officers, to seek the public good. It will dispose magistrates to act as the fathers of the commonwealth with that care and concern for the public good that the father of a family has for the family, watchful against any public dangers, forward to improve their power to promote the public benefit, not being governed by selfish views in their administrations, seeking only or mainly to enrich themselves, or make themselves great, and advance themselves on the spoils of others as wicked rulers very often do." *WJE*, 8:261–62.

[268] *WJE*, 8:261.

[269] *WJE*, 8:264. The practical ends of Edwards's view of disinterested benevolence are evident. Edwards provides another example of loving one's neighbor: "Now this is contrary to selfishness; for it is not of such a nature as confines the heart to self but leads it forth to others as well as self, and in like manner as it does to self. It disposes persons to look on their neighbor as being, as it were, one with self, and not only to consider our own circumstances and necessities, but to consider the wants of our neighbors as we do our own; not only to have regard to our own

Finally, in the sermon *Christians a Chosen Generation*, preached in 1731, Edwards writes, "They should exercise a spirit of free, universal, and disinterested love and beneficence and Christian charity, which is a noble disposition."[270] Edwards equates disinterested benevolence with the need to do good. It is a love that is both sacrificial and active. So, it is no surprise that Christians should give themselves to the "self-denying duties of religion."[271]

In light of the social and activist stimuli located in Edwards's understanding of benevolence, sense needs to be made for Edwards's agreement with institutionalized slavery.[272] If selfless love is to be extended to all, a fair question to ask is why Edwards supported the institution. Edwards's proslavery position and opposition to the slave trade will be discussed next.

The Issue of Slavery

The hierarchical nature of prerevolutionary, colonial society was discussed in chapter three. Edwards embraced this reality. In *CF*, Edwards mentions the necessity of hierarchical ordering in light of the virtue of humility:

> Humility will tend to prevent a leveling behavior. They who are under the influence of a humble spirit will not be opposite to giving to others the honor which is due to them. They will be willing that their superiors should be known and acknowledged in their place, and it will not seem hard to them. They will not desire that all should be upon a level; for they know it is best that some should be above others and should be honored and submitted to as such, and therefore they are willing to comply with it agreeable to those precepts: Rom. 13:7, "Render therefore to all their duties: tribute to whom tribute is due; custom to

desires but to the desires of others, and to make their case our own, and to do to them as we would that they should do to us." *WJE*, 8:265.

[270]Jonathan Edwards, "Christians a Chosen Generation," in *Sermons and Discourses, 1730–1733*, ed. Mark Valeri, vol. 17, *The Works of Jonathan Edwards* (New Haven, CT: Yale University Press, 1999), 289. For the date of this sermon, see Mark Valeri, Introduction to "Christians a Chosen Generation," in *Sermons and Discourses, 1730–1733*, ed. Mark Valeri, vol. 17, *The Works of Jonathan Edwards* (New Haven, CT: Yale University Press, 1999), 273.

[271]*WJE*, 17:289.

[272]A number of insights and primary/secondary source references for the following section on Edwards and slavery come from a paper I wrote for a doctoral seminar, "Seminar in Theological Method," taken in the Spring of 2014.

> whom custom; fear to whom fear; honor to whom honor." Titus 3:1, "Put them in mind to be subject to principalities and powers, to obey magistrates."[273]

Clearly Edwards valued deference to authority. While there is biblical support for respecting those in such positions, Edwards erred by applying this logic to institutionalized slavery. It stems from his social and cultural situatedness.[274] Sherard Burns notes, the "only life that Edwards knew was one in which the enslavement of Africans was an acceptable practice."[275] Certainly, growing up being served by those enslaved was key to his view of slave-owning as normative.[276] It is no surprise that this conviction of his continued into adulthood, especially considering his social position in the broader community. Kenneth P. Minkema observes, as "a member of the social elite, Edwards was representative of the slaveowning class in New England."[277]

An important consideration of Edwards's slave-owning is the lack of priority given to the matter. His attention was elsewhere. As a revivalist minister, the most important thing for Edwards was that the spiritually lost become saved. Even after the Great Awakening, Edwards concerned himself with the thought of revival.[278] The importance of revivalism for Edwards has a connection to his racial thought beyond institutionalized slavery. This is highlighted in his ministry to the Native Americans in Stockbridge during the latter years of his life. McClymond and McDermott state,

[273] *WJE*, 8:242–43.

[274] Marsden notes, "We can consider Edwards' attitudes toward slavery in the context of his hierarchical assumptions," stemming from his prerevolutionary setting. George M. Marsden, *Jonathan Edwards: A Life* (New Haven, CT: Yale University Press, 2003), 255.

[275] Sherard Burns, "Trusting the Theology of a Slave Owner," in *A God Entranced Vision of All Things: The Legacy of Jonathan Edwards*, ed. John Piper and Justin Taylor (Wheaton, IL: Crossway Books, 2004), 156.

[276] McGever explains, "Enslaving was a part of Jonathan Edwards's family heritage. Both sets of his grandparents were enslavers. Jonathan and his wife, Sarah, grew up in homes where they were served by slaves. An enslaved man named Ansars, and perhaps others, served Jonathan and his parents during his childhood." Sean McGever, *Ownership: The Evangelical Legacy of Slavery in Edwards, Wesley, and Whitefield* (Downers Grove: InterVarsity Press, 2024), 29.

[277] Kenneth P. Minkema, "Jonathan Edwards on Slavery and the Slave Trade," *William & Mary Quarterly* 54, no. 4 (1997): 826.

[278] McClymond and McDermott observe: "Beginning in the late 1730s and continuing through the Great Awakening and beyond, Edwards prophesied that the world was on the verge of a massive religious revival." Michael J. McClymond and Gerald R. McDermott, *The Theology of Jonathan Edwards* (New York: Oxford University Press, 2012), 552.

"Perhaps Edwards's greatest stimuli to mission generally—and Indian mission in particular—were his extraordinary historical optimism and fervent expectation of imminent revival."[279] The expectation was for revivals or awakenings to reach across the globe, leading to the salvation of people from all nations.[280] Nonetheless, he viewed Native Americans as socially and culturally inferior. Minkema and Harry S. Stout assert that Edwards "considered Indian cultures as inferior and Indian religions as satanic. Separated from knowledge of the true religion, Indians were despicable."[281] Yet he recognized salvific potential in them. An extended quote illustrates Edwards's belief of salvation for Native Americans:

> And there has been this alteration abiding on multitudes all over the land, for a year and [a] half, without any appearance of a disposition to return to former vice and vanity. And under the influences of this work, there have been many of the remains of those wretched people and dregs of mankind, the poor Indians, that seemed to be next to a state of brutality, and with whom, till now, it seemed to be to little more purpose to use endeavors for their instruction and awakening, than with the beasts; whose minds have now been strangely opened to receive instruction, and have been deeply affected with the concerns of their precious souls, and have reformed their lives, and forsaken their former stupid, barbarous and brutish way of living; and particularly that sin to which they have been so exceedingly addicted, their drunkenness; and are become devout and serious persons; and many of them to appearance brought truly and greatly to delight in the things of God, and to have their souls very much engaged and entertained with the great things of the Gospel. And many of the poor Negroes also have been in like manner wrought upon and changed.[282]

For Edwards, turning to Christ for Native Americans also meant turning away from what he believed to be an uncivilized way of life. So religious

[279]McClymond and McDermott, *The Theology of Jonathan Edwards*, 552.

[280]McClymond and McDermott, *The Theology of Jonathan Edwards*, 552.

[281]Kenneth P. Minkema and Harry S. Stout, "The Edwardsean Tradition and the Antislavery Debate, 1740–1865," *Journal of American History* 92, no. 1 (2005): 51.

[282]Jonathan Edwards, "Some Thoughts Concerning the Revival," in *The Great Awakening*, ed. C. C. Goen, vol. 4, *The Works of Jonathan Edwards* (New Haven, CT: Yale University Press, 2009), 329–30.

conversion from non-Christian religion also meant social and cultural transformation. Yet Edwards viewed both Native Americans and Africans as equals both spiritually and in their humanity. In fact, "Edwards in his regular preaching did not draw metaphysical differences between races."[283] Instead Edwards believed all men have the same nature: "For men are made in the image of God . . . we are all nearly allied one to another by nature: we have all the same nature, like faculties, like dispositions, like desires of good, like needs, like aversion to misery, and are made of one blood."[284] This relates to the issue of personal virtue. Rachel Wheeler notes, for Edwards, "Europeans were not inherently more virtuous than Indians. Any superiority evident in European society could be explained by the advantages of having long had access to true religion through the written revelation of the gospel."[285] Thus, while "Edwards shared the overwhelming white consensus that Indian culture was inferior and even despicable," there was potential to improve both religiously and culturally.[286] It seems that Edwards gave little to no effort to embracing cultural distinctives, including the language used by Native Americans. McClymond and McDermott assert that Edwards "refused to learn their language, claiming that his time would be spent more profitably teaching them English and that they themselves agreed with his decision."[287] The agreement with Edwards could have stemmed from the understanding by Native Americans of Edwards's authoritarian position as head of the mission where they resided.[288] Additionally, "Perhaps some Indians also wondered why Edwards encouraged his own son to learn Mahican and how such an industrious scholar could not make some effort to learn the language of those he hoped to win to Christian faith."[289] In short, Edwards failed to value any aspects of their culture. Ministry to both Native Americans and Africans came from a posture of social and cultural superiority.

[283]Minkema, "Jonathan Edwards on Slavery and the Slave Trade," 829. Marsden gives a similar assertion: "Edwards explicitly denied that there was any inherent inferiority among different peoples in God's eye." Marsden, *Jonathan Edwards*, 258.

[284]*WJE*, 17:376.

[285]Rachel Wheeler, "Lessons from Stockbridge: Jonathan Edwards and the Stockbridge Indians," in *Jonathan Edwards at 300: Essays on the Tercentenary of His Birth*, ed. Harry S. Stout, Kenneth P. Minkema, and Caleb J. D. Maskell (Lanham, MD: University Press of America, 2005), 134.

[286]McClymond and McDermott, *The Theology of Jonathan Edwards*, 561.

[287]McClymond and McDermott, *The Theology of Jonathan Edwards*, 561.

[288]McClymond and McDermott, *The Theology of Jonathan Edwards*, 561.

[289]McClymond and McDermott, *The Theology of Jonathan Edwards*, 561.

Edwards's approval of institutionalized slavery sheds further light not only on his priority for European cultural civility, but also on certain religious convictions. He viewed the institution of slavery modeled in the colonies as something the Bible allowed.[290] The humane treatment of slaves was key for its allowance. Minkema explains, "Edwards acknowledged that slavery could be a cruel and sinful thing, as when Europeans encouraged Africans to seize fellow Africans and sell them into slavery, yet slaveowning was justified if the slave was purchased legally and treated decently."[291] An awareness of Edwards's views of slavery and the slave trade come from a draft letter he wrote to defend a minister who had a number of parishioners opposing his slave-owning practice.[292] Edwards discusses what he felt was the hypocrisy of those opposing slave-owning by highlighting their support of the slave-trade: "How ill does it suit for a man to cry out of another for taking money that is stolen, and then taking it of him in that wherein the injustice consists. If the slaves are unjustly theirs, then their slavery is unjustly theirs, and this they are partakers of."[293] Minkema points out that while those opposing Benjamin Doolittle were not themselves enslavers, Edwards showed "that they directly or indirectly profited from slavery and slave trading or consumed slave-made products."[294] Consequently, those that opposed slave-owning "are partakers of a far more cruel slavery than that which they object against in those that have slaves here."[295] For Edwards, the opponents were complicit in slave-owning by gaining and/or contributing to the institution financially by purchasing material goods through the trade.

[290]Marsden, *Jonathan Edwards*, 257.

[291]Minkema, "Jonathan Edwards on Slavery and the Slave Trade," 825–26. For an examination of Edwards's slave-owning history and views on slavery, see Kenneth P. Minkema, "Jonathan Edwards's Defense of Slavery," *Massachusetts Historical Review* 4 (2002): 23–59.

[292]Minkema, "Jonathan Edwards on Slavery and the Slave Trade," 823–24. For a detailed analysis of Edwards's draft letter, see Minkema, "Jonathan Edwards on Slavery and the Slave Trade," 823–34.

[293]Jonathan Edwards, "Draft Letter on Slavery," in *Letters and Personal Writings*, ed. George S. Claghorn, vol. 16, *The Works of Jonathan Edwards* (New Haven, CT: Yale University Press, 1998), 72. Minkema notes, "While they denounced any who actually owned slaves, Edwards submitted, they continued to profit from slave labor and to consume products of the transatlantic slave system." Minkema, "Jonathan Edwards on Slavery and the Slave Trade," 826.

[294]Minkema, "Jonathan Edwards's Defense of Slavery," 36.

[295]*WJE*, 16:72.

In 1731, Edwards purchased a slave named Venus from a man named Richard Perkins on the seaport of Newport, Rhode Island.[296] Regardless of the reservations he may have had with domestic slavery as an institution, he had no problem owning slaves.[297] According to Minkema, Edwards "owned several slaves: Joseph and Lee, a woman named Venus, purchased in 1731, and, listed in the inventory of his estate in 1758, a 'negro boy' named Titus."[298] It was part and parcel of his social nobility, willing to spend a significant amount of his income to own slaves.[299] Edwards's agreement with institutionalized slavery is surprising given his likely awareness of the despondent state of slaves, for slave owners were conscious "that Africans were unhappy in their servile condition."[300] Edwards must have known their unhappiness as those enslaved, especially in light of witnessing the slave trade at Newport to purchase Venus. Despite this, he continued with his

[296]Minkema, "Jonathan Edwards's Defense of Slavery," 24, 26. Newport is the place Hopkins would later develop his abolitionist stance. Minkema explains how Newport "was the very place, some four decades later, where Edwards's disciple Samuel Hopkins, horrified by the spectacle of slave auctions, would begin his campaign against slavery." Minkema, "Jonathan Edwards's Defense of Slavery," 24–25. Regarding Venus, because "there is no further mention of Venus in any of Edwards's letters, personal accounts, or church records," Minkema speculates that "she may have died since it was not uncommon for even 'seasoned' slaves to succumb to a disease when exposed to a new environment. If she did not die, Edwards apparently sold or traded her in fairly short order, for the only slave known to be in his household by 1736 was Leah, a women named after the first, unloved wife of the biblical patriarch Jacob." Minkema, "Jonathan Edwards's Defense of Slavery," 30. For the possibility of Venus being given the name Leah some years later, see McGever, *Ownership*, 99.

[297]Minkema, "Jonathan Edwards on Slavery and the Slave Trade," 825.

[298]Minkema, "Jonathan Edwards on Slavery and the Slave Trade," 825. Romer concisely describes Edwards's slave-owning history: "He traveled to Newport, Rhode Island in 1731 to purchase Venus, bought further slaves during the next two decades, and after his dismissal from the ministry of Northampton in 1750, he and his family moved to Stockbridge, thirty-five miles west of Northampton, where he served as minister and missionary to the Indians, taking with them a slave, Rose. . . . His 1758 estate inventory included 'a negro boy named Titus', probably Rose's son, as part of his 'quick stock.' " Robert H. Romer, *Slavery in the Connecticut Valley of Massachusetts* (Florence, MA: Levellers Press, 2009), 162.

[299]As Minkema states, "Within Northampton, a small but growing number of elites typically owned one or two slaves—a female for domestic chores and a male for fieldwork—and Edwards was willing to commit a substantial part of his annual salary to establish his membership in this select group." Minkema, "Jonathan Edwards's Defense of Slavery," 28. Regarding the purchase price for Venus and Edwards's salary, see Minkema, "Jonathan Edwards's Defense of Slavery," 51, n. 24. For an example of slave-owning by an immediate family member, see Edwards's letter to his daughter Esther in 1757. Specifically, Edwards tells Esther, "If you think of selling Harry, your mother desires you not to sell him, without letting her know it." Jonathan Edwards, "To Esther Edwards Burr," in *Letters and Personal Writings*, ed. George S. Claghorn, vol. 16, *The Works of Jonathan Edwards* (New Haven, CT: Yale University Press, 1998), 731.

[300]Marsden, *Jonathan Edwards*, 256.

proslavery position, even with the experience of overseeing the process of slaves being manumitted.[301]

In light of Edwards's shortcomings concerning his dealings with Native Americans and Africans, he did have a progressive attitude towards race given his social and cultural milieu. Minkema and Stout note that despite the deprecation of Native American culture, Edwards "exhibited a real sympathy for Indians, and during his tenure at the Indian mission at Stockbridge, he formed a bond with them."[302] The social, cultural, and religious inferiority of Native Americans for Edwards in no way hindered his love and care for them as their pastor. Furthermore, as mentioned earlier, he did not believe that there is any inherent inferiority in Native Americans or Africans as human beings. As a result, both need to be treated with respect. Edwards also included Africans and Native Americans as full members of his Northampton church.[303]

For slavery, while Edwards condoned the practice, his views were unlike the consensus voice of his time. While Edwards defended a minister's right to own slaves, he did denounce the transatlantic slave trade. Edwards writes,

> For if they still continue to cry out against those who keep negro slaves as partakers of injustice in making them slaves, and continue still themselves notwithstanding to be parkakers of their slavery, let 'em own that their objections are not conscientious, but merely to make difficulty and trouble for their neighbors. Whether or no other nations have any power or business to disenfranchise all the nations of Africa. And if they should, whether or no this would not be a greater encroachment on their liberties than even the opposers of this trade themselves do suppose this trade, making those slaves which they offer to sale.

[301]For comments on Jonathan and Sarah's involvement in the manumission of a married couple that were formerly enslaved by Sarah's deceased step-mother, see Minkema, "Jonathan Edwards's Defense of Slavery," 42–43; McGever, *Ownership*, 99.

[302]Minkema and Stout, "The Edwardsean Tradition and the Antislavery Debate, 1740–1865," 51.

[303]Marsden, *Jonathan Edwards*, 258. While it is not known whether enslaved Africans sat with white parishioners during Sunday services, the fact that they were recognized as communicant members is significant given Edwards's time period. For a discussion on congregational seating for enslaved Africans, see Lorenzo J. Greene, *The Negro in Colonial New England: 1620–1776* (1942; repr., Eastford, CT: Martino, 2016), 283–84.

> It would have a much greater tendency to sin, to have liberty to disenfranchise whole nations.[304]

Edwards connects this statement with a discussion on the Israelites in the Old Testament and God's allowance for the mistreatment of those from other nations.[305] Edwards then asserts, "God's winking at some things that were early was of old, in those times of darkness, which intimates that [God] don't wink at such things now under the gospel."[306] This means that for Edwards, "Israel's distinction was at an end and all humankind was now subject to the same moral law."[307] Because there is no limitation placed on the term neighbor, "the moral law applies to treatment of all nations."[308] Thus, for Edwards, "European nations had no right to steal from the Africans."[309]

In light of his progressive posture towards the slave trade, I agree with Minkema that Edwards is a figure that "represents a transitional stage in the development of antislavery thought among elites between complete advocacy of slavery and the immediatism of his first-generation, New Divinity disciples."[310] As Hopkins and other New Divinity disciples pushed for abolition in the Revolutionary years, it was Edwards who established a theological foundation for such a movement. Challenging Perry Miller's claim that Edwards's thinking was stagnant over the course of his life, McClymond and McDermott assert that Edwards's "thinking shifted repeatedly in response to changing circumstances in the Northampton church, the American colonies, and the transatlantic social and intellectual contexts."[311] During the latter years of his life in Stockbridge, it seems Edwards embraced a stronger global perspective as his interests in non-European cultures grew.

[304] *WJE*, 16:73.

[305] *WJE*, 16:75; Minkema, "Jonathan Edwards on Slavery and the Slave Trade," 828.

[306] *WJE*, 16:75.

[307] Minkema, "Jonathan Edwards on Slavery and the Slave Trade," 828.

[308] *WJE*, 16:75; Marsden, *Jonathan Edwards*, 257.

[309] Marsden, *Jonathan Edwards*, 257.

[310] Minkema, "Jonathan Edwards on Slavery and the Slave Trade," 824–25.

[311] McClymond and McDermott, *The Theology of Jonathan Edwards*, 77. Discussing the development of Edwards's ethical thought, McClymond and McDermott explain that "the 1730s and 1740s show Edwards gravitating toward a conception of the Christian life that highlighted ethical practice, perseverance through difficulties, self-sacrifice on behalf of others, and, at times, a quasi-mystical impetus toward self-abnegation and the annihilation of the self within what Edwards called 'a holy and pure love' of God." McClymond and McDermott, *The Theology of Jonathan Edwards*, 83.

Given the sovereignty of God, he began to contemplate the work of God in foreign cultures and religions:

> What we are calling a cultural-historical turn denotes Edwards's late-life preoccupation with "other" cultures—i.e., other than Anglo-American, English-language, and Protestant. Moreover, he was not only interested in identifying God's work within non-Christian cultures and religions but also in the secular aspects of Western civilization. This was an arena where few—if any—of Edwards's theological contemporaries would have looked to describe and depict a redemptive history.[312]

Edwards's racial and religious thoughts progressed toward the end of his life. His theological progress paved the way for the New Divinity opposition to slavery and the slave trade.[313]

To conclude, there are a number of tensions that need to be dealt with knowing Edwards condoned institutionalized slavery. Going back to the draft letter, Edwards defended a fellow pastor who embraced "Arminian leanings" for his right to own slaves.[314] Given that Edwards's opposition to Arminian theology is unquestioned, he placed a higher priority on slave-owning. It was societally acceptable to own slaves and Edwards viewed "his primary job as defending the authority of a fellow minister."[315] Edwards's agreement with slavery and opposition to slave-trading is another tension. As Burns states, to "condone slavery contradicts condemning the trade since the existence of slaves in the States is owing to rejection of the moral law and also the fact that the institution demands the trade."[316] Last, he compromised on fully applying his theology of love to enslaved Africans by condoning the institution.

[312]McClymond and McDermott, *The Theology of Jonathan Edwards*, 87. For more on this topic, see Gerald R. McDermott, *Jonathan Edwards Confronts the Gods: Christian Theology, Enlightenment Religion, and Non-Christian Faiths* (New York: Oxford University Press, 2000).

[313]As Saillant explains, even though "Edwards himself was a slaveowner, a number of those who affiliated themselves to his theology, along with others with a more general connection to Calvinism . . . became leaders in eighteenth-century abolitionism." John Saillant, "African American Engagements with Edwards in the Era of the Slave Trade," in *Jonathan Edwards at 300: Essays on the Tercentenary of His Birth*, ed. Harry S. Stout, Kenneth P. Minkema, and Caleb J. D. Maskell (Lanham, MD: University Press of America, 2005), 144.

[314]Marsden, *Jonathan Edwards*, 256.

[315]Marsden, *Jonathan Edwards*, 256.

[316]Burns, "Trusting the Theology of a Slave Owner," 153.

Conclusion

Both the philosophical and theological aspects of Edwards's virtue theory contain elements for the expression of moral activism in society. This is because Edwards's ethical thought is rooted in benevolence. Simply put, one is to love God and love others. This is possible by way of the Spirit uniting believers to God and others as part of a divinely created system. The believer loves with a God-given love, which is selfless in nature. Because it is from God, the nature of this love is supernatural, extending itself outward in order to glorify God and seek the good of others. Consequently, genuine benevolence will result in acts of justice and service for the betterment of those in need. Where Edwards errs is in his failure to fully apply his doctrine of benevolence to enslaved Africans by condoning institutionalized slavery. While he showed improvement in racial thought and attitude, especially in the latter years of his life, he never changed his stance on slavery. Nonetheless, his ethical thought was used by Hopkins for abolitionism. Where Edwards failed by condoning slavery, Hopkins succeeded by supporting the cessation of the institution. Hopkins's agreement with Edwards's virtue theory and more consistent application of Edwards's doctrine of benevolence to advocate for the abolition of slavery and the slave trade will be discussed next.

Chapter 5: A Comparative Analysis

This chapter demonstrates Hopkins's congruence with Edwards's virtue theory. More specifically, Hopkins's agreement with Edwards's ethical theology and faithful application of Edwards's doctrine of benevolence for abolitionism are established.[1] Consequently, it shows that Hopkins derived social concern and activism from Edwards's doctrine.

[1]According to scholarly opinion, *TV* was the source from Edwards that influenced Hopkins's doctrine of disinterested benevolence and consequently, his abolitionism. For example, McDermott and Story state: "His own son Jonathan Edwards Jr., and his foremost disciple, Samuel Hopkins, were early, outspoken abolitionists, and Hopkins's abolitionism was inspired by his reading of Edwards's treatise *The Nature of True Virtue*." Gerald R. McDermott and Ronald Story, eds., *The Other Jonathan Edwards: Selected Writings on Society, Love, and Justice* (Amherst: University of Massachusetts Press, 2015), 3. In another example, Swift notes: "The theological basis for Hopkins' attack on slavery had been articulated in Jonathan Edwards' *Nature of True Virtue*, with its stress on 'love of being in general' (*i.e.*, impartial love of all beings)." David E. Swift, "Samuel Hopkins: Calvinist Social Concern in Eighteenth Century New England," *Journal of Presbyterian History* 47, no. 1 (1969): 41. However, I do not believe *TV* was the only source that Hopkins drew from. Nor was *TH* the only work that was instrumental for Hopkins's abolitionism. As will be shown in this chapter, examining Hopkins's broader corpus beyond *TH* provides additional evidence of Hopkins's congruence with Edwards's virtue theory. In regards to the practical outworking of their respective ethics, other writings clearly show Hopkins's social concern and activism and consequently, a dependence on a broader understanding of Edwards's doctrine of benevolence found outside of *TV*. Also see Heejoon Jeon, "Jonathan Edwards and the Anti-Slavery Movement," *Journal of the Evangelical Theological Society* 63.4 (2020): 773–88; Heejoon Jeon, "The Role of Sanctification in the Ethics of Jonathan Edwards" (PhD diss., Trinity International University, 2019).

Benevolence to God *and* Neighbor

Hopkins, in defense of Edwards, responded to William Hart (and other opponents) who in 1771 polemically countered Edwards's virtue theory, in particular Edwards's doctrine of benevolence to Being in general.[2] Hart states his position, arguing that Edwards's doctrine and "the doctrines built upon them, extremely disgust inlightened and virtuous men, and perplex the simple, and confound their understanding, and involve practical religion . . . in a cloud, and give it so mysterious an appearance, that they are tempted to suspect there is nothing real in it," pointing to Edwards's theory as overly philosophical and impractical in nature.[3] Thus for Hart, "Edwards's ethical theory was too abstruse and cryptic for it to be an effective spur to moral living."[4]

Hopkins defends Edwards and his theory of virtue in *TH*. He specifically addresses Hart's polemic in the appendix to the work in order to "vindicate Mr. Edwards," recognizing that "Mr. Edwards had given a right idea and definition of true virtue, and that it is of importance he should be vindicated, and Mr. Hart's objections answered," thus defending Edwards's doctrine of benevolence to Being in general.[5] While there is agreement of Hopkins's motivation to defend Edwards's doctrine, scholarly opinion has given a picture of change or divergence. Holbrook asserts that "Hopkins had shifted Edwards's emphasis from Being in general as the principle of ultimate reality to the view of Being in general as a collection of beings, composed of God and his creation."[6] Similarly, Conforti in his oft cited *Samuel Hopkins & the New Divinity Movement* argues that Hopkins viewed Edwards's virtue theory as deficient, seeking to "correct Edwards by redefining Being in general as

[2]Peter Dan Jauhiainen, "An Enlightenment Calvinist: Samuel Hopkins and the Pursuit of Benevolence" (PhD diss., University of Iowa, 1997), 248, 250. For Hart's work against Edwards, see William Hart, *Remarks on President Edwards's Dissertations Concerning the Nature of True Virtue: Shewing That He Has given a Wrong Idea, and Definition of Virtue, and Is Inconsistent with Himself* (New Haven, CT: T. and S. Green, 1771).

[3]Hart, *Remarks on President Edwards's Dissertations Concerning the Nature of True Virtue*, 45–46.

[4]Jauhiainen, "An Enlightenment Calvinist," 249.

[5]Samuel Hopkins, "An Inquiry into the Nature of True Holiness," in *The Works of Samuel Hopkins, D.D.*, vol. 3 (Boston: Doctrinal Tract and Book Society, 1854), 67.

[6]Clyde A. Holbrook, *The Ethics of Jonathan Edwards: Morality and Aesthetics* (Ann Arbor: University of Michigan Press, 1973), 119.

'God and our neighbors,' that is, God and mankind."[7] In a recent work, Noll also sees a change by Hopkins in regards to Edwards's understanding of benevolence to Being in general, claiming, "What was for Edwards an aesthetic principle with ethical implications became for Hopkins a practical principle with aesthetic connotations."[8] And in a more recent work, Kidd, like Conforti, believes Hopkins viewed Edwards's theory as "deficient," thus altering benevolence to Being in general to loving God and neighbor.[9] Thus the consensus opinion is that Hopkins changed Edwards's doctrine, indicating that Edwards did not have neighbor or creatures in his definition but rather a philosophically oriented description of God. The language and argumentation are philosophical, but it does not negate the fact that Edwards also had in mind a system of existence in his definition as argued in chapter four.

So, is Hopkins's definition all that different from Edwards's doctrine? Hopkins for his work *TH* argues that he does "not pretend to be an original" apart from Edwards.[10] Rather, in defending Edwards and his definition of virtue in *TV*, Hopkins believes Edwards "has given the same account of holiness for substance, though under a different name," maintaining agreement with his mentor.[11] Hopkins continues: "All I can pretend to, as an improvement on him, is to have explained some things more fully than he did, and more particularly stated the opposition of holiness to self-love, and shown that this representation of holiness is agreeable to the Scripture; and to have answered some objections he has not mentioned, and made a number of inferences."[12] Hopkins says that he aims to improve on Edwards's work, but nowhere does he mention any idea of reworking Edwards's virtue theory due to deficiencies. He does mention how Edwards gives the same definition of holiness but "under a different name." Jauhiainen importantly notes that Hopkins, responding to "criticisms that his mentor's treatise was too abstract and metphysical," did away with "much of the philosophical

[7]Joseph A. Conforti, *Samuel Hopkins and the New Divinity Movement: Calvinism, the Congregational Ministry, and Reform in New England Between the Great Awakenings* (Grand Rapids: Christian University Press, 1981), 110–11.

[8]Mark A. Noll, *America's God: From Jonathan Edwards to Abraham Lincoln* (New York: Oxford University Press, 2002), 274.

[9]Thomas S. Kidd, *The Great Awakening: The Roots of Evangelical Christianity in Colonial America* (New Haven, CT: Yale University Press, 2007), 229.

[10]Hopkins, *TH*, 6.

[11]Hopkins, *TH*, 7.

[12]Hopkins, *TH*, 7.

language of *True Virtue* in favor of a greater dependence upon biblical terminology."[13] Jauhiainenx continues: "Expressions such as 'virtue' and 'Being in general' were often replaced with 'holiness' and 'God and neighbor.'"[14] This is compelling given Edwards's moral sense opponents for the *Two Dissertations*, Hopkins's goal in defending Edwards's virtue theory in *TH*, and simply using the word holiness instead of virtue for the title of his work. Evidence of Hopkins's agreement with Edwards's doctrine of benevolence to Being in general substantiates the argument for consistency in meaning and difference in language between the two figures.

In regards to Hopkins's understanding of Christian love, Jauhiainen argues, "Benevolence was the dominant rule which governed both his ethical behavior and his reconstruction of Reformed doctrine."[15] This assertion is without debate given the emphasis Hopkins places on benevolence for the moral life. Hopkins defines benevolence by connecting it to God's moral character: "When it is said that the moral character of God, or his holiness, consists in love, in which sense 'God is love,' universal, infinite benevolence or good will is meant by love, and all that which this necessarily implies."[16] As will be discussed later, the ideas of holiness and love are unified. A holy God is a God of love and this love is universal as it is extended to all creatures. The nature of this love for Hopkins is selfless or disinterested. It is contrary to selfishness as "true religion and all holy exercise" consists in "disinterested

[13]Jauhiainen, "An Enlightenment Calvinist," 257. This makes sense due to Hart's agenda. Conforti notes that Hart believed "Edwards had replaced the biblical God with the abstract metaphysical concept of 'Being in general.' Furthermore, Hart argued, a penchant for metaphysics and aesthetics had led Edwards to deny that social morality was true virtue and to 'involve practical religion . . . in a cloud.' Most of Edwards's dissertation was vitiated, Hart suggested, because he had confused aesthetics with ethics." Joseph A. Conforti, "Samuel Hopkins and the New Divinity: Theology, Ethics, and Social Reform in Eighteenth-Century New England," *William and Mary Quarterly* 34, no. 4 (1977): 575. Jauhiainen's point about Hopkins's intended audience is helpful in light of Hart's assertion that Edwards replaced "the biblical God," stating: "Whereas Edwards responded to the theories of the British moralists, Hopkins had a different audience in mind—critics who accused his mentor of departing from biblical standards. Thus he supplemented Edwards's philosophical approach with the traditional terminology of the Bible and Calvinism." Jauhiainen, "An Enlightenment Calvinist," 261. It was not an alteration of Edwards's thought, but rather a strategic alteration of his language by Hopkins in order to apologetically respond to opponents who claimed Edwards substituted the God revealed in Scripture with a philosophical concept of God.

[14]Jauhiainen, "An Enlightenment Calvinist," 257–58.

[15]Jauhiainen, "An Enlightenment Calvinist," 232.

[16]Samuel Hopkins, "The Being and Perfections of God," in *The Works of Samuel Hopkins, D.D.*, vol. 1 (Boston: Doctrinal Tract and Book Society, 1854), 49.

affection."[17] It is the same message Edwards gives when discussing selfless benevolence that seeks the good of others. The practical expressions of such disinterestedness are holy because they are Spirit produced. Taking into account the "words and actions" of believers, "they may reasonably conclude that they are born of the Spirit of God, and that their religion consists in disinterested affection."[18] Such benevolence is evidence of genuine faith. This echoes what Edwards says in *RA*, in particular Christian practice as evidence of genuine affections.

Like Edwards, Hopkins discusses Christian love by distinguishing love of benevolence and love of complacence.[19] Edwards says, "Love of *benevolence* is that affection or propensity of the heart to any being, which causes it to incline to its well-being, or disposes it to desire and take pleasure in its happiness."[20] In the same manner, explaining the love of benevolence, Hopkins points to the benefit of others: "The love of benevolence is good will to beings capable of good, or happiness, and consists in desiring and pursuing their good, or rejoicing in their possessing it."[21] Energy is extended to help one's neighbor for his betterment. By love of complacence, Hopkins has in mind "the pleasure and delight we take in the person and character of an intelligent being, as beautiful and excellent."[22] Elsewhere, Hopkins writes about love of complacence as "love of complacency in moral beauty and excellence," pointing to aesthetics in relation to morality.[23] It is love for one's moral beauty and excellence rather than intentional action to meet the needs of others. Edwards says the same thing in *TV*, asserting that love of complacence has to do with love to an individual for his beauty. In other

[17]Samuel Hopkins, "The Application of Redemption," in *The Works of Samuel Hopkins, D.D.*, vol. 1 (Boston: Doctrinal Tract and Book Society, 1854), 392.

[18]Hopkins, "The Application of Redemption," 395. Hopkins uses the word "affection" and "benevolence" as synonymous terms in this context. Immediately following the referenced quote, Hopkins states "that this disinterested benevolence will further evidence itself in religious, holy joy in God, his works, and revealed designs, in which there is no selfishness, but the contrary." Hopkins, "The Application of Redemption," 395. Hopkins makes clear that disinterestedness is selflessness.

[19]Hopkins, *TH*, 15.

[20]Jonathan Edwards, "The Nature of True Virtue," in *Ethical Writings*, vol. 8 (New Haven, CT: Yale University Press, 1989), 542.

[21]Hopkins, *TH*, 15.

[22]Hopkins, *TH*, 15–16.

[23]Samuel Hopkins, "The Apostasy of Man, and the Evil Consequence to Him," in *The Works of Samuel Hopkins, D.D.*, vol. 1 (Boston: Doctrinal Tract and Book Society, 1854), 236.

words, the moral beauty one possesses is cause for an individual to express benevolence to him.

Also like Edwards, Hopkins's virtue theory has God as the greatest being in the universe. Hopkins states that "universal benevolence or love to being in general must have God, who is infinitely the greatest and most excellent, and the sum of all being and perfection, for its object, and is exercised towards him in loving him with all the heart, with all the soul, with all the mind, and with all the strength."[24] The creature is to have supreme regard for his Creator: "They must be heartily devoted to the glory of God, to his honor, interest, and kingdom, as the supreme object of their desire and affection."[25] As creatures are a result of the creating activity of God, the being with most excellence is clear. Hopkins makes evident the distinction of God from his creation, namely creatures: "Benevolence regards him as at the head of the universe, infinitely great, omnipotent, and supreme; all the creation being as nothing, compared with him, and absolutely in his hands, and at his control, made and used for him; he being the only necessary and all-important Being, his interest, honor, and glory being the supreme end of all," viewing God as the only divine being and therefore, most important.[26] It is not a denigration of creatures but rather an elevation of God when compared to creation. It makes sense, then, that "God is infinitely the greatest part of existence," being set apart from his creation.[27] Edwards makes the same point in *TV*, explaining how God has most ownership of all existence as the greatest being. Because God is supreme, he has the greatest portion of existence.

Discussing the "moral world," Hopkins states that "God himself must be considered as included in this everlasting, moral kingdom, as the supreme Head and eternal King of it; and he, being infinitely greater, more important, and worthy of regard than any or all creatures, must, therefore, be the end

[24]Hopkins, *TH*, 18.

[25]Samuel Hopkins, "How Christians Work Out Their Own Salvation: Sermon II," in *The Works of Samuel Hopkins, D.D.*, vol. 3 (Boston: Doctrinal Tract and Book Society, 1854), 595. This sermon series was written in 1798. See Samuel Hopkins, "How Christians Work Out Their Own Salvation: Sermon I," in *The Works of Samuel Hopkins, D.D.*, vol. 3 (Boston: Doctrinal Tract and Book Society, 1854), 581.

[26]Samuel Hopkins, "The Decrees of God the Foundation of Piety: Sermon I," in *The Works of Samuel Hopkins, D.D.*, vol. 2 (Boston: Doctrinal Tract and Book Society, 1854), 711. This sermon series was written in 1789. See Hopkins, "The Decrees of God the Foundation of Piety: Sermon I," 703.

[27]Samuel Hopkins, "On Christian Practice," in *The Works of Samuel Hopkins, D.D.*, vol. 2 (Boston: Doctrinal Tract and Book Society, 1854), 204.

of all that is done; that is, he must make himself the highest and last end," viewing himself as the head of creation.[28] This is why Hopkins can say that God has "supreme regard to himself and the highest happiness and glory of his kingdom," recognizing that there is no greater being.[29] This is the same message Edwards gives in *CEW*, viewing God as the being with most worth and thus, a being who has most regard for himself. Hopkins and Edwards agree that creatures within the system are to be regarded as those authored by God but with proper esteem compared to God who is most worthy. Consequently, the end of creation must be God himself given who is and the status he occupies.

In light of God as the greatest being, creatures are to make the glory of God their "supreme end" in everything they do.[30] Edwards makes clear in *CEW* that God makes himself and his glory the end of creation. He also discusses how man is created for God's glory. Hopkins agrees with his mentor. As a result of God's glory, "the greatest manifestation and display of the divine character and perfections, includes the greatest possible good of the created universe; for in producing and effecting this, the omnipotence, infinite wisdom and goodness of God are acted out and manifested to the greatest advantage to be seen by creatures."[31] God demonstrates his perfections and thus, his character. This will encourage believers to pursue God's glory as their end.[32] Edwards in like manner discusses the communication of divine attributes in *CEW* for the benefit of creatures.

As mentioned earlier, Hopkins, like Edwards, also believes in a system of existence that is made up of God and creatures. Hopkins in *TH* equates "Universal being" with "God and all intelligent creatures."[33] Earlier he points to holiness "as comprehending Creator and creatures," viewing God and creatures as united.[34] Referring to divine love, Hopkins makes clear the union of God with creatures and the singular nature of love expressed. Hopkins explains, "This love, of which God and the creature are the objects, is, in the nature of it, one and the same undivided affection, differing only

[28]Hopkins, "The Decrees of God the Foundation of Piety: Sermon I," 705.

[29]Hopkins, *TH*, 20.

[30]Samuel Hopkins, "The Decrees of God the Foundation of Piety: Sermon III," in *The Works of Samuel Hopkins, D.D.*, vol. 2 (Boston: Doctrinal Tract and Book Society, 1854), 741.

[31]Hopkins, "The Decrees of God the Foundation of Piety: Sermon III," 741–42.

[32]Hopkins, "The Decrees of God the Foundation of Piety: Sermon III," 741.

[33]Hopkins, *TH*, 16.

[34]Hopkins, *TH*, 10.

as it is exercised towards different objects, on various occasions, and in diverse circumstances."[35] Edwards gives this message in *TV*, emphasizing divine and creaturely union. God expresses the same love to himself and creatures. Hopkins's dependence on Edwards regarding the unition of God and creatures in the universal system of existence and singularity of love is clear. Hopkins then discusses its relation to the system of existence: "It consists in *universal benevolence*, or benevolence to being in general capable of happiness, and all that affection and exercise of heart which is necessarily included in this."[36] Like Edwards, Hopkins discusses the system of existence ontologically, defining the system as including God and creatures. The language of "benevolence to being in general" is adopted by Hopkins as is the universal nature of divine love as God encompasses the created order.

Hopkins elaborates on the idea of divine and creaturely union: "Holiness is that by which intelligent beings are united together in the highest, most perfect, and beautiful union. It consists in that harmony of affection and union of heart by which the intelligent system becomes *one*, so far as holiness prevails; which fixes every being, by his own inclination and choice, in his proper place, so as in the best manner to promote the good of the whole."[37] God extends holiness, or love, to creatures for his glory and their good: "The holiness of God primarily consists in *love*, or benevolence to himself and to the creature, in the exercise of which, he seeks his own glory and the happiness of the creature; or, in one word, he seeks the good of the universe, as comprehending both Creator and creatures."[38] Holiness and benevolence are inseparable realities which unite creatures together. Hopkins makes this evident by viewing "holy love" as that which "unites the heart to universal existence, so far as it comes into view, and is the most cordial friendship to all without exception," stressing the impartial outworking of benevolence.[39]

[35] Hopkins, "The Application of Redemption," 375.

[36] Hopkins, "The Application of Redemption," 375.

[37] Hopkins, *TH*, 10. Union among creatures not only leads to moral beauty but also creaturely happiness: "There is no moral beauty or happiness among intelligent beings without harmony and union of heart." Hopkins, *TH*, 10.

[38] Samuel Hopkins, "Sin through Divine Interposition an Advantage to the Universe: Sermon III," in *The Works of Samuel Hopkins, D.D.*, vol. 2 (Boston: Doctrinal Tract and Book Society, 1854), 527. This sermon series was written in 1759. See Samuel Hopkins, "Sin through Divine Interposition an Advantage to the Universe: Preface," in *The Works of Samuel Hopkins, D.D.*, vol. 2 (Boston: Doctrinal Tract and Book Society, 1854), 495.

[39] Hopkins, *TH*, 17. Hopkins makes clear the inseparable relationship between holiness and benevolence in light of 1 Cor 13: "That all true holiness consists in disinterested, benevolent affection, and what is implied in this, is evident from what St. Paul says, (1 Cor. xiii.) Here the

Hopkins connects this impartial love to the system of existence and creaturely unity. Hopkins writes, "Disinterested, impartial benevolence to being in general that is capable of good and happiness, regards and wishes well to every being and creature in the system, according to the degree of his existence, worth and capacity of happiness, so far as all this comes into the view of the benevolent person, and so far as the good and happiness of each is, or appears to be, consistent with the greatest good of the whole."[40] Edwards stresses the need to seek the good of the whole in *TV*. Love is to be extended to every individual in the system with the need to benefit all. It needs to have the interest of the whole in mind. In like manner, Hopkins writes:

> This leads to observe, further, that this love, which is the new creation, or the new creature, has not only the Supreme Being for its object, but creatures, also, who are capable of happiness. It wishes well to every such creature so far as their good and happiness is consistent with the greatest public general good, and no farther; for universal benevolence seeks the greatest good of the whole, and, therefore, is ready to give up, not to desire, but to renounce, the good and happiness of individuals, when and as far as it is inconsistent with the greatest good of the whole, all beings and all things taken into view.[41]

Hopkins's concern for the whole is clear: "True benevolence always seeks the greatest good of the whole, and is a disposition to give up the less good for the greater."[42] It is consistent with Edwards's thoughts in *CEW* of the system as a whole being greater than the individual parts. It is a call to sacrifice self-interest for the interests of others.[43] Discussing selflessness, Hopkins explains that this "charity, this benevolent, disinterested affection,

apostle speaks of charity as comprising all real holiness, or true religion, by which he means that love to God and our neighbor which the law of God requires." Hopkins, *TH*, 50. Edwards's influence is evident in light of the *CF* sermons.

[40]Hopkins, "The Application of Redemption," 379–80. The "benevolent man is a friend to universal being, capable of good; he wishes well to all; therefore, he who regards the good of being in general, and promotes the general good, or expresses his benevolence by doing good to any particular being, is the proper object of grateful love," valuing both the individual and the whole. Hopkins, "The Decrees of God the Foundation of Piety: Sermon I," 715.

[41]Hopkins, "The Application of Redemption," 377.

[42]Hopkins, *TH*, 60.

[43]Hopkins, *TH*, 60.

is the only bond of holy union among intelligent beings," emphasizing creaturely unity.[44]

In light of union with God and others, Hopkins highlights divine communication as a necessary prerequisite for creaturely holiness. Edwards makes the idea of God's self-communication explicit in *CEW*. God communicates himself to creatures which make up the system of existence. For Edwards, divine communication occurs by way of God communicating his attributes. Likewise, upon discussing the display of God's perfections, Hopkins explains: "This exhibition and display of the divine perfections necessarily implies and involves, as essential to it, the communication of his own holiness and happiness to the greatest possible degree, which consists in effecting or producing the greatest possible moral excellence and felicity in his creation, or by his works."[45] What is communicated to creatures is God himself. Because believers are now in Christ, they have holiness residing within: "This is the moral image of God; the divine nature communicated and implanted; or Christ formed in the soul."[46] As a result, the believer is joined to God himself.

Discussing holiness and the law of love, Hopkins says since "the divine holiness is expressed in the law, in requiring love, so the creature, by exercising this same love, is a partaker of God's holiness, or of the divine nature," being united with God.[47] It is the very holiness of God that resides within the Christian.[48] Hopkins explains: "We have the greatest certainty of this, in that holiness in the creature is, in Scripture, called the image of God, and that by which they partake of the divine nature, and is represented to be the Holy Spirit of God, or God's holiness, dwelling and acting in them, by which God dwells in them, and they dwell in God."[49] It is by way of the Spirit that believers are in union with God as they experience his presence. It is God himself: "And if holiness in creatures is of the same nature and kind, being a participation of the divine nature, and consists in the Spirit of God imparted to the soul, and dwelling in it," believers have assurance

[44]Hopkins, *TH*, 50.

[45]Samuel Hopkins, "The Decrees of God," in *The Works of Samuel Hopkins, D.D.*, vol. 1 (Boston: Doctrinal Tract and Book Society, 1854), 73.

[46]Samuel Hopkins, "Saving Faith," in *The Works of Samuel Hopkins, D.D.*, vol. 1 (Boston: Doctrinal Tract and Book Society, 1854), 446.

[47]Hopkins, *TH*, 37.

[48]Hopkins, *TH*, 11.

[49]Hopkins, *TH*, 11.

of genuine holiness.[50] And as the believer, by way of the indwelling Spirit, loves others, his expressions of love flow from God's holiness.[51] This is why Hopkins can say that, "Love to God, and love to our fellow-creatures, is of the same nature and kind, and differs only as it is exercised towards different objects. It consists most essentially in benevolence or good will to being in general."[52] The universal system of existence is made evident as is the singular nature of divine love, which Edwards affirmed.

Self-Regard and the Role of Happiness

The selfless nature of Hopkins's doctrine of disinterested benevolence is clear. What contributed to the self-denying thrust of his doctrine was his concern of selfishness in regards to the moral life.[53] Thus, Hopkins stressed selfless benevolence, which has led to claims of Hopkins lacking self-regard in his doctrine. Jauhiainen importantly notes: "Hopkins's radical stress on self-denial has led interpreters to claim that he stripped entirely any regard to self from his theory of benevolence."[54] This is one of the reasons why scholars have tended to portray Hopkins as diverging from Edwards's doctrine.[55] For example, Post argues that in "contrast to Edwards, Hopkins argued that the test of Christian love is absolute disinterest in one's own well-being."[56] As a result, Post states: "Selfless love for God of the sort proposed by Hopkins fails to recognize that the structure of personal and social existence requires a theology of love that allows for the self to participate in the good of communion."[57] According to Post, because Hopkins's understanding of selflessness was so extreme, no space was given for proper self-regard in his understanding of benevolence. In another example, Davidson similarly claims that Hopkins espoused "an inhuman rejection of even natural self-

[50]Hopkins, *TH*, 11–12.

[51]Hopkins, *TH*, 37.

[52]Hopkins, "The Apostasy of Man, and the Evil Consequence to Him," 236.

[53]Jauhiainen, "An Enlightenment Calvinist," 235.

[54]Jauhiainen, "An Enlightenment Calvinist," 235.

[55]Jauhiainen, "An Enlightenment Calvinist," 236.

[56]Stephen Garrard Post, *Christian Love and Self-Denial: An Historical and Normative Study of Jonathan Edwards, Samuel Hopkins, and American Theological Ethics* (Lanham: University Press of America, 1987), vii. This has largely to do with Hopkins's understanding of damnation for the glory of God, which will be discussed in the next section.

[57]Post, *Christian Love and Self-Denial*, xi–xii.

love."[58] There is no regard for one's wellbeing. Contrarily, I agree with Jauhiainen's assertion that "Hopkins's theology of disinterested benevolence *did*, in fact, include a place for the love of self, and for the most part, his doctrine was consistent with Edwards's."[59] The role of happiness is key for Hopkins's view of self-regard.

Edwards understands self-regard in a twofold sense: one that embraces personal happiness and one that is private or selfish in nature. In terms of self-regard, Hopkins asserts, "It is true, indeed, as has been shown, that the most disinterested affection does not exclude proper regard to our own being and interest, but necessarily includes it."[60] How is this the case given Hopkins's priority on loving the other? As everyone is called to extend love to all, every individual in the system will, as a result, have their own interests met. A lengthy quote by Hopkins illustrates the point:

> By many there is not a proper distinction made, and kept in view, between self-love, and that regard which the benevolent person must have for himself and his interest and happiness, which is necessarily included in disinterested affection. Disinterested, impartial benevolence to being in general that is capable of good and happiness, regards and wishes well to every being and creature in the system, according to the degree of his existence, worth and capacity of happiness, so far as all this comes into the view of the benevolent person, and so far as the good and happiness of each is, or appears to be, consistent with the greatest good of the whole. And as he himself is one individual part of the whole, he must of necessity be the object of this disinterested, impartial benevolence, and his own interest and happiness must be regarded and desired, as much as that of his neighbor, or any individual of the whole society; not because it is *himself*, but because he is included in the whole, and his happiness is worth as much, and as desirable as that of his neighbor, other circumstances being equal.[61]

[58]Bruce W. Davidson, "The Four Faces of Self-Love in the Theology of Jonathan Edwards," *Journal of the Evangelical Theological Society* 51, no. 1 (2008): 99.

[59]Jauhiainen, "An Enlightenment Calvinist," 236.

[60]Hopkins, *TH*, 61.

[61]Hopkins, "The Application of Redemption," 379–80. In light of the distinction between selfishness and self-regard, Hopkins equates self-love with selfishness: "To distinguish between self-love and selfishness, is to attempt to make a distinction where there is no difference;

Hopkins, like Edwards, believes it is necessary to distinguish self-love, which is selfishness, and a proper regard for self as a participant in the system of existence. An individual exuding selfless love for others will have his needs and interests met as well, being in union with other creatures. Personal happiness and joy are just as valuable as that of his neighbor as benevolence is extended to all impartially. Hopkins argues in like manner elsewhere, distinguishing selfishness from proper self-regard:

> But when the distinction is properly made, and the matter plainly stated, the mistake is discovered, and it appears that disinterested benevolence will take all proper and sufficient care of every individual in the system, and will desire and seek the best interest and happiness of all, and of the benevolent person himself, so far as is consistent with the greatest good of the whole; and that this is not self-love, but the same disinterested, impartial benevolence, when it takes into view his own happiness, and values and seeks it as much as that of his neighbor.[62]

By recognizing the distinction, personal happiness is embraced. Hopkins also notes: "Many do not appear to distinguish between self-love, and a desire or love of happiness, — or a capacity of pleasure and enjoyment, and of being pleased with and choosing one object rather than another. These are quite distinct and different things."[63] Clearly Hopkins does not devalue personal delight in his promotion of selfless love.

As highlighted, Hopkins makes clear the need to benefit the whole when advocating one's own well-being:

> The person who exercises disinterested good will to being in general must have a proper and proportionable regard to himself, as he belongs to being in general, and is included in it as a necessary part of it. It is impossible he should love being in general, or universal being, and not love himself, because he is included in universal being. And the more he has of a disinterested, universal benevolence, and the stronger his exercises of it

unless by self-love be meant disinterested benevolence. Disinterested affection and self-love are very distinct and opposite affections, and the latter, in every degree of it, cannot be distinguished from selfishness; for these are two words for one and the same thing." Hopkins, "The Application of Redemption," 380–81.

[62]Hopkins, "The Application of Redemption," 380.

[63]Hopkins, "The Application of Redemption," 379.

> are, the more regard will he have to his own being, and the more fervently will he desire and seek his own interest and happiness. But here it must be observed, that he will not desire and seek it as his own, or because it is his own interest, considered as distinct and detached from the interest of the whole, or of being in general, but as included in it. Thus disinterested benevolence to being in general loves our neighbor as ourselves; in which there is nothing selfish, but ourselves are loved as included in the general object of disinterested love.[64]

The desire for personal benefit must be in accordance with the good of others if it is to be regarded as genuine benevolence. Otherwise it would be for selfish considerations. The consequences are clear: "The least degree of selfish love necessarily destroys all due proportion, and sets up a selfish interest detached from that of others, and injurious to the whole."[65] Hopkins continues, expanding on the effects of selfishness: "It is, in the very nature of it, an enemy to the harmony and happiness of the whole, and breaks in upon it, and tends to spread confusion and evil through the whole, in opposition to universal benevolence; and is inconsistent with our loving our neighbor as ourselves; but, by the supposition, loves self and nothing else."[66] When seeking self-regard apart from a selfless love for others, people are hurt in the process. Rather, individuals are to seek the good of the whole and be others focused:

> Disinterested benevolence is pleased with the public interest, — the greatest good and happiness of the whole. This is the highest good to the benevolent person. In this he places his happiness, and not in the interest and happiness of any individual, or of himself, any further than it is consistent with the greatest interest and happiness of the whole, and really included in it, and serves to promote it.[67]

Personal concern is not only encouraged, but beneficial. As Hopkins states, proper regard "for ourselves, our own interest and happiness, which is necessarily included in universal benevolence, is not only a proper and

[64]Hopkins, "The Apostasy of Man, and the Evil Consequence to Him," 240–41.

[65]Hopkins, "The Apostasy of Man, and the Evil Consequence to Him," 241.

[66]Hopkins, "The Apostasy of Man, and the Evil Consequence to Him," 241.

[67]Hopkins, "The Application of Redemption," 379.

reasonable regard, but is discerning, wise, and judicious, and seeks our true interest."[68] It is wise because, unlike self-love, it seeks self-interest and happiness in the correct place, which is in union with other creatures.[69] Contrarily, "self-love is partial and unreasonable in its own nature, and in every degree of it, and blinds men to their own true interest and happiness, and seeks happiness where it is not to be found, and as certainly and effectually renders them miserable, as if it were ill will to themselves."[70]

In sum, the believer places his happiness in God and others. Hopkins makes evident the connection of God to the creature's happiness. The communication of God's character and glory are tied with the creature's good and therefore, his happiness.[71] And because God finds joy in the creature's happiness, the creaturely desire for happiness is encouraged. God is the object and source of his happiness.[72] Referring to the problem of selfishness, Hopkins says the believer "places his happiness, not in his own private interest, but in a good more worthy to be sought, viz. the glory of God and the prosperity of his church and kingdom."[73] Creaturely joy is found in God, his glory, and good of the whole. Creatures experiencing happiness through practice further illustrates the point. In light of "Christian practice, and the character of a true Christian," Hopkins says that "Christianity is in the best manner suited to make those happy in this world and forever who cordially embrace and practise it, and to render society, whether public or more private, beautiful and happy."[74] There is joy in seeing others benefited through Christian service. Such posture requires humility: "A person who humbles himself renounces that self-exaltation and honor, in comparison with other beings, which pride and selfishness seek, and places his honor and happiness in abasing himself, and becoming the servant of all, by exalting God, and promoting his glory, and serving his fellow-creatures, ministering to their greatest good in the exercise of universal benevolence," exemplifying humility as he finds happiness in glorifying God and serving

[68]Hopkins, "The Application of Redemption," 386.

[69]Hopkins, "The Application of Redemption," 386.

[70]Hopkins, "The Application of Redemption," 386.

[71]Hopkins, "The Decrees of God," 73.

[72]Hopkins, "The Being and Perfections of God," 58, 59.

[73]Hopkins, *TH*, 60.

[74]Hopkins, "On Christian Practice," 206.

others.[75] Importantly, one does not express love to his neighbor in order to experience personal happiness, but rather extends love to his neighbor for his neighbor's sake.[76] Happiness is a result of such benevolence. Edwards explains this reality in both *TV* and *CEW*, believing a creature's happiness consists in the happiness of others as he extends benevolence. Hence, such self-regard is selfless.

Selfishness and Self-Enlargement

The reason scholars claim that Hopkins rejected the notion of self-regard is because of his doctrine of the willingness to be damned for God's glory. Post says, "Christian love, for Hopkins, meant self-denial without limits."[77] Similarly, Davidson claims, "Samuel Hopkins, Edwards's most devoted disciple, came to take the most extreme view, holding that a saint must be willing to be damned for the glory of God, a view Edwards himself had explicitly rejected as self-contradictory and unbiblical."[78] Yet Hopkins's promotion of self-regard needs to be taken into account. It is not a complete denial of personal concern in order to glorify God but rather an emphasis of selfless benevolence in light of selfish self-love. Discussing the scholarly tendency to view Hopkins's doctrine as inhibiting any amount of self-regard, Jauhianen explains: "Hopkins's advocacy of the willingness to be damned has been cited as evidence that he advocated such an extreme state of disinterestedness that there was little room left for any legitimate regard to self. Such a view overstates the importance of this teaching in his overall doctrine of universal benevolence and neglects his affirmation of the interests of the self as distinguished from selfishness."[79] This argument is likely, taking into account creaturely benefit as a participant in the system of existence along with finding happiness in God and the betterment of others.

[75]Hopkins, *TH*, 54.

[76]Hopkins makes the point clear: "The ground and reason of a person's taking pleasure in the happiness of his neighbor is his disinterested good will to him, and not this pleasure the cause of his good will to his neighbor." Hopkins, *TH*, 55. He continues: "Nothing but disinterested benevolence will give him a share in his neighbor's good; this is the ground and cause of his enjoying it, and not a desire of enjoying this happiness the ground of his benevolence." Hopkins, *TH*, 56.

[77]Post, *Christian Love and Self-Denial*, viii.

[78]Davidson, "The Four Faces of Self-Love in the Theology of Jonathan Edwards," 89.

[79]Jauhiainen, "An Enlightenment Calvinist," 282–83.

The reason for the view of Edwards's rejection of Hopkins's doctrine is because of the joy a believer experiences when loving God supremely. Edwards explains in Miscellany entry 530:

> Hence 'tis impossible for any person to be willing to be perfectly and finally miserable for God's sake, for this supposes love to God to be superior to self-love in the most general and extensive sense of self-love, which enters into the nature of love to God. It may be possible, that a man may be willing to be deprived of all his own proper separate good for God's sake; but then he is not perfectly miserable but happy, in the delight that he hath in God's good: for he takes greater delight in God's good, for the sake of which he parts with his own, than he did in his own. So that the man is not perfectly miserable, he is not deprived of all delight, but he is happy.[80]

The happiness a believer experiences in loving God is far greater than any potential loss of joy by putting God ahead of himself. Thinking otherwise is illogical in light of a believer's joy in God. Edwards continues:

> But if a man is willing to be perfectly miserable for God's sake, then he is willing to part with all his own separate good. But he must be willing also to be deprived of that which is indirectly his own, viz. God's good; which supposition is inconsistent with itself. For to be willing to be deprived of this latter sort of good, is opposite to that principle of love to God itself, from whence such a willingness is supposed to arise. Love to God, if it be superior to any other principle, will make a man forever unwilling, utterly and finally to be deprived of this part of his happiness, which he has in God's being blessed and glorified; and the more he loves him the more unwilling he will be. So that this supposition, that a man can be willing to be perfectly and utterly miserable out of love to God, is inconsistent with itself.[81]

Because the believer finds joy in loving God, it is impossible for one to be void of self-regard. Hence, scholars view Edwards as rejecting Hopkins's

[80]Jonathan Edwards, *Misc 530*, in *The "Miscellanies," 501-832*, ed. Ava Chamberlin, vol. 18, *The Works of Jonathan Edwards* (New Haven, CT: Yale University Press, 2000), 75.

[81]"Micellanies," no. 530, in *WJE*, 18:75.

doctrine of the willingness to be damned for the glory of God. Again, it is important to note Hopkins's posture towards selfishness in regards to his doctrine.

In *A Dialogue Between a Calvinist and a Semi-Calvinist*, Hopkins discusses the importance of self-sacrifice for the good of others. If one is called by God to suffer and even be damned for the betterment of others and their salvation, then that is what he should desire. It is a charge to trust in the sovereignty of God, willing to sacrificially accept God's will for his glory.[82] It is important to note that Hopkins's doctrine "served a rhetorical function of challenging Christians to examine the sincerity of their benevolence. To what lengths were they willing to go in submitting to God?"[83] Believers are called to love and obey God at all costs. Yet, it does not mean that a creature divests himself of all personal concern. Hopkins means that a believer ought to be willing to suffer such consequences as eternal damnation in order to obey God, live a holy life, and seek the salvation and good of others. The point is obedience and sacrificial living, not literal damnation. Edwards would agree, given his understanding of selfless benevolence and thus, the need to sacrifice oneself for the good of others.[84]

Both Edwards and Hopkins also advocate solidarity with one's neighbor by receiving him via self-enlargement as an act of benevolence. In speaking of the heart, Edwards explains how love "enlarges it and extends it to others. A man's self is as it were extended and enlarged by love. Others so far as beloved do, as it were, become parts of himself; so that wherein their interest is promoted he looks on his own as promoted, and wherein their interest is touched his is touched."[85] For Edwards, space is made in the heart and conscience to draw others in, resulting in benevolent unity. Discussing "compounded self-love" in opposition to selfish self-love, Edwards states:

> There is a compounded self-love, which is exercised in the delight that a man has in the good of another, it is the value that he sets upon that delight. This I call compounded self-love, be-

[82] Samuel Hopkins, "A Dialogue Between a Calvinist and a Semi-Calvinist," in *The Works of Samuel Hopkins, D.D.*, vol. 3 (Boston: Doctrinal Tract and Book Society, 1854), 143–57.

[83] Jauhiainen, "An Enlightenment Calvinist," 280.

[84] Jauhiainen notes: "Although Edwards repudiated the willingness to be damned for the glory of God, this doctrine was implied in his theory of true virtue, which required a disinterested love to being in general." Jauhiainen, "An Enlightenment Calvinist," 277.

[85] Jonathan Edwards, "Charity and Its Fruits," in *Ethical Writings*, ed. Paul Ramsey, vol. 8, *The Works of Jonathan Edwards* (New Haven, CT: Yale University Press, 1989), 263.

> cause it arises from a compounded principle. It arises from the necessary nature of a perceiving and willing being, whereby he loves his own pleasure or delight; but not from this alone. But it supposes also another principle that determines the exercise of this principle, and makes that to become its object which otherwise cannot: a certain principle uniting this person with another, that causes the good of another to be its good. The first arises simply from his own being, whereby that which agrees immediately and directly with his own being, is his good; the second arises also from a principle uniting him to another being, whereby the good of that other being does in a sort become his own. This second sort of self-love is not entirely distinct from love to God, but enters into its nature.[86]

Edwards stresses union with other creatures as a result of selfless love, embracing and taking in the wellbeing of others as his own. In like manner, Hopkins argues: "But universal benevolence—Christian love—spreads happiness wherever it flourishes. It enlarges and ennobles the mind, and puts the benevolent person in possession of the good and happiness of others, so that he enjoys it all in a great degree, and rejoices with those who rejoice."[87] The one extending benevolence receives him whom he loves. He embraces and finds joy in his neighbor's well-being and happiness.

Social Concern and Activism

Because scholars have portrayed Edwards's ethics as solely philosophical, aesthetic, and/or theological in nature, they have argued that Edwards lacked social concern in his virtue theory. This leads to the view of Hopkins's departure from Edwards, given Hopkins's activist ethics.

According to Conforti, because Edwards's ethical thought was overly aesthetic, there is a void of any social and activist motivation located in his theory.[88] Edwards's philosophical approach to virtue "placed theological obstacles in the way of evangelical activism," thus failing to address the practical dimension of ethics.[89] Specifically, Hopkins's doctrine of disin-

[86]"Micellanies," no. 530, in *WJE*, 74–75.

[87]Hopkins, "The Application of Redemption," 398.

[88]Conforti, "Samuel Hopkins and the New Divinity," 575.

[89]Conforti, "Samuel Hopkins and the New Divinity," 577.

terested benevolence was novel compared to Edwards's understanding of virtue, which Hopkins sought to make better.[90] This view continues to be espoused. In a recent work, William B. Evans represents the traditional claim that Hopkins changed Edwards's doctrine of benevolence to Being in general.[91] Edwards "presents a highly theocentric view of ethics and virtue" and "closely associates ethics and aesthetics," thus endorsing an impractical virtue theory.[92] On the other hand, Hopkins "had a deep interest in the practical dimensions of piety, and Edwards' conception of virtue seemed to provide an insufficient basis for social ethics."[93] As a result, Evans believes "Edwards' theocentric universe has given way to anthropocentrism," signaling a change by Hopkins towards a pragmatic approach to ethics.[94] It is a result of viewing the *Two Dissertations*, namely *TV*, in isolation from Edwards's theological ethics represented in his sermons.[95] Thus, according to Evans, Hopkins redefined Edwards's understanding of "virtue as *disinterested* benevolence, and its application both to human beings and especially to God," moving from the impractical to the practical.[96] Finally, Kling contrasts what he believes to be Hopkins's activist ethic versus Edwards's "aesthetic" account of virtue that culminates in a "holy consciousness."[97] Consequently, Edwards's virtue theory differs markedly from that of Hopkins's disinterested understanding of benevolence.[98]

A key to the argument of ethical congruence between the two figures is Hopkins's awareness and dependence of Edwards's doctrine of benevolence. The scholarly consensus is that Hopkins drew from *TV* for his doctrine of disinterested benevolence. Jauhiainen, who argues for Hopkins's overall faithfulness to Edwards's virtue theory, claims similarly that Hopkins's

[90]Conforti, "Samuel Hopkins and the New Divinity," 574, 576.

[91]William B. Evans, *Imputation and Impartation: Union with Christ in American Reformed Theology* (Milton Keynes, UK: Paternoster, 2008), 115.

[92]Evans, *Imputation and Impartation*, 115.

[93]Evans, *Imputation and Impartation*, 115.

[94]Evans, *Imputation and Impartation*, 116.

[95]McDermott establishes evidence of social concern in Edwards's ethical thought by mining what were, at the time, Edwards's unpublished sermons. See Gerald R. McDermott, *One Holy and Happy Society: The Public Theology of Jonathan Edwards* (University Park, PA: Penn State University Press, 1992).

[96]Evans, *Imputation and Impartation*, 129.

[97]David W. Kling, *Edwards and the Edwardseans: Jonathan Edwards, the New Divinity, and the Making of a Theological Culture* (Eugene, OR: Pickwick Publications, 2024), 142.

[98]Kling, *Edwards and the Edwardseans*, 142.

understanding of disinterested benevolence came from two main sources: "debate with Old Calvinists over the state of unregenerate endeavors" and Edwards's *TV*.[99] I believe there were additional sources that Hopkins drew from, specifically as they pertain to Edwards's understanding of benevolence.

Hopkins was aware of the *CF* sermons, likely urging Bellamy to transcribe them.[100] Ramsey importantly notes, from his reading of Tryon Edwards's preface to his "nineteenth-century edition of the charity sermons," that Hopkins and Joseph Bellamy determined that the *CF* sermons should be published, and that Bellamy began the formal publication process.[101] He points to a quote in Tryon Edwards's preface, which is also in the Yale edition.[102] Tryon Edwards writes, "After his death they were selected for publication by Dr. Hopkins and Dr. Bellamy; and by the latter were in part copied out and prepared for the press, when for some reason he was interrupted in their preparation, so that now for the first time they are given to the public."[103] Ramsey also points out a letter that Hopkins wrote to Bellamy in regards to a "joint publishing project," which "*might* be a reference to the partial copy of the charity sermons by Bellamy," indicating Hopkins's desire for the sermons to become public.[104] Given the content of the letter, Ramsey asserts that "Hopkins's language is consistent" with the notion that Hopkins was referring to the *CF* sermons in his letter to Bellamy.[105] If this is the case, Hopkins had intimate knowledge of the content. And having received from Sarah the rest of Edwards's manuscripts after his death, it is safe to conclude that Hopkins was aware of Edwards's sermons and consequently, a broader understanding of Edwards's doctrine of benevolence.

[99] Jauhiainen, "An Enlightenment Calvinist," 240–41. Another example is Lucas's view that Bellamy and Hopkins, "along with later Edwardsians, used *The Nature of True Virtue* to forge a powerful theological basis for social reform in the nineteenth century." Sean Michael Lucas, *God's Grand Design: The Theological Vision of Jonathan Edwards* (Wheaton, IL: Crossway, 2011), 117–18.

[100] Paul Ramsey, "Editor's Introduction," in *Ethical Writings*, vol. 8, *The Works of Jonathan Edwards* (New Haven, CT: Yale University Press, 1989), 3–5.

[101] *WJE*, 8:3.

[102] *WJE*, 8:3.

[103] Tryon Edwards, "Tryon Edwards' Introduction," in *Ethical Writings*, ed. Paul Ramsey, vol. 8, *The Works of Jonathan Edwards* (New Haven, CT: Yale University Press, 1989), 125–26.

[104] *WJE*, 8:3–4.

[105] *WJE*, 8:4–5.

Hopkins also witnessed firsthand the benevolent temper Edwards had as a person. According to Hopkins, Edwards showed great "Liberality, and Charity to the Poor and Distressed. He was much in recommending this, both in his public Discourses and private Conversation."[106] Clearly Hopkins was aware of Edwards's "public Discourses" on the social and activist expressions of charity. Moreover, it was Edwards's conviction that local churches should have funds set aside for such ministry, ready to contribute to members in need.[107] His voice carried weight as his life was marked by such benevolence.[108] Thus, we can conclude that Hopkins knew of Edwards's activism both from his doctrine and personal life.

Given the above discussion, it seems like a stretch that Hopkins only drew from *TV*, modifying Edwards's ethics for his purposes in establishing his practically oriented doctrine of disinterested benevolence. Scholars agree that disinterested benevolence for Hopkins "was not just an abstract theological tenet but a way of life, finding concrete expression in his self-denying service to his parishioners in Newport."[109] Yet they consistently limit the discussion of Hopkins's understanding of disinterested benevolence to *TH* and *A Dialogue Between a Calvinist and a Semi-Calvinist* for his understanding of the willingness to be damned for God's glory. Other sources by Hopkins found in his *System of Doctrines* and sermons provide additional evidence of Hopkins's understanding of selfless, activist love. This is significant given that Hopkins championed abolitionism from the Revolutionary years to the end of his life. As shown in chapter four, Edwards endorsed social concern and activism by way of his doctrine of benevolence. The following discussion will show Hopkins's agreement with Edwards's view, thus providing a case for Hopkins's derivation of social concern and activism from his mentor's doctrine.

In sermon one of *CF*, Edwards mentions that acts of justice are a result of serving one's neighbor in all ways. Like Edwards, a result of disinterested love for Hopkins is embracing justice. Concern for the interests of one's

[106] Samuel Hopkins, *The Life and Character of the Late Reverend, Learned, and Pious Mr. Jonathan Edwards, President of the College of New Jersey* (Northampton, MA: S. & E. Butler, 1804), 45. This source and reference was identified by reading McDermott's discussion on the topic. See McDermott, *One Holy and Happy Society*, 115.

[107] Hopkins, *The Life and Character of the Late Reverend, Learned, and Pious Mr. Jonathan Edwards, President of the College of New Jersey*, 45.

[108] Hopkins, *The Life and Character of the Late Reverend, Learned, and Pious Mr. Jonathan Edwards, President of the College of New Jersey*, 45–46.

[109] Jauhiainen, "An Enlightenment Calvinist," 234.

neighbor should be a natural expression of Christian benevolence. Hopkins explains, "The exercise and practice of righteousness or justice towards our neighbor implies a benevolent regard to him and his interest. Where this is not there is no exercise and practice of justice in the heart, whatever is the external conduct; for justice consists in doing to our neighbor as we would he should do to us, or, in other words, loving our neighbor as ourselves."[110] Acts of justice are a result of an inward condition where justice is present. This is a result of the Spirit's work, for Christians desire God's "Spirit to dwell in them, and form their hearts to every Christian exercise and duty, and doing all in the name of Christ, in the exercise of a cordial love of his whole character," modeling the character of Christ.[111] Likewise, Edwards discusses God as the source of such benevolent acts, such as deeds of justice, in sermons one, two, and three of *CF*. God is the source of the moral life as the believer seeks the betterment of others.

Because benevolence lies in the Christian's heart, justice is a natural expression of benevolence. Hopkins makes this clear by discussing the inseparable connection of love with other attributes: "Take away love and goodness, and there will be neither wisdom, truth, faithfulness, nor justice, for they have no existence but in the exercise of love; and love implies all these, and necessarily acts out so as to form a character properly denoted by these names, as it appears to creatures in different relations, and respects different objects."[112] As one loves, acts of justice will occur where necessary. This will be extended to all people impartially. Hopkins states that Christians "are careful and exact to do justice to all with whom they have any connection, and are conscientiously concerned and engaged not to injure any person either in their thoughts, words, or actions, in any of his interests, of worldly property or character, of body or soul," but rather have a neighbor's best interest in mind.[113] Not only are they to extend justice impartially, but also all acts flowing from love, whether to meet material or

[110]Hopkins, *TH*, 28.

[111]Hopkins, "How Christians Work Out Their Own Salvation: Sermon II," 595. Hopkins also discusses how the "moral nature" lies within the heart: "True faith, or a real belief of thc truths of the gospel, is of a moral nature, and, therefore, has its foundation and seat in the heart; so that exercise of heart is necessarily implied in it, and essential to it; for every thing of a moral nature belongs to the heart, and that in which no disposition or exercise of the heart is implied has nothing of a moral nature; and is neither good nor evil in a moral sense," so virtuous actions stem from that which is in the heart, namely benevolence. Hopkins, "How Christians Work Out Their Own Salvation: Sermon I," 590.

[112]Hopkins, *TH*, 38.

[113]Hopkins, "How Christians Work Out Their Own Salvation: Sermon II," 599.

spiritual needs: "And they are not only concerned and careful to do justice to all, but they love mercy, and wish and endeavor to do all the good they can unto all men, embracing all opportunities to promote their best interest, both temporal and eternal, whether they be friends or enemies."[114] Doing good and giving to others impartially is what Edwards discusses in sermon four of *CF*. Moreover, to be concerned for both the spiritual and material needs of others are common themes throughout Edwards's sermons. The concern for spiritual revivals/awakenings is testament to Edwards's concern for the spiritual state of unbelievers.

Hopkins urges ministry to meet both the physical and temporal needs of others. Hopkins explains,

> They must live in the exercise and expression of benevolence and kindness to them, being ready and careful to minister to the relief and comfort of their bodies, by giving them food and raiment, and affording them any help of which any of them shall stand in need, and by exercising and manifesting a particular concern and friendship for them, and complacency in them, in the exercise and practice of that brotherly love which is peculiar to Christians.[115]

The believer is to help provide daily sustenance for those in need, such as food and clothing. Edwards in his sermons highlights the need for believers to give what they have to others that are in need.[116] Hopkins notes, Christians are about "being liberal and bountiful to the poor and distressed, to the utmost of their ability," graciously providing what is needed.[117] Likewise, Edwards had much to say about caring for the poor. In sermon one of *CF*, Edwards makes clear that believers are to show regard towards those that are poor. In *Duty of Charity to the Poor*, Edwards says giving to those in need is a result of loving one's neighbor. He also highlights giving to the poor in the sermon, *Much in Deeds of Charity*. A final example is from Edwards's notebook, "Signs of Godliness," which shows the act of providing for the poor to be a result of benevolence. Like Edwards, Hopkins stresses

[114]Hopkins, "How Christians Work Out Their Own Salvation: Sermon II," 599.

[115]Hopkins, "How Christians Work Out Their Own Salvation: Sermon II," 600.

[116]For example, see Jonathan Edwards, "True Nobleness of Mind," in *Sermons and Discourses, 1723–1729*, ed. Kenneth P. Minkema, vol. 14, *The Works of Jonathan Edwards* (New Haven, CT: Yale University Press, 1997), 238.

[117]Hopkins, "The Application of Redemption," 394.

service to the poor. Christians are called to give great effort to helping those with physical ailments and material needs: "Giving all the assistance and relief in their power to others who are suffering under temporal bodily wants and distresses; being disposed to do good, ready to distribute, willing to communicate, and minister to the help and comfort of others, as far as they have ability and opportunity."[118] It is not just concern for one's spiritual state, but rather a concern for both "the temporal and eternal interest of all," looking to also provide materially.[119] Giving an illustration of a judge who has a disinterested posture rather than a selfish one for deciding a case, Hopkins explains how his interests will be to serve those in disadvantaged situations:

> Such a judge, when he renounces all selfish considerations, and espouses the cause of the widow and fatherless, and delivers them from the hand of oppressors, has an interest which he seeks, but not an interest which selfishness prompts him to pursue; and the more he interests himself in the cause of the poor, helpless widow, and the greater pleasure he takes in helping her, the more disinterested are his exertions and conduct, and the more is self-love counteracted and mortified.[120]

Edwards also discusses the need to serve those that are downtrodden. He talks about serving those that are hurting in sermon one of *CF* and helping those in difficult situations in the sermon *Bringing the Ark of Zion a Second Time*. Like Edwards, within Hopkins's doctrine of disinterested benevolence are clear stimuli for meeting the needs of those in an oppressed state. To serve those in helpless situations is the opposite of selfish living.

Furthermore, Hopkins emphasizes the need to help others in all ways possible. It is the same idea Edwards gives in sermon one of *CF* where he encourages service to one's neighbor through every duty needed. Like Edwards, it is action stemming from union with God and creatures: "It is that love which unites men to God and the Redeemer, and forms them to all the acts of piety, and gives them the highest enjoyment, which at the same time unites them to each other, and forms them to all social duties and enjoyments."[121] The ways in which one helps others are many,

[118]Hopkins, "On Christian Practice," 195.

[119]Hopkins, "On Christian Practice," 196.

[120]Hopkins, *TH*, 30.

[121]Hopkins, "On Christian Practice," 207.

including actions to meet societal needs. The result of such living is delight for the believer. Edwards established such thinking by championing both societal and national concern in sermon seven of *CF*. This has implications for expressions of benevolence. For Hopkins, if Christian love is "acted out in its proper nature and perfection, or, love to God and our neighbor made perfect in all its genuine exercises and expressions," genuine benevolence is present.[122] And only this "universal, disinterested benevolence" will "form men to such exercises and conduct."[123] The Christian will adapt, expressing these acts of benevolence to fit required responses. It depends on the needs of the person being served:

> Christian practice includes the faithful and punctual performance of all relative duties, founded in the different relations and stations in which persons stand in this life. These are various, and call for different and various duties, but may be all comprehended in the different relations included in superiors, inferiors, and equals. Love will form the Christian to the duties required in those different relations, and they all consist in expressing this love in all proper ways in those different relations.[124]

Hopkins argues that Christians "must be careful to speak and conduct towards all with becoming decency and respect, whether superiors, inferiors, or equals; and to set good examples before all, of humility, temperance, sobriety, meekness, and kindness; being ready to every good work, practising patience, forgiveness, and long-suffering, endeavoring to live in peace with all men, as far as shall be in their power."[125] Appropriate benevolent actions are to be extended to others regardless of one's personal and social rank. It is a result of believers "loving God with all their heart, and loving their neighbor as themselves. Christian practice consists in expressing and acting out this affection on all occasions, in every suitable way, in obedience to all the holy laws of God."[126] Edwards champions the need for Christians to

[122]Hopkins, *TH*, 29.

[123]Hopkins, *TH*, 31.

[124]Hopkins, "On Christian Practice," 198.

[125]Hopkins, "How Christians Work Out Their Own Salvation: Sermon II," 600.

[126]Hopkins, "On Christian Practice," 182. Similarly, Hopkins explains how Christians embrace "the dictates of Christian love, and so as shall be most for the honor of Christ and the good of every individual of the church. This is included in the exercise of piety towards God, as well as his duty to his fellow-Christians; and his love to God will induce him to speak and act, in all

engage in practice. In *RA*, Edwards recognizes practice as the primary sign of a holy life. In sermon ten of *CF*, Edwards shows how practice is a result of divine grace. The believer will express his holiness by the way he lives. And in *Much in Deeds of Charity*, Edwards provides another example of the need to engage in benevolent actions in all ways possible.

The diverse and strategic ways in which love is to be expressed has, for Hopkins, a connection to the divine law. Though Edwards does not stress the law as much as Hopkins, there is obvious agreement upon the need to love God and neighbor, which Edwards says sums up the law of God. This is illustrated in sermon one of *CF*. Upon discussing the foundational nature of love for virtuous actions, Hopkins explains, "The law of God, then, leads us to consider holiness as consisting in universal disinterested good will, considered in all its genuine exercises and fruits, and acted out in all its branches towards God and our neighbor," flowing out of a disposition of disinterested benevolence.[127] The legal character of Hopkins's doctrine of disinterested benevolence is evident. By obeying the divine law, one loves God and others. As a result, benevolent acts to meet the needs of one's neighbor takes place. Again, Hopkins explains the connection of love with the divine law: "As the law of God requires *love*, and nothing but love, considered as comprehending all the proper and genuine fruits and expressions of it; so the new creature, or that which is born of God, consists wholly in love, as it is conformity to the law of God," and thus conformity to divine love.[128] This connection of the law, as Hopkins understands it, and love, also has a connection to social needs:

> Christian practice consists, in part, in a proper conduct towards our fellow-men, or in that conduct of which our neighbor is the more immediate object, and is employed in relative and social duties; and this consists wholly in obeying the law of love, in loving our neighbor as ourselves, and in expressing and acting

companies and on all occasions, for the honor of God, and so as to recommend Christianity to all, being constantly concerned that his conversation should be as becometh the gospel of Christ." Hopkins, "How Christians Work Out Their Own Salvation: Sermon II," 599. The manner and time in which benevolence should be expressed is dependent on the needs of his neighbor.

[127]Hopkins, *TH*, 38.

[128]Hopkins, "The Application of Redemption," 375.

> out this love in the most natural and proper manner, in words and actions, on all occasions, and at all times.[129]

The believer is to obey the "law of love," engaging in benevolent acts to his neighbor in order to meet his specific needs. The character of Hopkins's disinterested benevolence is evident as sacrifice is required. One is to love his neighbor regardless of what is required and when it is required. This calls for humility as one elevates his neighbor as he seeks to serve him:

> A person who humbles himself renounces that self-exaltation and honor, in comparison with other beings, which pride and selfishness seek, and places his honor and happiness in abasing himself, and becoming the servant of all, by exalting God, and promoting his glory, and serving his fellow-creatures, ministering to their greatest good in the exercise of universal benevolence; and so obtains true exaltation and honor, which is most contrary to selfishness and pride.[130]

This attitude is found in sermons five, six, and eight of *CF*. Humility stemming from Christian benevolence is opposite of human pride and therefore, opposite of selfishness. Hopkins reiterates the need for selfless benevolence, serving his neighbor in all needed ways while bringing glory to God. In fact, the glory of God encompasses the good of one's neighbor as the believer lives selflessly for God and others:

> So he, who, in the exercise of holy love, pursues the glory of God and the highest interest and happiness of his kingdom, which includes the greatest good of his fellow-creatures, pursues the best, the most important interest, and has the most noble, refined pleasure in the exercise of this affection; yet in all this he is wholly disinterested, as he opposes selfishness and all regard to self, which is not implied in being thus devoted to the greatest general good, and forsakes the whole interest which self-love seeks, for the kingdom of God's sake.[131]

Hopkins again equates selfishness with self-love. To have one's neighbor in view is contrary to a selfish disposition. For a Christian, "the public

[129]Hopkins, "On Christian Practice," 194.

[130]Hopkins, *TH*, 54.

[131]Hopkins, *TH*, 30–31.

interest now appears to him to be infinitely greater," as he aims "to promote the greatest common good; and that self-love which is contrary to this, is enmity to the greatest good of the public, and to the good of society, and, therefore, enmity against God."[132] For both Edwards and Hopkins, selflessness is required in order to exude social concern.

In general, selfless benevolence will lead a believer to express kindness towards others. This is a theme which runs throughout the *CF* sermon series. Quoting 1 John 4:12, Hopkins explains that "by loving one another, while we see and converse with each other, with the love of benevolence and kindness in doing good to others, our love to God is expressed in the best and most perfect manner; especially as we herein imitate God, and follow him as his dear children."[133] As friendships are formed amongst Christians, "acts of beneficence and kindness" will take place as believers express "love and friendship in all proper ways," placing the needs of others before their own.[134] And referring to 1 John 3:17, Hopkins states, "It is to be observed, that the love to our brother here spoken of is the love of good will, expressed in showing kindness to him," illustrating the practical nature of genuine benevolence.[135]

Finally, Hopkins believed it was necessary that benevolence be extended to one's enemies. Edwards makes this clear in the sermon *The Spirit of the True Saints Is a Spirit of Divine Love*. An enemy is also considered a neighbor. Hopkins states, "The love to our neighbor, which God's law requires, is certainly universal, disinterested good will, since it is a love which will dispose us to do good unto all men, and must extend to our greatest enemies; for no love but this will do so."[136] Because enemies are considered neighbors, Christians are to love them "with cordial, friendly desires of their good and happiness, leading us to do them all the good

[132]Hopkins, "The Application of Redemption," 396.

[133]Hopkins, *TH*, 42.

[134]Hopkins, "On Christian Practice," 200. This also has implications for Christians to also bear the burdens of those in difficult situations. Discussing the close relationship between Christians, Hopkins explains, "Now, the more love and benevolence we have for our friends, the higher sympathy shall we have with them under their troubles, and their burdens and calamities will necessarily become ours in some measure; so that the higher degree of love and friendship we have for them, the more shall we suffer with them when they are in trouble." Samuel Hopkins, "A Discourse on Christian Friendship," in *The Works of Samuel Hopkins, D.D.*, vol. 2 (Boston: Doctrinal Tract and Book Society, 1854), 660. This discourse was written in 1767 and preached in six sermons. See Hopkins, "A Discourse on Christian Friendship," 625.

[135]Hopkins, *TH*, 35.

[136]Hopkins, *TH*, 35.

we can."[137] Doing so provides evidence of authentic Christianity. Believers are to go further and accept ill treatment from their enemies in order to exude disinterested love. This is an idea Edwards gives in the sermon *Living Peaceably One With Another*. Similarly, Hopkins explains:

> We hope we have that benevolent, universal love to all our fellow-men which is peculiar to Christians, which leads us to wish them the greatest good they are capable of enjoying in this life and in the world to come, and to do good as far as we have an opportunity; and we hope we love even our enemies, so that whatever evil they do, or attempt or desire to do us, this does not make us to cease to wish them well, and to do them all the good we can, and to pray heartily for their welfare; always studying and endeavoring, if it be possible, to live in peace with all men.[138]

Not only are believers to bear harm from enemies as an act of benevolence, but they must also seek to benefit them in all ways. Hopkins explains further what it means for a Christian to do good to his enemy:

> They must exercise a benevolent love to their worst enemies, whatever injuries they may have received from them; they must wish them well, do good to them, and pray for them in particular, while they are praying for all men; and if at any time they are convinced that they have injured any of their fellow-men, they must not rest till they have made all the reparation or restitution which is in their power, whatever mortification, cost, and pains this may require.[139]

Peace is to be sought at all costs, especially if a believer has harmed another individual in any way. In the end, love for enemies was demonstrated supremely in Christ. Hopkins states, "His love to men was, in the highest degree, disinterested benevolence, as it was love to enemies, and such a regard for their good as to lead him to be willing to take their misery on

[137]Hopkins, "The Application of Redemption," 384.

[138]Samuel Hopkins, "The Reason of the Christian's Hope, Which He Ought Always to Be Ready to Give," in *The Works of Samuel Hopkins, D.D.*, vol. 3 (Boston: Doctrinal Tract and Book Society, 1854), 717. This sermon was written in 1801. See Hopkins, "The Reason of the Christian's Hope, Which He Ought Always to Be Ready to Give," 689.

[139]Hopkins, "How Christians Work Out Their Own Salvation: Sermon II," 599–600.

himself, and bear it all, that they might escape and live forever."[140] Hopkins continues, stating that this type of love "is the highest instance of pure, disinterested benevolence that ever was known, and it is commonly spoken of as such, and the excellency of it is owned to consist very much in its being in such a striking degree disinterested love and goodness."[141] Love for enemies, as modeled by Christ, points to genuine, selfless love. Upon discussing selfishness, Hopkins explains,

> Therefore love to enemies is here enjoined as essential to the character of a disciple of Christ, so that no love which does not imply this disinterested benevolence, or love to enemies, is the love in which holiness consists, by which the true disciples of Christ are distinguished from others, every thing else which does not imply this being found with sinners. According to this, disinterested benevolence, or that love which will extend to enemies, is the holy love which distinguishes the true disciples of Christ from all others, and nothing will pass for true holiness in Christ's account but such love and what is implied in it.[142]

The character of this love, which reaches out to enemies, is God produced. It is what separates the Christian from those void of the Spirit. Edwards would agree, believing that the source of the benevolent life is the triune God.

To conclude, Hopkins aligned with Edwards's ethical theology. Both exuded clear social concern and activism in their respective doctrines of benevolence. Given the points of agreement between the two figures, we can conclude that Edwards's understanding of benevolence influenced Hopkins and his doctrine of disinterested benevolence. Thus, the social, activist stimuli in Edwards's doctrine encouraged Hopkins's abolitionism. Hopkins's opposition to slavery and the slave trade will be discussed next.

The Issue of Slavery

Hopkins's abolitionist posture began during his ministry in Newport, Rhode Island. He was first a pastor in Great Barrington, Massachusetts before agree-

[140]Hopkins, *TH*, 44–45.

[141]Hopkins, *TH*, 45.

[142]Hopkins, *TH*, 49.

ing to become the pastor at the First Congregational Church of Newport.[143] Essig sums up the impact the seaport had on Hopkins when witnessing the selling of slaves. Upon his arrival to Newport, Hopkins "began to make visits to the docks of a major slavetrading port, and there he beheld the ships unloading Africans onto the piers. It was perhaps this experience that first made Hopkins directly aware of the horrors of the slave trade and started him on his antislavery career."[144]

Specifically, after twenty-five years in Great Barrington, Massachusetts, Hopkins, like Edwards, was dismissed by his congregation from his pastorate.[145] Soon after arriving to Newport, Hopkins "began to denounce slavery from the pulpit and make house-to-house visitations to gather support for his views."[146] The inhumanity of the trade certainly made its mark

[143]James D. Essig, *The Bonds of Wickedness: American Evangelicals Against Slavery, 1770–1808* (Philadelphia: Temple University Press, 1982), 15.

[144]Essig, *The Bonds of Wickedness*, 15. Lovejoy notes that "it was at Newport that he commenced his antislavery campaign and at the same time absorbed Revolutionary ideas." David S. Lovejoy, "Samuel Hopkins: Religion, Slavery, and the Revolution," *New England Quarterly* 40, no. 2 (1967): 231. Conforti highlights Hopkins's rural experience from his pastorate in Great Barrington and the new, merchant class environment of Newport: "Hopkins's repudiation of the new morality and the self-love ethical theories upon which it was based originated in his rural upbringing and twenty-five year pastorate in the back-country. It was intensified by his experience of the worldly society and commercial economy of Newport, with its mercantile involvement in the slave trade and the production of rum which was used to secure human cargo on the coast of Africa. To the rustic theologian, committed to a simple and even ascetic socio-religious tradition, Newport appeared a symbol of what America was in danger of becoming — a society comprised of avaricious, self-centered individuals." Conforti, *Samuel Hopkins and the New Divinity Movement*, 125. Clearly the selfishness and materialism of the seaport was cause for discomfort. Hopkins himself makes this clear: "The inhabitants of Rhode Island, especially those of Newport, have had by far the greater share in this traffic of all these United States. This trade in the human species has been the first wheel of commerce in Newport, on which every other movement in business has chiefly depended. That town has been built up, and flourished in times past, at the expense of the blood, the liberty, and happiness of the poor Africans; and the inhabitants have lived on this, and by it have gotten most of their wealth and riches." Samuel Hopkins, "The Slave Trade and Slavery," in *The Works of Samuel Hopkins, D.D.*, vol. 2 (Boston: Doctrinal Tract and Book Society, 1854), 615.

[145]Essig, *The Bonds of Wickedness*, 89. According to Essig, reasons for his dismissal were "his strict communion policy" and "abstract" theologizing. Essig, *The Bonds of Wickedness*, 89. For a discussion of Hopkins's ministry to Native Americans in Great Barrington, see Swift, "Samuel Hopkins," 33–37.

[146]Essig, *The Bonds of Wickedness*, 90. For an example of an early antislavery sermon manuscript from Hopkins, see Samuel Hopkins and Jonathan D. Sassi, *"This Whole Country Have Their Hands Full of Blood This Day": Transcription and Introduction of an Antislavery Sermon Manuscript Attributed to the Reverend Samuel Hopkins* (Worcester: American Antiquarian Society, 2004). Sassi points out that the manuscript shows "that Hopkins's position went beyond his well-known *Dialogue*; that additional aspects of New Divinity theology fueled his attack; that the experience of living in Newport informed his position; and that his reading of other authors contributed

on Hopkins as he saw slaves being unloaded from the ships. He ended up being "the most outspoken antislavery advocate" amongst his New Divinity colleagues.[147] This is significant given that Hopkins was once a slave owner.[148] Importantly, he did manumit a slave sometime prior to 1770.[149] Yet Hopkins's transformation "into a dedicated antislavery reformer occurred between 1770–1773, the same years in which he developed his doctrine of disinterested benevolence."[150]

Clearly Hopkins's abolitionist stance arose from his doctrine of disinterested benevolence. Also, the equalitarianism of Revolutionary America had an impact on Hopkins as he believed, from his understanding of benevolence, that all men are equal and deserving of selfless love.[151] Disinterested benevolence will be extended to those who need "benevolence most, that is, the oppressed of mankind. And who, of all beings, asked Hopkins, were most oppressed and most needed universal good will but Negroes whose slavery was an offense to Christian benevolence?"[152] No one else needed more selfless benevolence than enslaved Africans, who lived in a state of subjugation.

As his doctrine of disinterested benevolence along with republican ideology influenced Hopkins's abolitionist posture, he sought to advocate for

to his development in ways heretofore unrecognized." Hopkins and Sassi, *This Whole Country Have Their Hands Full of Blood This Day*, 62.

[147]Kidd, *The Great Awakening*, 228.

[148]Before arriving at Newport in 1770, "Hopkins had not publicly or privately expressed any disapproval of or moral uneasiness with the slave trade or slavery." Conforti, *Samuel Hopkins and the New Divinity Movement*, 126. It is not surprising, then, that "for several years of Hopkins's residence at Great Barrington a black female servant lived in his household." Conforti, *Samuel Hopkins and the New Divinity Movement*, 126. Swift also notes: "Hopkins had evidently given little thought to the slave issue before he came to Newport. Indeed, he had owned a slave and sold him in Albany for $100 while pastor at Great Barrington." Swift, "Samuel Hopkins," 42. This is testament to the powerful influence of culture, given the changing socio-political landscape during the Revolutionary years, and personal experience.

[149]Sean McGever, *Ownership: The Evangelical Legacy of Slavery in Edwards, Wesley, and Whitefield* (Downers Grove: InterVarsity Press, 2024), 154.

[150]Conforti, *Samuel Hopkins and the New Divinity Movement*, 126. As demonstrated in this chapter, other sources beyond *TH* (1773) show Hopkins's understanding of disinterested benevolence. His *System of Doctrines* and sermons provide additional evidence of the ways disinterested benevolence is to be expressed. Given that Hopkins advocated for the abolition of slavery and the slave trade from his early years in Newport to the end of his life, I believe he continued to develop his doctrine of disinterested benevolence as evidenced in the mentioned works.

[151]Lovejoy, "Samuel Hopkins," 234.

[152]Lovejoy, "Samuel Hopkins," 233–34.

the rights of slaves.[153] Rightful equality was not being extended to enslaved Africans. Hopkins expresses this conviction in his *A Dialogue Concerning the State of the Africans*, addressed to the Continental Congress. Hopkins communicates to the members that slavery and the slave trade are evil realities that should be eradicated. From the beginning, Hopkins makes clear that slavery is sinful. He connects the culpability of slave-owning with the colonial struggle for liberty from Britain. Hopkins explains that "if the slavery in which we hold the blacks is wrong, it is a very great and public sin, and, therefore, a sin which God is now testifying against in the calamities he has brought upon us; consequently, must be reformed before we can reasonably expect deliverance, or even sincerely ask for it."[154] In Hopkins's mind, the only way for the colonies to experience liberty was for freedom to be brought to slaves. Only then would God allow the colonies to gain independence from the motherland. Slavery is a "scene of inhumanity, oppression, and cruelty — exceeding every thing of the kind that has ever been perpetrated by the sons of men — is suited to excite; and awaken us to a proper indignation against the authors of this violence and outrage done to their fellow-men, and to feelings of humanity and pity towards our brethren who are the miserable sufferers."[155] Hopkins espouses equalitarian sentiment as he considers enslaved Africans as fellow human beings and brothers.

The purchasing and selling of slaves also sustained and supported the slave trade.[156] This was a reality Edwards failed to see as he condoned institutionalized slavery while denouncing the slave trade. Furthermore, it is wrong to justify the slave trade and slavery by claiming that slaves are

[153]Kidd notes: "As the revolutionary crisis grew, Hopkins began to see slavery as sin, a symptom of the greed and acquisitiveness of American society, and a profound contradiction of the expressed ideals of American republicanism." Kidd, *The Great Awakening*, 230.

[154]Samuel Hopkins, "A Dialogue Concerning the Slavery of the Africans," in *The Works of Samuel Hopkins, D.D.*, vol. 2 (Boston: Doctrinal Tract and Book Society, 1854), 551. In an article published in 1784, Hopkins elaborates on this issue: "And as it is so important and necessary — in order to do justice to the injured Africans, and promote the public good, and our acting a consistent part, who have been such mighty advocates for *our own liberty* — that liberty should be restored to them, ought we to think much of a little expense, or of doing more than we think is our equal part, in order to answer such important ends?" Samuel Hopkins, "On the Slave Trade," in *The Works of Samuel Hopkins, D.D.*, vol. 2 (Boston: Doctrinal Tract and Book Society, 1854), 747. Colonists desiring their own liberty from Britain should also desire the liberty of enslaved Africans, as promoting such freedom is for the good of the whole.

[155]Hopkins, *DS*, 552–53.

[156]Hopkins, *DS*, 560.

presented with the gospel and introduced to Christianity.[157] If the motive was to truly "Christianize" the slaves, then the land from which they were taken should be "Christianized."[158] Hopkins argues that Christ "commands us to go and preach the gospel to all nations, to carry the gospel to them, and not to go and with violence bring them from their native country without saying a word to them, or to the nations from whom they are taken, about the gospel or any thing that relates to it."[159]

Enslaved Africans need to be considered as equals to white colonists.[160] They deserved freedom, not subjugation. For Hopkins, enslaved Africans are "by nature and by right on a level with our brethren and children, and those of our neighbors, and that benevolence which loves our neighbor as ourselves, and is agreeable to truth and righteousness, we should begin to feel towards them, in some measure at least, as we should towards our children and neighbors in the case above supposed, and be as much engaged for their relief."[161] Like Edwards, Hopkins did not believe there were any metaphysical differences between whites and Africans. Yet unlike Edwards, Hopkins did not denigrate non-European culture. And clearly, he did not believe slavery should be allowed.

While not discounting other sins, Hopkins did view the sin of slavery as especially egregious. Hopkins explains:

> But that this is a sin most particularly pointed out, and so contrary to our holy religion in every view of it, and such an open violation of all the laws of righteousness, humanity, and charity, and so contrary to our professions and exertions in the cause of liberty, that we have no reason to expect, nor can sincerely ask deliverance, so long as we continue in a disposition to hold fast this iniquity.[162]

As mentioned, the sin of slavery will continue to prohibit the freedom of the colonies. God will not honor such sin which is contrary to disinterested

[157]Hopkins, *DS*, 557.

[158]Hopkins, *DS*, 557.

[159]Hopkins, *DS*, 557.

[160]Hopkins, *DS*, 574.

[161]Hopkins, *DS*, 574.

[162]Hopkins, *DS*, 586.

benevolence. Thus the call is for the emancipation of slaves.[163] Valerie sums up Hopkins's *DS* well: "He insisted that genuinely revolutionary sensibilities would not countenance slavery and that disinterested benevolence should force slave owners and traders to sacrifice their own interests for the common good. Americans, he argued, could not consistently complain against imperial oppression while trading and owning slaves."[164] In short, disinterested benevolence towards African slaves requires the eradication of slavery and the slave trade.

In like manner, Hopkins addresses slave owners in *An Address to the Owners of Negro Slaves in the American Colonies*, again highlighting the evil of slave owning and the need for emancipation. As he did in *DS*, Hopkins points out the contradiction of the colonist's desire for freedom while enslaving Africans, which is a more severe form of enslavement.[165] Hopkins again emphasizes racial equality as he refers to those enslaved as brothers.[166] Justice is needed in light of their oppression: "Are not the African slaves among us the poor, the strangers, the fatherless, who are oppressed and vexed, and sold for silver?"[167] The consequences of condoning such a practice are clear: "And will not God visit and punish such oppression? Are you willing to be the instruments of bringing judgments and ruin on this land, and on yourselves and families, rather than let the oppressed go out free?"[168] The only way for peaceful living is by extending mercy to the oppressed.[169]

Hopkins makes clear that the inhumane treatment of slaves is contrary to the principles of Christianity.[170] Both slavery and the slave trade are works of Satan as "wicked men" subjugate "their fellow men."[171] In light of

[163]Hopkins, *DS*, 588.

[164]Mark Valeri, *Law and Providence in Joseph Bellamy's New England: The Origins of the New Divinity in Revolutionary America* (New York: Oxford University Press, 1994), 163.

[165]Samuel Hopkins, "An Address to the Owners of Negro Slaves in the American Colonies," in *The Works of Samuel Hopkins, D.D.*, vol. 2 (Boston: Doctrinal Tract and Book Society, 1854), 590.

[166]Hopkins, "An Address to the Owners of Negro Slaves in the American Colonies," 590.

[167]Hopkins, "An Address to the Owners of Negro Slaves in the American Colonies," 592.

[168]Hopkins, "An Address to the Owners of Negro Slaves in the American Colonies," 592.

[169]Hopkins, "An Address to the Owners of Negro Slaves in the American Colonies," 594.

[170]Samuel Hopkins, "A Discourse upon the Slave Trade and the Slavery of the Africans," in *The Works of Samuel Hopkins, D.D.*, vol. 2 (Boston: Doctrinal Tract and Book Society, 1854), 602.

[171]Hopkins, *DSS*, 604–5.

witnessing the oppression of enslaved Africans in Newport, Hopkins believed it was an evil that needed to be eradicated immediately. As a solution to the hardships they would continue to face, Hopkins espoused the notion of sending freed Africans back to Africa:

> Let us consult and determine what we may do in favor of the blacks among us, especially those who are free, in protecting them from oppression and injuries, by encouraging and assisting them to industry and a prudent management of their worldly affairs, attempting to reform the vicious, to instruct the ignorant, and promote morality, virtue, and religion among them, and providing for the education of their children in useful learning, that they may be raised to an acknowledged equality with the white people, and some of them, of the most promising abilities and piety, be fitted to preach the gospel to their brethren in Africa, and that numbers may be the better prepared to move to that region, and settle there, and set an example of industry and wisdom in cultivating the land of that fertile country, and of the practice of Christianity, which will have the best tendency to civilize those now barbarous nations, to spread the light of the gospel among them, and persuade them to be Christians.[172]

While Hopkins championed the full emancipation of African slaves, he did not envision their freedom in the American colonies.[173] His perspective was not only informed by personal concern for Africans, but also by evangelistic considerations, desiring the gospel to be brought to Africa.[174] Hopkins explains:

[172]Hopkins, *DSS*, 608. Saillant points out how Hopkins also saw it as an opportunity for white colonists to exercise selfless benevolence: "Indeed, Hopkins understood the effort to christianize Africa through the 'return' of black Americans as a crucial opportunity for benevolent whites to exercise their virtue. Having forced the termination of slavery and the slave trade, they would then prepare blacks to 'return' to Africa." John Saillant, "Slavery and Divine Providence in New England Calvinism: The New Divinity and a Black Protest, 1775–1805," *New England Quarterly* 68, no. 4 (1995): 595.

[173]Sherard Burns, "Trusting the Theology of a Slave Owner," in *A God Entranced Vision of All Things: The Legacy of Jonathan Edwards*, ed. John Piper and Justin Taylor (Wheaton, IL: Crossway Books, 2004), 166.

[174]Cowing and Burns provide examples of differing perspectives. Cowing, mentioning Hopkins's millennialist emphasis, states: "He wanted to send the Negroes back to Africa, not to avoid miscegenation but to evangelize the natives of the Dark Continent before the Second Coming." Cedric B. Cowing, *The Great Awakening and the American Revolution: Colonial Thought in the 18th Century* (Chicago: Rand McNally, 1971), 115. Burns points to other possible factors: "While they all shared an understanding that the immediate effects of abolitionism were the

> Is there not good reason to believe, that if this nation, the inhabitants in the United States of America, both high and low, rulers and ruled, had a proper view and sense of the unrighteousness of the slave trade and the slavery of the Africans, and of the sore calamity and misery of millions of our fellow-men in Africa, the West Indies, and on this continent, as the effect of this iniquity, not only a stop would be put to this trade, and all the slaves among us be set free as fast as possible, but such a strong compassion would be excited towards these injured, miserable men, and desire and zeal to make all possible compensation to them, and render them happy, that no exertions or expense would be thought too much which would be required to transport those to Africa who should be disposed to go and settle there, and to furnish them with every thing necessary and convenient for their being settled there in the best circumstances suited to promote their temporal and eternal happiness, and of the nations on that vast continent? How happy, if we, as a people and nation, should cheerfully unite in this from motives of justice and benevolence, and a desire that the gospel may be preached to every creature![175]

By sending freed Africans, given the gospel in the colonies, back to Africa with financial and material support, Hopkins believed Africa could then bear

spiritual and physical freedom of the Africans, it was their understanding of the long-term solution that created separation. To Hopkins and Edwards, Jr., the long-term solution was expatriation. While they conceived of freedom for the Africans, they had not intended that such freedom be exercised in the colonies, fearing a number of things, most notably intermarrying and retribution." Burns, "Trusting the Theology of a Slave Owner," 166. While evangelization, concern for intermarrying, and fear of retribution could all be reasons for Hopkins's stance, it seems that Cowing's perspective on the need for evangelization is likely given the gospel emphasis of the discourse. It is also important to note Hopkins's concern for non-Europeans and their habitual oppression by white colonists. Swift, "Samuel Hopkins," 35. Jauhiainen notes Hopkins's compassion towards Africans due to the personal and economic disadvantages they would continue to face at the hands of the colonists. Jauhiainen, "An Enlightenment Calvinist," 323–25. Nonetheless, the fact that Hopkins did not envision a society where whites and freed Africans would live together is surprising, given his doctrine of disinterested benevolence. Perhaps it was a concern for unhappy slaves due to constant oppression and a desire to see them back in their homeland for their sake. Perhaps there was some thought of necessary racial separation. Because Hopkins only discussed the need for the continent of Africa to have Christian witness, the need to support freed Africans both personally and materially for their voyage back, and sadness for the continued oppression of Africans, other reasons are left for speculation.

[175] Hopkins, *DSS*, 608–9.

Christian witness. Consequently, while Hopkins fought for the abolition of slavery and the slave trade, he did not envision a society where whites and freed Africans could coexist together due to increasing racial prejudice.[176] That would be a reality in the future: "The slave trade, and all slavery, shall be totally abolished, and the gospel shall be preached to all nations; good shall be brought out of all the evil which takes place, and all men shall be united into one family and kingdom under Christ the Savior; and the meek shall inherit the earth, and delight themselves in the abundance of peace."[177] In the end, If Africa can be reached with the gospel, there is optimism for worldwide evangelism. According to Hopkins, what is needed first is the eradication of institutionalized slavery and slave trade for the kingdom to be established on earth.[178]

Conclusion

Overall, Hopkins aligned with Edwards's virtue theory. Both evidenced the philosophical, theocentric, and activist dimensions of ethics. Both believed God created an inclusive system where every individual is represented. As a result, benevolence is to be extended to all human beings. Both believed proper self-regard is selfless in nature, embracing the betterment and happiness of others. Both believed love results in neighborly unity. Both believed in the singular nature of a supreme love for God and ensuing love for others. Both believed that God, by way of the Spirit, is the source of a holy life. And both had clear stimuli for social concern and activism in their respective doctrines of benevolence. Thus, Hopkins did not diverge and

[176]Conforti, *Samuel Hopkins and the New Divinity Movement*, 148.

[177]Hopkins, *DSS*, 609.

[178]Conforti, *Samuel Hopkins and the New Divinity Movement*, 144, 153–54. Unlike Hopkins, Edwards believed world evangelization and missions could grow amid the institution of slavery. Hopkins succeeded by applying his doctrine of disinterested benevolence to the slavery issue while Edwards failed to fully apply his doctrine of benevolence to those enslaved by condoning the institution. As discussed in chapter 4, Edwards viewed all people as spiritual equals irrespective of race. The fact that Edwards allowed enslaved Africans to be full communicant members of his Northampton church is key. In the end, the conviction and pursuit to reach the world with the gospel was the same for both men. Yet because of Edwards's proslavery position, they diverged in practice regarding slavery. For recent examples of Edwards's preaching to enslaved Africans and Native Americans, see John A. Grigg, "Missions" in *The Oxford Handbook of Jonathan Edwards*, eds. Douglas A. Sweeney and Jan Stievermann (Oxford: Oxford University Press, 2021), 416–30; John Saillant, "Ministry to the Bound and Enslaved" in *The Oxford Handbook of Jonathan Edwards*, eds. Douglas A. Sweeney and Jan Stievermann (Oxford: Oxford University Press, 2021), 431–45.

change Edwards's doctrine of benevolence to Being in general, but was in agreement with his mentor. Moreover, a broader understanding of Edwards's doctrine of benevolence influenced Hopkins and his doctrine of disinterested benevolence. This is confirmed by congruence. It was Hopkins's dependence on and resultant derivation of social activism from Edwards's doctrine of benevolence that encouraged Hopkins's abolitionism. As a result, Hopkins was more consistent with Edwards's ethical theology as they diverged in practice regarding the issue of slavery.

CHAPTER 6: CONCLUSION

IN THIS STUDY, I PROVIDED a comparative examination of Edwards's and Hopkins's virtue theories. More specifically, I examined Hopkins's doctrine of disinterested benevolence in relation to Edwards's doctrine of benevolence to provide evidence of congruence between the two figures. I highlighted a number of reasons for the need of this study in chapters one and two. In summary, there have been and continue to be claims of Hopkins's departure from Edwards's virtue theory. Edwards has been portrayed as one who lacked social concern and activism due to the philosophical and/or theocentric nature of his ethical thought. Thus, Hopkins's practically oriented doctrine of disinterested benevolence is seen as diverging from his mentor's theory. Yet Hopkins, like Edwards, exuded philosophical and theocentric dimensions in his virtue theory. And Edwards, like Hopkins, stressed social activism in his ethical thought. In short, both have philosophical, theocentric, and activist dimensions in their respective virtue theories. Though Hopkins was in agreement with his mentor, they differed in regards to their stance on slavery.

To evidence congruence between Edwards and Hopkins, I first established a holistic account of Edwards's virtue theory in chapter four by highlighting the philosophical, theocentric, and activist aspects. Scholars have tended to focus on the philosophical and/or God-centered aspects to delineate Edwards's ethical thought until recent revisionist accounts have brought attention to the practical side of his virtue theory. I then established Hopkins's virtue theory by showing the philosophical, God-centered, and practical aspects, providing a holistic account of Hopkins's theory as well. This is important because Hopkins has been portrayed as an ethical pragmatist, with little attention being given to the philosophical and/or theocentric dimensions to his virtue theory. In the end, while there is some diversity, Hopkins maintained the inherent integrity of Edwards's virtue theory.

In order to understand Edwards's proslavery stance and Hopkins's abolitionism in light of agreement, I showed Hopkins's congruence with Edwards's ethical theology by way of Edwards's doctrine of benevolence. I provided evidence of clear social and activist stimuli located in Edwards's doctrine that Hopkins used to derive social concern and activism for his abolitionist stance. In chapter three, I established the social and cultural realities that influenced both figures in their respective historical milieus. Because slavery was largely unquestioned in prerevolutionary America and because antislavery sentiment grew during the Revolutionary years, Edwards and Hopkins ended up on opposite ends of the slavery issue. Where Edwards failed, Hopkins succeeded by faithfully applying his mentor's doctrine of benevolence via disinterested benevolence to fight for the eradication of both the slave trade and institutionalized slavery.

To conclude, I have argued in this study that Hopkins was more consistent with Edwards's ethical theology by faithfully applying Edwards's doctrine of benevolence to fight for the abolition of institutionalized slavery and the slave trade. Hopkins's congruence and derivation of social concern and activism from Edwards's doctrine of benevolence substantiate this claim.

Additional comparative studies of Edwards and Hopkins would be advantageous for identifying areas of continuity and discontinuity between the two figures. A study of continuity could be an examination of their Trinitarian thought. As God is the source of the moral life, this can also be connected to their virtue theories. A study of discontinuity could be an examination of their soteriologies. While Edwards embraced more of a penal substitutionary view, Hopkins held to a governmental theory of the atonement.

Bibliography

Primary Sources

Edwards, Jonathan. *A History of the Work of Redemption*. Edited by John F. Wilson. Vol. 9. *The Works of Jonathan Edwards*. New Haven, CT: Yale University Press, 1989.

Edwards, Jonathan. *Apocalyptic Writings*. Edited by Stephen J. Stein. Vol. 5. *The Works of Jonathan Edwards*. New Haven, CT: Yale University Press, 1977.

Edwards, Jonathan. *Ecclesiastical Writings*. Edited by David D. Hall. Vol. 12. *The Works of Jonathan Edwards*. New Haven, CT: Yale University Press, 1994.

Edwards, Jonathan. *Ethical Writings*. Edited by Paul Ramsey. Vol. 8. *The Works of Jonathan Edwards*. New Haven, CT: Yale University Press, 1989.

Edwards, Jonathan. *Freedom of the Will*. Edited by Paul Ramsey. Vol. 1. *The Works of Jonathan Edwards*. New Haven, CT: Yale University Press, 2009.

Edwards, Jonathan. *Original Sin*. Edited by Clyde A. Holbrook. Vol. 3. *The Works of Jonathan Edwards*. New Haven, CT: Yale University Press, 1970.

Edwards, Jonathan. *Religious Affections*. Edited by John E. Smith. Vol. 2. *The Works of Jonathan Edwards*. New Haven, CT: Yale University Press, 2009.

Edwards, Jonathan. *Sermons and Discourses, 1720–1723*. Edited by Wilson H. Kimnach. Vol. 10. *The Works of Jonathan Edwards*. New Haven, CT: Yale University Press, 1992.

Edwards, Jonathan. *Sermons and Discourses, 1723–1729*. Edited by Kenneth P. Minkema. Vol. 14. *The Works of Jonathan Edwards*. New Haven, CT: Yale University Press, 1997.

Edwards, Jonathan. *Sermons and Discourses, 1730–1733*. Edited by Mark Valeri. Vol. 17. *The Works of Jonathan Edwards*. New Haven, CT: Yale University Press, 1999.

Edwards, Jonathan. *Sermons and Discourses, 1739–1742*. Edited by Harry S. Stout, Nathan O. Hatch, and Kyle P. Farley. Vol. 22. *The Works of Jonathan Edwards*. New Haven, CT: Yale University Press, 2003.

Edwards, Jonathan. *Sermons and Discourses, 1743–1758*. Edited by Wilson H. Kimnach. Vol. 25. *The Works of Jonathan Edwards*. New Haven, CT: Yale University Press, 2006.

Edwards, Jonathan. *The Great Awakening*. Edited by C. C. Goen. Vol. 4. *The Works of Jonathan Edwards*. New Haven, CT: Yale University Press, 2009.

Edwards, Jonathan. *The "Miscellanies," 501-832*. Edited by Ava Chamberlain. Vol. 18. *The Works of Jonathan Edwards*. New Haven, CT: Yale University Press, 2000.

Edwards, Jonathan. *The "Miscellanies," 833-1152*. Edited by Amy Plantinga Pauw. Vol. 20. *The Works of Jonathan Edwards*. New Haven, CT: Yale University Press, 2002.

Edwards, Jonathan. *The "Miscellanies," 1153-1360*. Edited by Douglas A. Sweeney. Vol. 23. *The Works of Jonathan Edwards*. New Haven, CT: Yale University Press, 2004.

Edwards, Jonathan. *The "Miscellanies," a-500*. Edited by Thomas A. Schafer. Vol. 13. *The Works of Jonathan Edwards*. New Haven, CT: Yale University Press, 1994.

Edwards, Jonathan. *Writings on the Trinity, Grace, and Faith*. Edited by Sang Hyun Lee. Vol. 21. *The Works of Jonathan Edwards*. New Haven, CT: Yale University Press, 2002.

Hopkins, Samuel. *The Works of Samuel Hopkins, D.D.* 3 vols. Boston: Doctrinal Tract and Book Society, 1854.

Books

Ahlstrom, Sydney E. *A Religious History of the American People*. 2nd ed. New Haven: Yale University Press, 2004.

Almond, Philip C. *Heaven and Hell in Enlightenment England*. Cambridge: Cambridge University Press, 1994.

Ames, William. *The Marrow of Theology*. Translated by John Dykstra Eusden. Boston: Pilgrim, 1968.

Arminius, Jacobus. *Arminius Speaks: Essential Writings on Predestination, Free Will, and the Nature of God*. Edited by John D. Wagner. Eugene, OR: Wipf & Stock, 2011.

Arminius, Jacobus. *The Writings of James Arminius*. Translated by James Nichols and W. R. Bagnall. 3 vols. Grand Rapids: Baker, 1977.

Audi, Robert. *The Cambridge Dictionary of Philosophy*. New York: Cambridge University Press, 2015.

Axtell, James. *The Invasion Within: The Contest of Cultures in Colonial North America*. New York: Oxford University Press, 1985.

Bailey, Richard A. *Race and Redemption in Puritan New England*. New York: Oxford University Press, 2011.

Bailyn, Bernard. *The Ideological Origins of the American Revolution*. Cambridge, MA: Belknap Press of Harvard University Press, 1967.

Baldwin, Alice M. *The New England Clergy and the American Revolution*. New York: F. Ungar, 1958.

Beeman, Richard R. *The Varieties of Political Experience in Eighteenth Century America*. Philadelphia: University of Pennsylvania Press, 2004.

Bezzant, Rhys S. *Jonathan Edwards and the Church*. Oxford: Oxford University Press, 2014.

Bombaro, John J. *Jonathan Edwards's Vision of Reality: The Relationship of God to the World, Redemption History, and the Reprobate*. Eugene, OR: Pickwick, 2012.

Bonwick, Colin. *The American Revolution*. Charlottesville, VA: University Press of Virginia, 1991.

Bozeman, T. Dwight. *To Live Ancient Lives: The Primitivist Dimension in Puritanism*. Chapel Hill: University of North Carolina Press, 1988.

Brand, David C. *Profile of the Last Puritan: Jonathan Edwards, Self-Love, and the Dawn of the Beatific*. Atlanta, GA: Scholars Press, 1991.

Bremer, Francis J., ed. *Puritanism: Transatlantic Perspectives on a Seventeenth-Century Anglo-American Faith*. Boston: Massachusetts Historical Society, 1993.

Bremer, Francis J. *The Puritan Experiment: New England Society from Bradford to Edwards*. Hanover, NH: University Press of New England, 1995.

Bremer, Francis J., and Tom Webster, eds. *Puritans and Puritanism in Europe and America: A Comprehensive Encyclopedia*. 2 vols. Santa Barbara, CA: ABC-CLIO, 2006.

Brooke, John Hedley. *Science and Religion: Some Historical Perspectives*. Cambridge: Cambridge University Press, 1991.

Brown, Robert E. *Jonathan Edwards and the Bible*. Bloomington: Indiana University Press, 2002.

Buckley, Kerry W. *A Place Called Paradise: Culture and Community in Northampton, Massachusetts, 1654–2004*. Boston: University of Massachusetts Press, 2004.

Bumsted, J. M. *What Must I Do to Be Saved? The Great Awakening in Colonial America*. Hinsdale, IL: Dryden Press, 1976.

Bushman, Richard L. *From Puritan to Yankee: Character and the Social Order in Connecticut, 1690–1765*. Cambridge: Harvard University Press, 1967.

Caldwell III, Robert W. *Communion in the Spirit: The Holy Spirit as the Bond of Union in the Theology of Jonathan Edwards*. Milton Keynes, UK: Paternoster, 2006.

Calloway, Colin G., and Neal Salisbury. *Reinterpreting New England Indians and the Colonial Experience*. Boston: Colonial Society of Massachusetts, 2009.

Cassirer, Ernst. *The Philosophy of the Enlightenment*. Princeton, NJ: Princeton University Press, 1951.

Chai, Leon. *Jonathan Edwards and the Limits of Enlightenment Philosophy*. New York: Oxford University Press, 1998.

Cherry, Conrad. *Nature and Religious Imagination: From Edwards to Bushnell*. Philadelphia: Fortress Press, 1980.

Cherry, Conrad. *The Theology of Jonathan Edwards: A Reappraisal*. Bloomington, IN: Indiana University Press, 1990.

Cho, Hyun-Jin. *Jonathan Edwards on Justification: Reformed Development of the Doctrine in Eighteenth-Century New England*. Lanham, MD: University Press of America, 2012.

Clark, Christopher. *The Roots of Rural Capitalism: Western Massachusetts, 1780–1860*. Ithaca, NY: Cornell University Press, 1990.

Clebsch, William A. *American Religious Thought: A History*. Chicago: University of Chicago Press, 1973.

Cochran, Elizabeth A. *Receptive Human Virtues: A New Reading of Jonathan Edwards's Ethics*. University Park, PA: Penn State University Press, 2011.

Conforti, Joseph A. *Jonathan Edwards, Religious Tradition, and American Culture*. Chapel Hill: University of North Carolina Press, 1995.

Conforti, Joseph A. *Samuel Hopkins and the New Divinity Movement: Calvinism, the Congregational Ministry, and Reform in New England Between the Great Awakenings*. Grand Rapids: Christian University Press, 1981.

Conkin, Paul Keith. *The Uneasy Center: Reformed Christianity in Antebellum America*. Chapel Hill: University of North Carolina Press, 1995.

Corrigan, John. *The Hidden Balance: Religion and the Social Theories of Charles Chauncy and Jonathan Mayhew*. Cambridge: Cambridge University Press, 1987.

Coughtry, Jay. *The Notorious Triangle: Rhode Island and the African Slave Trade, 1700–1807*. Philadelphia: Temple University Press, 1981.

Cowing, Cedric B. *The Great Awakening and the American Revolution: Colonial Thought in the 18th Century*. Chicago: Rand McNally, 1971.

Cragg, Gerald R. *From Puritanism to the Age of Reason: A Study of Changes in Religious Thought within the Church of England, 1660 to 1700*. Cambridge: Cambridge University Press, 1950.

Cragg, Gerald R. *Reason and Authority in the Eighteenth Century*. Cambridge: Cambridge University Press, 1964.

Cragg, Gerald R. *The Church and the Age of Reason, 1648–1789*. Grand Rapids: Eerdmans, 1960.

Crane, Elaine Forman. *A Dependent People: Newport, Rhode Island in the Revolutionary Era*. New York: Fordham University Press, 1985.

Crisp, Oliver. *Jonathan Edwards on God and Creation*. New York: Oxford University Press, 2012.

Crisp, Oliver D., and Douglas A. Sweeney, eds. *After Jonathan Edwards: The Courses of the New England Theology*. New York: Oxford University Press, 2012.

Dallimore, Arnold A. *George Whitefield: The Life and Times of the Great Evangelist of the Eighteenth-Century Revival*. London: Banner of Truth Trust, 1970.

Danaher, William J. *The Trinitarian Ethics of Jonathan Edwards*. Louisville, KY: Westminster John Knox, 2004.

Davis, David Brion. *Inhuman Bondage: The Rise and Fall of Slavery in the New World*. Oxford: Oxford University Press, 2006.

Davis, David Brion. *The Problem of Slavery in the Age of Revolution, 1770–1823*. Ithaca, NY: Cornell University Press, 1975.

Davis, David Brion. *The Problem of Slavery in Western Culture*. Ithaca, NY: Cornell University Press, 1966.

De Jong, Peter Y. *The Covenant Idea in New England Theology, 1620–1847*. Grand Rapids: Eerdmans, 1945.

Delattre, Roland A. *Beauty and Sensibility in the Thought of Jonathan Edwards: An Essay in Aesthetics and Theological Ethics*. New Haven, CT: Yale University Press, 1968.

Dodds, Elisabeth D. *Marriage to a Difficult Man: The Uncommon Union of Jonathan and Sarah Edwards*. Philadelphia: Westminster, 1971.

Dyrness, William A. *Reformed Theology and Visual Culture: The Protestant Imagination from Calvin to Edwards*. Cambridge: Cambridge University Press, 2004.

Elwood, Douglas J. *The Philosophical Theology of Jonathan Edwards*. New York: Columbia University Press, 1960.

Erdt, Terrence. *Jonathan Edwards, Art and the Sense of the Heart*. Amherst: University of Massachusetts Press, 1980.

Essig, James D. *The Bonds of Wickedness: American Evangelicals Against Slavery, 1770–1808*. Philadelphia: Temple University Press, 1982.

Evans, William B. *Imputation and Impartation: Union with Christ in American Reformed Theology*. Milton Keynes, UK: Paternoster, 2008.

Ferguson, John. *Memoir of the Life and Character of Rev. Samuel Hopkins, D.D.* Boston: L.W. Kimball, 1830.

Ferm, Robert L. *Jonathan Edwards the Younger, 1745–1801: A Colonial Pastor*. Grand Rapids: Eerdmans, 1976.

Fiering, Norman. *Jonathan Edwards's Moral Thought and Its British Context*. Chapel Hill: University of North Carolina Press, 1981.

Foster, Frank Hugh. *A Genetic History of the New England Theology*. New York: Garland, 1987.

Foster, Stephen. *Their Solitary Way: The Puritan Social Ethic in the First Century of Settlement in New England*. New Haven, CT: Yale University Press, 1971.

Franklin, John Hope. *From Slavery to Freedom: A History of Negro Americans*. 4th ed. New York: Knopf, 1974.

Gambrell, Mary Latimer. *Ministerial Training in Eighteenth-Century New England*. New York: AMS, 1967.

Gaustad, Edwin S. *The Great Awakening in New England*. New York: Harper, 1957.

Gay, Peter. *Deism: An Anthology*. Princeton, NJ: Van Nostrand, 1968.

Gay, Peter. *The Enlightenment: A Comprehensive Anthology*. New York: Simon & Schuster, 1985.

Gay, Peter. *The Enlightenment: An Interpretation*. Vol. 1. New York: Knopf, 1967.

Gay, Peter. *The Enlightenment: An Interpretation*. Vol. 2. New York: Knopf, 1969.

Gill, Robin. *The Cambridge Companion to Christian Ethics*. Cambridge: Cambridge University Press, 2001.

Grass, Günter. *Der Traum der Vernunft: Vom Elend der Aufklärung*. Darmstadt: Luchterhand, 1985.

Greene, Lorenzo J. *The Negro in Colonial New England: 1620–1776*. 1942. Reprint, Eastford, CT: Martino, 2016.

Guelzo, Allen C. *Edwards on the Will: A Century of American Theological Debate*. Middletown, CT: Wesleyan University Press, 1989.

Gura, Philip F. *A Glimpse of Sion's Glory: Puritan Radicalism in New England, 1620–1660*. Middletown, CT: Wesleyan University Press, 1984.

Gura, Philip F. *Jonathan Edwards: America's Evangelical*. New York: Hill and Wang, 2006.

Gustafson, James M. *Ethics From a Theocentric Perspective*. Chicago: University of Chicago Press, 1981.

Hall, Richard A. S. *The Contribution of Jonathan Edwards to American Culture and Society: Essays on America's Spiritual Founding Father (The Northampton Tercentenary Celebration, 1703–2003)*. Lewiston, NY: Edwin Mellen, 2008.

Hall, Richard A. S. *The Neglected Northampton Texts of Jonathan Edwards: Edwards on Society and Politics*. Vol. 52. *Studies in American Religion*. Lewiston, NY: Edwin Mellen, 1990.

Hammond, Geordan, and David Ceri Jones. *George Whitefield: Life, Context, and Legacy*. Oxford: Oxford University Press, 2016.

Hampe, Johann Christoph. *Ehre und Elend der Aufklärung gestern wie heute: Ein engagierter Vergleich*. Munich: Kaiser, 1971.

Haroutunian, Joseph. *Piety Versus Moralism: The Passing of the New England Theology*. New York: H. Holt, 1932.

Hart, D. G., Sean Michael Lucas, and Stephen J. Nichols, eds. *The Legacy of Jonathan Edwards: American Religion and the Evangelical Tradition*. Grand Rapids: Baker Academic, 2003.

Hart, William. *A Sermon of a New Kind, Never Preached, nor Ever Will Be; Containing a Collection of Doctrines, Belonging to the Hopkintonian Scheme of Orthodoxy*. New Haven, CT: T. and S. Green, 1769.

Hart, William. *Brief Remarks on a Number of False Propositions, and Dangerous Errors, Which Are Spreading in the Country; Collected out of Sundry Discourses Lately Publish'd, Wrote by Dr. Whitaker and Mr. Hopkins*. New London: T. and S. Green, 1769.

Hart, William. *Remarks on President Edwards's Dissertations Concerning the Nature of True Virtue: Shewing That He Has given a Wrong Idea, and Definition of Virtue, and Is Inconsistent with Himself*. New Haven, CT: T. and S. Green, 1771.

Hastings, Ross. *Jonathan Edwards and the Life of God: Toward an Evangelical Theology of Participation*. Minneapolis, MN: Fortress, 2015.

Hatch, Nathan O. *The Sacred Cause of Liberty: Republican Thought and the Millennium in Revolutionary New England*. New Haven, CT: Yale University Press, 1977.

Hatch, Nathan O., and Harry S. Stout, eds. *Jonathan Edwards and the American Experience*. New York: Oxford University Press, 1988.

Hauerwas, Stanley. *Character and the Christian Life: A Study in Theological Ethics*. San Antonio: Trinity University Press, 1975.

Haykin, Michael. *A Sweet Flame: Piety in the Letters of Jonathan Edwards*. Grand Rapids: Reformation Heritage Books, 2013.

Hazard, Paul. *La crise de la conscience européenne, 1680–1715*. Paris: Le Livre de Poche, 1994.

Hazard, Paul. *La pensée européenne au XVIIIe siècle: De Montesquieu à Lessing*. Paris: Hachette Littératures, 2006.

Heimert, Alan. *Religion and the American Mind: From the Great Awakening to the Revolution*. Cambridge: Harvard University Press, 1966.

Helm, Paul, and Oliver Crisp. *Jonathan Edwards: Philosophical Theologian*. Burlington, VT: Ashgate, 2003.

Hempton, David. *The Church in the Long Eighteenth Century*. New York: I. B. Tauris, 2011.

Henry, Stuart C. *George Whitefield: Wayfaring Witness*. New York: Abingdon, 1957.

Hillerbrand, Hans Joachim. *Encyclopedia of Protestantism*. New York: Routledge, 2004.

Hoffer, Peter Charles, ed. *The Marrow of American Divinity: Selected Articles on Colonial Religion*. New York: Garland, 1988.

Holbrook, Clyde A. *The Ethics of Jonathan Edwards: Morality and Aesthetics*. Ann Arbor: University of Michigan Press, 1973.

Holifield, E. Brooks. *Theology in America: Christian Thought from the Age of the Puritans to the Civil War*. New Haven, CT: Yale University Press, 2003.

Holmes, Stephen R. *God of Grace and God of Glory: An Account of the Theology of Jonathan Edwards*. Grand Rapids: Eerdmans, 2001.

Hopkins, Samuel. *Sketches of the Life of the Late Rev. Samuel Hopkins, D.D., Pastor of the First Congregational Church in Newport*. Edited by Stephen West. Hartford, CT: Hudson and Goodwin, 1805.

Hopkins, Samuel. *The Life and Character of the Late Reverend, Learned, and Pious Mr. Jonathan Edwards, President of the College of New Jersey*. Northampton, MA: S. & E. Butler, 1804.

Hopkins, Samuel, and Jonathan D. Sassi. *"This Whole Country Have Their Hands Full of Blood This Day": Transcription and Introduction of an Antislavery Sermon Manuscript Attributed to the Reverend Samuel Hopkins*. Worcester: American Antiquarian Society, 2004.

Howe, Daniel Walker. *Making the American Self: Jonathan Edwards to Abraham Lincoln*. Cambridge, MA: Harvard University Press, 1997.

Hudson, Winthrop S. *Religion in America*. 3rd ed. New York: Scribner, 1981.

Hutcheson, Francis. *An Inquiry into the Original of our Ideas of Beauty and Virtue; In Two Treatises*. Rev. ed. Indianapolis: Liberty Fund, 2008.

James, Sydney V. *Colonial Rhode Island: A History*. New York: Scribner, 1975.

Jenson, Robert W. *America's Theologian: A Recommendation of Jonathan Edwards*. New York: Oxford University Press, 1992.

Jones, James William. *The Shattered Synthesis: New England Puritanism before the Great Awakening*. New Haven, CT: Yale University Press, 1973.

Jordan, Don, and Michael Walsh. *White Cargo: The Forgotten History of Britain's White Slaves in America*. New York: New York University Press, 2008.

Kidd, Thomas S. *George Whitefield: America's Spiritual Founding Father*. New Haven, CT: Yale University Press, 2014.

Kidd, Thomas S. *God of Liberty: A Religious History of the American Revolution*. New York: Basic Books, 2010.

Kidd, Thomas S. *The Great Awakening: The Roots of Evangelical Christianity in Colonial America*. New Haven, CT: Yale University Press, 2007.

Kling, David William. *A Field of Divine Wonders: The New Divinity and Village Revivals in Northwestern Connecticut, 1792–1822*. University Park, PA: Pennsylvania State University Press, 1993.

Kling, David William. *Edwards and the Edwardseans: Jonathan Edwards, the New Divinity, and the Making of a Theological Culture*. Eugene, OR: Pickwick Publications, 2021.

Kling, David William, and Douglas A. Sweeney, eds. *Jonathan Edwards at Home and Abroad: Historical Memories, Cultural Movements, Global Horizons*. Columbia, SC: University of South Carolina Press, 2003.

Knight, Janice. *Orthodoxies in Massachussetts: Rereading American Puritanism*. Cambridge, MA: Harvard University Press, 1997.

Kreider, Glenn R. *Jonathan Edwards's Interpretation of Revelation 4:1–8:1*. Lanham, MD: University Press of America, 2004.

Kuklick, Bruce. *Churchmen and Philosophers: From Jonathan Edwards to John Dewey*. New Haven, CT: Yale University Press, 1985.

Kunneman, Harry, and Hent de Vries, eds. *Die Aktualität der "Dialektik der Aufklärung": Zwischen Moderne und Postmoderne*. Frankfurt am Main: Campus, 1989.

Leach, Douglas Edward. *Arms for Empire: A Military History of the British Colonies in North America, 1607–1763*. New York: Macmillan, 1973.

Lee, Sang Hyun. *The Philosophical Theology of Jonathan Edwards*. Princeton, NJ: Princeton University Press, 1988.

Lee, Sang Hyun. *The Princeton Companion to Jonathan Edwards*. Princeton, NJ: Princeton University Press, 2005.

Lee, Sang Hyun, and Allen C. Guelzo, eds. *Edwards in Our Time: Jonathan Edwards and the Shaping of American Religion*. Grand Rapids: Eerdmans, 1999.

Levin, David. *Jonathan Edwards: A Profile*. New York: Hill and Wang, 1969.

Livingston, James C. *Modern Christian Thought: The Enlightenment and the Nineteenth Century*. Minneapolis: Fortress Press, 2006.

Lovejoy, David S. *Samuel Hopkins: Religion, Slavery, and the Revolution*. Philadelphia: United Church Press, 1976.

Lucas, Paul R. *Valley of Discord: Church and Society along the Connecticut River, 1636–1725*. Hanover, NH: University Press of New England, 1976.

Lucas, Sean Michael. *God's Grand Design: The Theological Vision of Jonathan Edwards*. Wheaton, IL: Crossway, 2011.

Marsden, George M. *Jonathan Edwards: A Life*. New Haven, CT: Yale University Press, 2003.

Marty, Martin E. *Protestantism in the United States: Righteous Empire*. 2nd ed. New York: Scribner's, 1986.

Maxson, Charles Hartshorn. *The Great Awakening in the Middle Colonies*. Chicago: University of Chicago Press, 1920.

May, Henry F. *The Enlightenment in America*. New York: Oxford University Press, 1976.

McClymond, Michael J. *Encounters with God: An Approach to the Theology of Jonathan Edwards*. New York: Oxford University Press, 1998.

McClymond, Michael J., and Gerald R. McDermott. *The Theology of Jonathan Edwards*. New York: Oxford University Press, 2012.

McDermott, Gerald R. *Jonathan Edwards Confronts the Gods: Christian Theology, Enlightenment Religion, and Non-Christian Faiths*. New York: Oxford University Press, 2000.

McDermott, Gerald R. *One Holy and Happy Society: The Public Theology of Jonathan Edwards*. University Park, PA: Penn State University Press, 1992.

McDermott, Gerald R. *Seeing God: Jonathan Edwards and Spiritual Discernment*. Vancouver: Regent College Publishing, 2000.

McDermott, Gerald R., ed. *Understanding Jonathan Edwards: An Introduction to America's Theologian*. New York: Oxford University Press, 2009.

McDermott, Gerald R., and Ronald Story, eds. *The Other Jonathan Edwards: Selected Writings on Society, Love, and Justice*. Amherst: University of Massachusetts Press, 2015.

McGever, Sean. *Ownership: The Evangelical Legacy of Slavery in Edwards, Wesley, and Whitefield*. Downers Grove: InterVarsity Press, 2024.

McLoughlin, William G. *Revivals, Awakenings, and Reform: An Essay on Religion and Social Change in America, 1607–1977*. Chicago: University of Chicago Press, 1978.

McManus, Edgar J. *Black Bondage in the North*. Syracuse: Syracuse University Press, 2001.

Mead, Sidney E. *The Lively Experiment: The Shaping of Christianity in America*. New York: Harper & Row, 1963.

Melish, Joanne Pope. *Disowning Slavery: Gradual Emancipation and "Race" in New England, 1780–1860*. Ithaca, NY: Cornell University Press, 2015.

Miller, Perry. *Jonathan Edwards*. 1949. Reprint, Lincoln, NE: Bison Books, 2005.

Miller, Perry. *Nature's Nation*. Cambridge, MA: Harvard University Press, 1967.

Miller, Perry. *The New England Mind: From Colony to Province*. Cambridge, MA: Harvard University Press, 1953.

Mitchell, Louis J. *Jonathan Edwards on the Experience of Beauty*. Princeton, NJ: Princeton Theological Seminary, 2003.

Moody, Josh. *Jonathan Edwards and Justification*. Wheaton, IL: Crossway, 2012.

Moody, Josh. *Jonathan Edwards and the Enlightenment: Knowing the Presence of God*. Lanham, MD: University Press of America, 2005.

Moody, Josh. *The God-Centered Life: Insights from Jonathan Edwards for Today*. Vancouver: Regent College Publishing, 2007.

Morgan, Edmund S. *The Gentle Puritan: A Life of Ezra Stiles, 1727–1795*. New Haven, CT: Yale University Press, 1962.

Morgan, Edmund S. *Visible Saints: The History of a Puritan Idea*. New York: New York University Press, 1963.

Morimoto, Anri. *Jonathan Edwards and the Catholic Vision of Salvation*. University Park, PA: Pennsylvania State University Press, 1995.

Murray, Iain H. *Jonathan Edwards: A New Biography*. Carlisle, PA: Banner of Truth, 1987.

Nichols, Stephen J. *An Absolute Sort of Certainty: The Holy Spirit and the Apologetics of Jonathan Edwards*. Phillipsburg, NJ: P & R Publishing, 2003.

Nichols, Stephen J. *Heaven on Earth: Capturing Jonathan Edwards's Vision of Living in Between*. Wheaton, IL: Crossway, 2006.

Nichols, Stephen J. *Jonathan Edwards: A Guided Tour of His Life & Thought*. Phillipsburg, NJ: P & R Publishing, 2001.

Niebuhr, H. Richard. *The Kingdom of God in America*. Hamden, CT: Shoe String Press, 1956.

Nobles, Gregory H. *Divisions throughout the Whole: Politics and Society in Hampshire County, Massachusetts, 1740–1775*. New York: Cambridge University Press, 1983.

Noll, Mark A. *A History of Christianity in the United States and Canada*. Grand Rapids: Eerdmans, 1992.

Noll, Mark A. *America's God: From Jonathan Edwards to Abraham Lincoln*. New York: Oxford University Press, 2002.

Noll, Mark A. *Christians in the American Revolution*. Grand Rapids: Christian University Press, 1977.

Noll, Mark A. *God and Race in American Politics: A Short History*. Princeton, NJ: Princeton University Press, 2008.

Noll, Mark A. *The Old Religion in a New World: The History of North American Christianity*. Grand Rapids: Eerdmans, 2002.

Noll, Mark A. *The Rise of Evangelicalism: The Age of Edwards, Whitefield, and the Wesleys*. Downers Grove, IL: InterVarsity, 2003.

Noll, Mark A., Nathan O. Hatch, and George M. Marsden. *The Search for Christian America*. Westchester, IL: Crossway Books, 1983.

Oberg, Barbara, and Harry S. Stout, eds. *Benjamin Franklin, Jonathan Edwards, and the Representation of American Culture*. New York: Oxford University Press, 1993.

Ortlund, Dane C. *A New Inner Relish: Christian Motivation in the Thought of Jonathan Edwards*. Fearn, UK: Christian Focus, 2008.

Ortlund, Dane C. *Edwards on the Christian Life: Alive to the Beauty of God.* Wheaton, IL: Crossway, 2014.

Packer, J. I. *A Quest for Godliness: The Puritan Vision of the Christian Life.* Wheaton, IL: Crossway, 1990.

Pauw, Amy Plantinga. *The Supreme Harmony of All: The Trinitarian Theology of Jonathan Edwards.* Grand Rapids: Eerdmans, 2002.

Peckham, Howard H. *The Colonial Wars, 1689–1762.* Chicago: University of Chicago Press, 1964.

Peterson, Mark A. *The Price of Redemption: The Spiritual Economy of Puritan New England.* Stanford, CA: Stanford University Press, 1997.

Pettit, Norman. *The Heart Prepared: Grace and Conversion in Puritan Spiritual Life.* New Haven, CT: Yale University Press, 1966.

Piper, John. *God's Passion for His Glory: Living the Vision of Jonathan Edwards.* Wheaton: Crossway Books, 1998.

Piper, John, and Justin Taylor, eds. *A God Entranced Vision of All Things: The Legacy of Jonathan Edwards.* Wheaton, IL: Crossway, 2004.

Plantinga, Alvin, ed. *Faith and Philosophy: Philosophical Studies in Religion and Ethics.* Grand Rapids: Eerdmans, 1964.

Post, Stephen Garrard. *Christian Love and Self-Denial: An Historical and Normative Study of Jonathan Edwards, Samuel Hopkins, and American Theological Ethics.* Lanham: University Press of America, 1987.

Reardon, Bernard M. G. *Religion in the Age of Romanticism: Studies in Early Nineteenth Century Thought.* New York: Cambridge University Press, 1985.

Reardon, Bernard M. G. *Religious Thought in the Nineteenth Century.* London: Cambridge University Press, 1966.

Roberts, T. A. *The Concept of Benevolence: Aspects of Eighteenth-Century Moral Philosophy.* London: Macmillan, 1973.

Robinson, Donald L. *Slavery in the Structure of American Politics, 1765–1820.* New York: W. W. Norton, 1979.

Romer, Robert H. *Slavery in the Connecticut Valley of Massachusetts.* Florence, MA: Levellers Press, 2009.

Rupp, E. Gordon. *Religion in England, 1688–1791.* Oxford: Clarendon Press, 1986.

Sassi, Jonathan D. *A Republic of Righteousness: The Public Christianity of the Post-Revolutionary New England Clergy.* New York: Oxford University Press, 2001.

Schlesinger Jr., Arthur M., and Morton White. *Paths of American Thought.* Boston: Houghton Mifflin, 1963.

Schmidt, James. *What Is Enlightenment? Eighteenth-Century Answers and Twentieth-Century Questions*. Berkeley: University of California Press, 1996.

Schneewind, J. B. *The Invention of Autonomy: A History of Modern Moral Philosophy*. Cambridge: Cambridge University Press, 1998.

Schneider, Herbert W. *The Puritan Mind.* Ann Arbor, MI: University of Michigan Press, 1958.

Schweitzer, William M. *God Is a Communicative Being: Divine Communicativeness and Harmony in the Theology of Jonathan Edwards*. New York: T & T Clark, 2012.

Sewall, Samuel. *The Selling of Joseph: A Memorial.* Edited by Sidney Kaplan. Amherst: University of Massachusetts Press, 1969.

Simonson, Harold P. *Jonathan Edwards: Theologian of the Heart*. Grand Rapids: Eerdmans, 1974.

Smith, John E. *Jonathan Edwards: Puritan, Preacher, Philosopher*. Notre Dame: University of Notre Dame Press, 1992.

Stein, Stephen J. *The Cambridge Companion to Jonathan Edwards*. New York: Cambridge University Press, 2007.

Stephens, Bruce M. *God's Last Metaphor: The Doctrine of the Trinity in New England Theology*. Chico, CA: Scholars Press, 1981.

Stewart, James Brewer. *Holy Warriors: The Abolitionists and American Slavery*. Rev. ed. New York: Hill and Wang, 1997.

Storms, C. Samuel. *Signs of the Spirit: An Interpretation of Jonathan Edwards' Religious Affections*. Wheaton, IL: Crossway Books, 2007.

Story, Ronald. *Jonathan Edwards and the Gospel of Love*. Amherst: University of Massachusetts Press, 2012.

Stout, Harry S. *The New England Soul: Preaching and Religious Culture in Colonial New England*. New York: Oxford University Press, 1986.

Stout, Harry S., Kenneth P. Minkema, and Caleb J. D. Maskell, eds. *Jonathan Edwards at 300: Essays on the Tercentenary of His Birth*. Lanham, MD: University Press of America, 2005.

Strobel, Kyle. *Jonathan Edwards's Theology: A Reinterpretation*. New York: T & T Clark, 2013.

Strong, Douglas M. *Perfectionist Politics: Abolitionism and the Religious Tensions of American Democracy*. Syracuse, NY: Syracuse University Press, 1999.

Studebaker, Steven M., and Robert W. Caldwell III. *The Trinitarian Theology of Jonathan Edwards: Text, Context, and Application*. Burlington, VT: Ashgate, 2012.

Sweeney, Douglas A. *Jonathan Edwards and the Ministry of the Word: A Model of Faith and Thought*. Downers Grove, IL: IVP Academic, 2009.

Sweeney, Douglas A. *Nathaniel Taylor, New Haven Theology, and the Legacy of Jonathan Edwards*. New York: Oxford University Press, 2003.

Sweeney, Douglas A., and Allen C. Guelzo, eds. *The New England Theology: From Jonathan Edwards to Edwards Amasa Park*. Grand Rapids: Baker Academic, 2006.

Sweeney, Douglas A., and Jan Stievermann, eds. *The Oxford Handbook of Jonathan Edwards*. Oxford: Oxford University Press, 2021.

Sweet, John W. *Bodies Politic: Negotiating Race in the American North, 1730–1830*. Philadelphia: University of Pennsylvania Press, 2006.

Tise, Larry E. *Proslavery: A History of the Defense of Slavery in America, 1701–1840*. Athens, GA: University of Georgia Press, 1987.

Todd, Margo. *Christian Humanism and the Puritan Social Order*. Cambridge: Cambridge University Press, 1987.

Todorov, Tzvetan. *L'Esprit des Lumières*. Paris: Le Livre de Poche, 2007.

Tracy, Patricia J. *Jonathan Edwards, Pastor: Religion and Society in Eighteenth-Century Northampton*. New York: Hill and Wang, 1980.

Turner, James. *Without God, Without Creed: The Origins of Unbelief in America*. Baltimore: Johns Hopkins University Press, 1985.

Tyacke, Nicholas. *Anti-Calvinists: The Rise of English Arminianism, c. 1590–1640*. Oxford: Clarendon Press, 1987.

Valeri, Mark. *Heavenly Merchandize: How Religion Shaped Commerce in Puritan America*. Princeton, NJ: Princeton University Press, 2010.

Valeri, Mark. *Law and Providence in Joseph Bellamy's New England: The Origins of the New Divinity in Revolutionary America*. New York: Oxford University Press, 1994.

Valjavec, Fritz. *Geschichte der abendländischen Aufklärung*. Munich: Herold, 1961.

Viner, Jacob. *The Role of Providence in the Social Order: An Essay in Intellectual History*. Princeton, NJ: Princeton University Press, 1972.

Wallace, Dewey D. *Puritans and Predestination: Grace in English Protestant Theology, 1525–1695*. Chapel Hill: University of North Carolina Press, 1982.

Walters, Kerry S. *Rational Infidels: The American Deists*. Durango, CO: Longwood Academic, 1992.

Walters, Kerry S. *The American Deists: Voices of Reason and Dissent in the Early Republic*. Lawrence, KS: University Press of Kansas, 1992.

Warch, Richard. *School of the Prophets: Yale College, 1701–1740.* New Haven, CT: Yale University Press, 1973.

Welch, Claude. *Protestant Thought in the Nineteenth Century: 1799–1870.* Vol. 1. New Haven, CT: Yale University Press, 1972.

Welch, Claude. *Protestant Thought in the Nineteenth Century: 1870–1914.* Vol. 2. New Haven, CT: Yale University Press, 1985.

West, Stephen, ed. *Sketches of the Life of the Late, Rev. Samuel Hopkins, D.D., Pastor of the First Congregational Church in Newport, Written by Himself; Interspersed with Notes Extracted from His Private Diary.* Hartford, CT: Hudson and Goodwin, 1805.

White, Ryan. *The Hidden God: Pragmatism and Posthumanism in American Thought.* New York: Columbia University Press, 2015.

Whitefield, George. *The Sermons of George Whitefield.* Edited by Lee Gatiss. Vol. 1. Wheaton, IL: Crossway, 2012.

Whitefield, George. *The Sermons of George Whitefield.* Edited by Lee Gatiss. Vol. 2. Wheaton, IL: Crossway, 2012.

Whitefield, George, J. C. Ryle, and Richard Elliot. *Select Sermons of George Whitefield.* London: Banner of Truth Trust, 1958.

Whittemore, Robert C. *The Transformation of the New England Theology.* New York: Peter Lang, 1987.

Willey, Basil. *The Eighteenth-Century Background: Studies on the Idea of Nature in the Thought of the Period.* London: Chatto & Windus, 1940.

Wilson, Robert J. *The Benevolent Deity: Ebenezer Gay and the Rise of Rational Religion in New England, 1696–1787.* Philadelphia: University of Pennsylvania Press, 1984.

Wilson, Stephen A. *Virtue Reformed: Rereading Jonathan Edwards's Ethics.* Leiden: Brill, 2005.

Winslow, Ola Elizabeth. *Jonathan Edwards, 1703–1758: A Biography.* New York: Collier Books, 1961.

Wood, Gordon S. *The Creation of the American Republic, 1776–1787.* Chapel Hill: University of North Carolina Press, 1998.

Wood, Gordon S. *The Radicalism of the American Revolution.* New York: Vintage, 1993.

Yeager, Jonathan M. *Early Evangelicalism: A Reader.* Oxford: Oxford University Press, 2013.

Zakai, Avihu. *Exile and Kingdom: History and Apocalypse in the Puritan Migration to America.* Cambridge: Cambridge University Press, 1991.

Zakai, Avihu. *Jonathan Edwards's Philosophy of History: The Reenchantment of the World in the Age of Enlightenment*. Princeton, NJ: Princeton University Press, 2003.

Zakai, Avihu. *Jonathan Edwards's Philosophy of Nature: The Reenchantment of the World in the Age of Scientific Reasoning*. New York: T & T Clark, 2010.

Zilversmit, Arthur. *The First Emancipation: The Abolition of Slavery in the North*. Chicago: University of Chicago Press, 1967.

Zylla, Phillip Charles. *Virtue as Consent to Being: A Pastoral-Theological Perspective on Jonathan Edwards's Construct of Virtue*. Eugene, OR: Pickwick Publications, 2011.

Articles and Essays

Battles, Ford Lewis. "Bellamy Papers." *Hartford Quarterly* 7, no. 3 (1967): 64–91.

Bombaro, John J. "Dispositional Peculiarity, History, and Edwards's Evangelistic Appeal to Self-Love." *Westminster Theological Journal* 66, no. 1 (2004): 121–57.

Bombaro, John J. "Jonathan Edwards's Vision of Salvation." *Westminster Theological Journal* 65, no. 1 (2003): 45–67.

Brauer, Jerald C. "Types of Puritan Piety." *Church History* 56, no. 1 (1987): 39–58.

Breitenbach, William. "Piety and Moralism: Edwards and the New Divinity." In *Jonathan Edwards and the American Experience*, edited by Nathan O. Hatch and Harry S. Stout, 177–204. New York: Oxford University Press, 1988.

Breitenbach, William. "Religious Affections and Religious Affectations: Antinomianism and Hypocrisy in the Writings of Edwards and Franklin." In *Benjamin Franklin, Jonathan Edwards, and the Representation of American Culture*, edited by Barbara B. Oberg and Harry S. Stout, 13–26. New York: Oxford University Press, 1993.

Breitenbach, William. "The Consistent Calvinism of the New Divinity Movement." *William and Mary Quarterly* 41, no. 2 (1984): 241–64.

Breitenbach, William. "Unregenerate Doings: Selflessness and Selfishness in New Divinity Theology." *American Quarterly* 34, no. 5 (1982): 479–502.

Burns, Sherard. "Trusting the Theology of a Slave Owner." In *A God Entranced Vision of All Things: The Legacy of Jonathan Edwards*, edited by

John Piper and Justin Taylor, 145–71. Wheaton, IL: Crossway Books, 2004.

Bushman, Richard L. "Jonathan Edwards and Puritan Consciousness." In *Puritan New England: Essays on Religion, Society, and Culture*, edited by Francis J. Bremer and Alden T. Vaughan, 346–62. New York: St. Martin's Press, 1977.

Chamberlain, Ava. "The Theology of Cruelty: A New Look at the Rise of Arminianism in Eighteenth-Century New England." *Harvard Theological Review* 85, no. 3 (1992): 335–56.

Choi, Ki Joo. "The Role of Perception in Jonathan Edwards's Moral Thought: The Nature of True Virtue Reconsidered." *Journal of Religious Ethics* 38, no. 2 (2010): 269–96.

Cochran, Elizabeth A. "Consent, Conversion, and Moral Formation: Stoic Elements in Jonathan Edwards's Ethics." *Journal of Religious Ethics* 39, no. 4 (2011): 623–50.

Cochran, Elizabeth A. "Creaturely Virtues in Jonathan Edwards: The Significance of Christology for the Moral Life." *Journal of the Society of Christian Ethics* 27, no. 2 (2007): 73–95.

Cochran, Elizabeth A. "Ethics." In *The Oxford Handbook of Jonathan Edwards*, edited by Douglas A. Sweeney and Jan Stievermann, 281–95. Oxford: Oxford University Press, 2021.

Cochran, Joseph T. "Imitating the Virtue Ethic of Jonathan Edwards and William James." *Bulletin of Ecclesial Theology* 9, no. 2 (2022): 19–42.

Conforti, Joseph A. "Samuel Hopkins and the New Divinity: Theology, Ethics, and Social Reform in Eighteenth-Century New England." *William and Mary Quarterly* 34, no. 4 (1977): 572–89.

Conforti, Joseph A. "Samuel Hopkins and the Revolutionary Anti-Slavery Movement." *Rhode Island History* 38, no. 2 (1979): 38–49.

Danaher, William J. "Beauty, Benevolence, and Virtue in Jonathan Edwards's The Nature of True Virtue." *Journal of Religion* 87, no. 3 (2007): 386–410.

Davidson, Bruce W. "Not from Ourselves: Holy Love in the Theology of Jonathan Edwards." *Journal of the Evangelical Theological Society* 59, no. 3 (2016): 571–84.

Davidson, Bruce W. "The Four Faces of Self-Love in the Theology of Jonathan Edwards." *Journal of the Evangelical Theological Society* 51, no. 1 (2008): 87–100.

Delattre, Roland A. "Aesthetics and Ethics: Jonathan Edwards and the Recovery of Aesthetics for Religious Ethics." *Journal of Religious Ethics* 31, no. 2 (2003): 277–97.

Delattre, Roland A. "Beauty and Theology: A Reappraisal of Jonathan Edwards." *Soundings: An Interdisciplinary Journal* 51, no. 1 (1968): 60–79.

Delattre, Roland A. "The Theological Ethics of Jonathan Edwards: An Homage to Paul Ramsey." *Journal of Religious Ethics* 19, no. 2 (1991): 71–102.

Donnan, Elizabeth. "The New England Slave Trade after the Revolution." *New England Quarterly* 3, no. 2 (1930): 251–78.

Ellis, Joseph. "Habits of Mind and an American Enlightenment." *American Quarterly* 28, no. 2 (1976): 150–64.

Elsbree, Oliver Wendell. "Samuel Hopkins and His Doctrine of Benevolence." *New England Quarterly* 8, no. 4 (1935): 534–50.

Fiering, Norman. "Will and Intellect in the New England Mind." *William and Mary Quarterly* 29, no. 4 (1972): 516–58.

Foster, Stephen. "New England and the Challenge of Heresy, 1630 to 1660: The Puritan Crisis in Transatlantic Perspective." *William and Mary Quarterly* 38, no. 4 (1981): 624–60.

Frey, Sylvia R. "Slavery and Anti-Slavery." In *The Blackwell Encyclopedia of the American Revolution*, edited by Jack P. Greene and J. R. Pole, 379–91. Cambridge, MA: Blackwell Reference, 1991.

Goodwin, Gerald J. "The Myth of 'Arminian-Calvinism' in Eighteenth-Century New England." *New England Quarterly* 41, no. 2 (1968): 213–37.

Greene, Jack P. "Search for Identity: An Interpretation of the Meaning of Selected Patterns of Social Response in Eighteenth-Century America." *Journal of Social History* 3, no. 3 (1969): 189–220.

Greene, Lorenzo J. "Slave-Holding New England and Its Awakening." *Journal of Negro History* 13, no. 4 (1928): 492–533.

Grigg, John A. "Missions." In *The Oxford Handbook of Jonathan Edwards*, edited by Douglas A. Sweeney and Jan Stievermann, 416–30. Oxford: Oxford University Press, 2021.

Hatch, Nathan O. "The Origins of Civil Millennialism in America: New England Clergymen, War with France, and the Revolution." *William and Mary Quarterly* 31, no. 3 (1974): 407–30.

Holmes, Steve. "Edwards on the Will." *International Journal of Systematic Theology* 1, no. 3 (1999): 266–85.

Hoopes, James. "Jonathan Edwards's Religious Psychology." *Journal of American History* 69, no. 4 (1983): 849–65.

Hunsinger, George. "Dispositional Soteriology: Jonathan Edwards on Justification by Faith Alone." *Westminster Theological Journal* 66, no. 1 (2004): 107–20.

Jauhiainen, Peter Dan. "'Reasoning Out of the Scriptures': Samuel Hopkins, the Theological Enterprise, and the Deist Threat." *Journal of Presbyterian History* 79, no. 2 (June 1, 2001): 119–33.

Jauhiainen, Peter Dan. "Samuel Hopkins and Hopkinsianism." In *After Jonathan Edwards: The Courses of the New England Theology*, edited by Oliver Crisp and Douglas A. Sweeney, 107–17. New York: Oxford University Press, 2012.

Jeon, Heejoon. "Jonathan Edwards and the Anti-Slavery Movement." *Journal of the Evangelical Theological Society* 63, no. 4 (2020): 773–88.

Kling, David W. "New Divinity Schools of the Prophets, 1750–1825: A Case Study in Ministerial Education." *History of Education Quarterly* 37, no. 2 (1997): 185–206.

Knapp, Hugh Heath. "The Early Career of Samuel Hopkins and the End of the Awakening Style." *Bulletin of the Connecticut Historical Society* 39, no. 2 (1974): 54–64.

Lake, Peter. "Defining Puritanism-Again?" In *Puritanism: Transatlantic Perspective on a Seventeenth-Century Anglo-American Faith*, edited by Francis J. Bremer, 3–29. Boston: Massachusetts Historical Society, 1993.

Laurence, David. "Jonathan Edwards, Solomon Stoddard, and the Preparationist Model of Conversion." *Harvard Theological Review* 72, no. 3 (1979): 267–83.

Lovejoy, David S. "Samuel Hopkins: Religion, Slavery, and the Revolution." *New England Quarterly* 40, no. 2 (1967): 227–43.

MacEacheren, Elaine. "Emancipation of Slavery in Massachusetts: A Reexamination 1770–1790." *Journal of Negro History* 55, no. 4 (1970): 289–306.

Marsden, George M. "Biography." In *The Cambridge Companion to Jonathan Edwards*, edited by Stephen J. Stein, 19–37. New York: Cambridge University Press, 2007.

May, Henry F. "The Problem of the American Enlightenment." *New Literary History* 1, no. 2 (1970): 201–14.

McClymond, Michael J. "Spiritual Perception in Jonathan Edwards." *Journal of Religion* 77, no. 2 (1997): 195–216.

McDermott, Gerald R. "Jonathan Edwards and American Indians: The Devil Sucks Their Blood." *New England Quarterly* 72, no. 4 (1999): 539–57.

McDermott, Gerald R. "Poverty, Patriotism, and National Covenant: Jonathan Edwards and Public Life." *Journal of Religious Ethics* 31, no. 2 (2003): 229–51.

Mead, Sidney E. "American Protestantism During the Revolutionary Epoch." *Church History* 22, no. 4 (1953): 279–97.

Meyer, D. H. "The Uniqueness of the American Enlightenment." *American Quarterly* 28, no. 2 (1976): 165–86.

Miller, Perry. "Jonathan Edwards on the Sense of the Heart." *Harvard Theological Review* 41, no. 2 (1948): 123–45.

Miller, Perry. "Jonathan Edwards' Sociology of the Great Awakening." *New England Quarterly* 21, no. 1 (1948): 50–77.

Miller, Perry. "Jonathan Edwards' Sociology of the Great Awakening." In *The Marrow of American Divinity: Selected Articles on Colonial Religion*, edited by Peter Charles Hoffer, 94–121. New York: Garland, 1988.

Minkema, Kenneth P. "Jonathan Edwards in the Twentieth Century." *Journal of the Evangelical Theological Society* 47, no. 4 (2004): 659–87.

Minkema, Kenneth P. "Jonathan Edwards on Slavery and the Slave Trade." *William and Mary Quarterly* 54, no. 4 (1997): 823–34.

Minkema, Kenneth P. "Jonathan Edwards's Defense of Slavery." *Massachusetts Historical Review* 4 (2002): 23–59.

Minkema, Kenneth P., and Harry S. Stout. "The Edwardsean Tradition and the Antislavery Debate, 1740–1865." *Journal of American History* 92, no. 1 (2005): 47–74.

Morgan, Edmund S. "Slavery and Freedom: The American Paradox." *Journal of American History* 59, no. 1 (1972): 5–29.

Morgan, Edmund S. "The Puritan Ethic and the American Revolution." *William and Mary Quarterly* 24, no. 1 (1967): 4–43.

Morgan, Edmund S. "The Puritan Ethic and the American Revolution." In *Puritan New England: Essays on Religion, Society, and Culture*, edited by Alden T. Vaughan and Francis J. Bremer, 364–84. New York: St Martin's Press, 1977.

Morimoto, Anri. "An Edwardsian Lost and Found: The Legacy of Jonathan Edwards in Asia." In *After Jonathan Edwards: The Courses of the New England Theology*, edited by Oliver D. Crisp and Douglas A. Sweeney, 225–36. New York: Oxford University Press, 2012.

Murrin, John M. "No Awakening, No Revolution? More Counterfactual Speculations." *Reviews in American History* 11, no. 2 (1983): 161–171.

Noll, Mark. "God at the Center: Jonathan Edwards on True Virtue." *Christian Century* 110, no. 25 (1993): 854–58.

Noll, Mark A. "Moses Mather (Old Calvinist) and the Evolution of Edwardseanism." *Church History* 49, no. 3 (1980): 273–85.

O'Brien, Susan. "A Transatlantic Community of Saints: The Great Awakening and the First Evangelical Network, 1735–1755." *American Historical Review* 91, no. 4 (1986): 811–32.

Pauw, Amy Plantinga. "Heaven Is a World of Love: Edwards on Heaven and the Trinity." *Calvin Theological Journal* 30, no. 2 (1995): 393–401.

Pearson, Samuel C. "The Religion of John Locke and the Character of His Thought." *Journal of Religion* 58, no. 3 (1978): 244–62.

Piper, John. "A God-Entranced Vision of All Things: Why We Need Jonathan Edwards 300 Years Later." In *A God Entranced Vision of All Things: The Legacy of Jonathan Edwards*, edited by John Piper and Justin Taylor, 21–34. Wheaton, IL: Crossway Books, 2004.

Porter, Jean. "Virtue Ethics." In *The Cambridge Companion to Christian Ethics*, edited by Robin Gill, 96–111. Cambridge: Cambridge University Press, 2001.

Post, Stephen G. "Disinterested Benevolence: An American Debate Over the Nature of Christian Love." *Journal of Religious Ethics* 14, no. 2 (1986): 356–68.

Post, Stephen G. "The Inadequacy of Selflessness: God's Suffering and the Theory of Love." *Journal of the American Academy of Religion* 56, no. 2 (1988): 213–28.

Proudfoot, Wayne. "From Theology to a Science of Religions: Jonathan Edwards and William James on Religious Affections." *Harvard Theological Review* 82, no. 2 (1989): 149–68.

Rosenthal, Bernard. "Puritan Conscience and New England Slavery." *New England Quarterly* 46, no. 1 (1973): 62–81.

Rozbicki, Michal J. "The Cultural Development of the Colonies." In *The Blackwell Encyclopedia of the American Revolution*, edited by Jack P. Greene and J. R. Pole, 71–83. Cambridge, MA: Blackwell Reference, 1991.

Saillant, John. "African American Engagements with Edwards in the Era of the Slave Trade." In *Jonathan Edwards at 300: Essays on the Tercentenary of His Birth*, edited by Harry S. Stout, Kenneth P. Minkema, and Caleb J. D. Maskell, 141–51. Lanham, MD: University Press of America, 2005.

Saillant, John. "Ministry to the Bound and Enslaved." In *The Oxford Handbook of Jonathan Edwards,* edited by Douglas A. Sweeney and Jan Stievermann, 431–45. Oxford: Oxford University Press, 2021.

Saillant, John. "Slavery and Divine Providence in New England Calvinism: The New Divinity and a Black Protest, 1775–1805." *New England Quarterly* 68, no. 4 (1995): 584–608.

Sams, Henry W. "Self-Love and the Doctrine of Work." *Journal of the History of Ideas* 4, no. 3 (1943): 320–32.

Schafer, Thomas A. "Jonathan Edwards and Justification by Faith." *Church History* 20, no. 4 (1951): 55–67.

Simonson, Harold P. "Jonathan Edwards and His Scottish Connections." *Journal of American Studies* 21, no. 3 (1987): 353–76.

Smith, John E. "Jonathan Edwards: Piety and Practice in the American Character." *Journal of Religion* 54, no. 2 (1974): 166–80.

Smith, John E. "Testing the Spirits: Jonathan Edwards and the Religious Affections." *Union Seminary Quarterly Review* 37, no. 1 (1981): 27–37.

Spohn, William C. "Sovereign Beauty: Jonathan Edwards and the Nature of True Virtue." *Theological Studies* 42, no. 3 (1981): 394–421.

Spohn, William C. "Spirituality and Its Discontents: Practices in Jonathan Edwards's Charity and Its Fruits." *Journal of Religious Ethics* 31, no. 2 (2003): 253–76.

Spohn, William C. "Union and Consent with the Great Whole: Jonathan Edwards and the Nature of True Virtue." *Annual of the Society of Christian Ethics* 5 (1985): 19–32.

Stout, Harry S. "Religion, Communications, and the Ideological Origins of the American Revolution." *William and Mary Quarterly* 34, no. 4 (1977): 519–41.

Stout, Harry S. "The Great Awakening in New England Reconsidered: The New England Clergy." *Journal of Social History* 8, no. 1 (1974): 21–47.

Stout, Harry S. "The Puritans and Edwards." In *The Princeton Companion to Jonathan Edwards*, edited by Sang Hyun Lee. Princeton, NJ: Princeton University Press, 2005.

Sweeney, Douglas A. "Edwards and His Mantle: The Historiography of the New England Theology." *New England Quarterly* 71, no. 1 (1998): 97–119.

Swift, David E. "Samuel Hopkins: Calvinist Social Concern in Eighteenth Century New England." *Journal of Presbyterian History* 47, no. 1 (1969): 31–54.

Sykes, Norman. "The Theology of Divine Benevolence." *Historical Magazine of the Protestant Episcopal Church* 16, no. 3 (1947): 278–91.

Thuesen, P. J. "Jonathan Edwards as Great Mirror." *Scottish Journal of Theology* 50, no. 1 (1997): 39–60.

Valeri, Mark. "The Economic Thought of Jonathan Edwards." *Church History* 60, no. 1 (1991): 37–54.

Valeri, Mark. "The New Divinity and the American Revolution." *William and Mary Quarterly* 46, no. 4 (1989): 741–69.

Wainwright, William. "Jonathan Edwards and the Sense of the Heart." *Faith and Philosophy* 7, no. 1 (1990): 43–62.

Watts, Emily Stipes. "The Neoplatonic Basis of Jonathan Edwards' 'True Virtue.'" *Early American Literature* 10, no. 2 (1975): 179–89.

Westbrook, Robert B. "Social Criticism and the Heavenly City of Jonathan Edwards." *Soundings: An Interdisciplinary Journal* 59, no. 4 (1976): 396–412.

Westra, Helen Petter. "'Above All Others': Jonathan Edwards and the Gospel Ministry." *American Presbyterians* 67, no. 3 (1989): 209–19.

Wheeler, Rachel. "'Friends to Your Souls': Jonathan Edwards' Indian Pastorate and the Doctrine of Original Sin." *Church History* 72, no. 4 (2003): 736–65.

Wheeler, Rachel. "Lessons from Stockbridge: Jonathan Edwards and the Stockbridge Indians." In *Jonathan Edwards at 300: Essays on the Tercentenary of His Birth*, edited by Harry S. Stout, Kenneth P. Minkema, and Caleb J. D. Maskell, 131–40. Lanham, MD: University Press of America, 2005.

Wilson, Stephen A. "Jonathan Edwards's Virtue: Diverse Sources, Multiple Meanings, and the Lessons of History for Ethics." *Journal of Religious Ethics* 31, no. 2 (2003): 201–28.

Wilson, Stephen A. "The Possibility of a Habituation Model of Moral Development in Jonathan Edward's Conception of the Will's Freedom." *Journal of Religion* 81, no. 1 (2001): 49–77.

Wilson, Stephen A., and Jean Porter. "Taking the Measure of Jonathan Edwards for Contemporary Religious Ethics." *Journal of Religious Ethics* 31, no. 2 (2003): 183–99.

Zakai, Avihu. "The Age of Enlightenment." In *The Cambridge Companion to Jonathan Edwards*, edited by Stephen J. Stein, 80–99. New York: Cambridge University Press, 2007.

Unpublished

Breitenbach, William. “New Divinity Theology and the Idea of Moral Accountability.” PhD diss., Yale University, 1978.

Conforti, Joseph A. “Samuel Hopkins and the New Divinity Movement, 1740–1820: A Study in the Transformation of Puritan Theology and the New England Social Order.” PhD diss., Brown University, 1975.

Gleim, John. “Topographies of Difference: Joseph Bellamy, Samuel Hopkins, and the Uneven Theological Development of Late-Puritan New England.” PhD diss., Fordham University, 2020.

Jauhiainen, Peter Dan. “An Enlightenment Calvinist: Samuel Hopkins and the Pursuit of Benevolence.” PhD diss., University of Iowa, 1997.

Jeon, Heejoon. “The Role of Sanctification in the Ethics of Jonathan Edwards.” PhD diss., Trinity International University, 2019.

Knapp, Hugh Heath. “Samuel Hopkins and the New Divinity.” PhD diss., University of Wisconsin, 1971.

Post, Stephen Garrard. “Love and Eudaemonism: A Study in the Thought of Jonathan Edwards and Samuel Hopkins.” PhD diss., University of Chicago, 1983.

Richards, Phillip M. “The New Divinity: Puritanism as Ideology in the Eighteenth Century.” PhD diss., University of Chicago, 1988.

Van Halsema, Dick L. “Samuel Hopkins, 1721–1803: New England Calvinist.” PhD diss., Union Theological Seminary, 1956.

Index

Below is a brief index of significant names and topics.

abolition, 1, 6, 19, 50, 79, 80, 89–91, 93, 95, 97, 148, 150, 151, 172, 181, 183, 187, 189, 190, 192
Ahlstrom, Sydney E., 79
antislavery sentiment, 17, 86, 91, 192
Arminian, 60, 62, 63
awakenings, 58, 64

Bailyn, Bernard, 78
Bellamy, Joseph, 16, 171
benevolism, 117
betrayal thesis, 3, 4, 19, 33, 34
Brand, David C., 99
Breitenbach, William, 47–49

Cassirer, Ernst, 81
Choi, Ki Joo, 31
Christian benevolence, 1, 2, 36, 41–44, 46, 97, 122, 124, 138, 178, 183
church membership, 14, 78
Clebsch, William, 24, 62
Cochran, Elizabeth, 30, 31
Cochran, Joseph T., 98, 105
Conforti, Joseph, 8, 34, 35, 37, 99, 152, 153, 169
conversion, 14, 43, 60, 76, 144
Corrigan, John, 39
Cowing, Cedric B., 54
Cragg, Gerald R., 81
Crane, Elain Forman, 86
creaturely participation, 49, 115, 116

Danaher, William J., 23, 26, 29–31
Davidson, Bruce, 29, 161, 166
Davis, David Brion, 71, 90
Deism, 6, 60–62, 83
Delattre, Roland, 24–26
disinterested benevolence, 3, 6, 17–19, 37, 49, 151, 161, 162, 164, 170–172, 175–178, 180, 181, 183, 186, 188, 190–192
disinterested love, 20, 36, 48, 141, 164, 172, 180, 181
disposition, 22, 37, 98, 102, 105–107, 110, 112, 115, 123, 126, 127, 129, 136, 137, 141, 143, 144, 159, 177, 178, 185
doctrine of benevolence, 3, 5–7, 9, 11, 18–21, 34, 37, 38, 48, 49, 95, 97, 150–152, 170–172, 190, 192
Doolittle, Benjamin, 145

Elsbree, Oliver, 36, 37
Elsbree,Oliver, 37
Elwood, Douglas, 27, 32
ethical theology, 5, 6, 9, 20, 21, 23, 32, 34, 35, 95, 97, 126, 181, 190, 192

Fiering, Norman, 26, 27, 39, 123
Foster, Frank Hugh, 3
Franklin, John Hope, 70, 88

Goen, C. C., 59
Great Awakening, 8, 12–14, 39, 58, 60, 72, 142
Guelzo, Allen C., 4, 15, 16

habits, 16, 76, 81, 89, 106
Hall, Richard, 40
Haroutunian, Joseph, 4, 33–35, 37, 39
Hart, William, 34, 152
Hawley, Joseph, 59
Hempton, David, 81
Holbrook, Clyde A., 1, 2, 26, 152
Holifield, E. Brooks, 15, 19
Hutcheson, Francis, 98

institutionalized slavery, 2, 5–8, 50, 70–73, 78–80, 86, 88–90, 92, 97, 141, 142, 145, 146, 149, 150, 184, 189, 192

Jauhiainen, Peter, 8, 12, 18, 19, 48, 49, 153, 154, 162, 170
Jauhianen, Peter Dan, 166

Kidd, Thomas S., 57, 69, 94
King Philip's War, 70
Kling, David, 19, 170
Kuklick, Bruce, 17

Lovejoy, David S., 8, 36
Lucas, Sean, 46

Marsden, George, 58, 64
Marty, Martin E., 76
McClymond, Michael, 28, 142, 144, 148
McDermott, Gerald, 41, 42, 61, 142, 144, 148
McGloughlin, William, 39
Melish, Joanne Pope, 90
Miller, Perry, 23, 24, 32, 38, 148
Minkema, Kenneth P., 145–148
moral inability, 16, 17
moral necessity, 16, 17
moral sense, 27, 28, 30, 61, 98–100, 103, 117, 154
Morgan, Edmund S., 78
motives, 16, 98, 185, 188

natural ability, 15–17
natural necessity, 15, 16
New England Theology, 3–5, 12, 34
Noll, Mark, 19, 57, 72, 84, 153

Ortlund, Dane, 44

Park, Edwards Amasa, 3, 20
Pequot War, 70
Perkins, Richard, 146
Porter, Jean, 27
Post, Stephen G., 8, 35–37, 161, 166

Ramsey, Paul, 23, 24, 26, 27, 32, 46, 105, 133, 171
Renaissance, 70
responsibility, 14–16, 31, 41, 42, 55, 84
revival, 12, 13, 17, 22, 39, 53, 57–59, 142, 143, 174
Robinson, Donald L., 76
Romer, Robert H., 71, 91, 94
Rozbicki, Michal, 63

Saillant, John, 83
Schneider, Herbert, 38
Smith, John E., 22
Spohn, William C., 6, 25, 26
Stewart, James, 92
Stoddard, Solomon, 58
Story, Ronald, 43
Stout, Harry, 147
Sweeney, Douglas, 3, 16

Tise, Larry E., 75
Tracy, Patricia, 64

virtue theory, 2, 5, 7, 8, 23, 24, 26, 29–35, 38, 40, 49, 95, 97, 122, 150, 152–154, 156, 169, 170, 189, 191, 192

Westbrook, Robert, 38
Wheeler, Rachel, 144
Whitefield, George, 60
Wilson, Stephen, 27
Wood, Godrdon S., 84
Wood, Gordon S., 65, 72

Zakai, Avihu, 55, 60
Zilversmit, Athur, 92

www.ingramcontent.com/pod-product-compliance
Lightning Source LLC
LaVergne TN
LVHW020711110826
845149LV00012B/2217

* 9 7 9 8 9 9 4 5 9 3 3 0 1 *